THE CONFUSION OF COMMAND

Lieutenant General Sir Thomas D'Oyly Snow KCB KCMG

The Confusion of Command

The War Memoirs of Lieutenant General Sir Thomas D'Oyly Snow

1914–1915

Edited and Presented by
Dan Snow and Mark Pottle

Frontline Books, London

The Confusion of Command

This edition published in 2011 by Frontline Books, an imprint of Pen & Sword Books Limited,
47 Church Street, Barnsley, S. Yorkshire, S70 2AS
www.frontline-books.com

ISBN: 978-1-84832-575-3

For more information on our books, please visit
www.frontline-books.com, email info@frontline-books.com
or write to us at the above address.

Typeset by JCS Publishing Services Ltd, www.jcs-publishing.co.uk
in perpetua font (12.5pt on 15pt)

Printed in the UK by CPI Mackays

CONTENTS

ILLUSTRATIONS

Maps

Plate Section

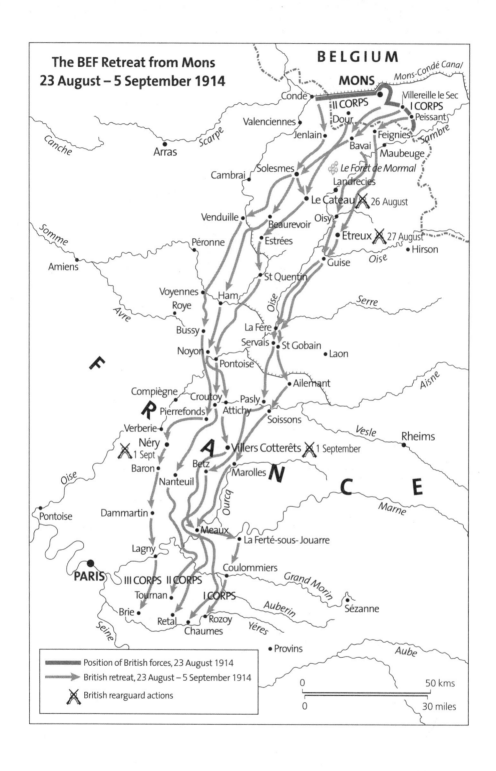

The BEF Retreat from Mons
23 August – 5 September 1914

BELGIUM

Mons-Condé Canal

MONS

Condé   Villereille le Sec

II CORPS   I CORPS

Valenciennes   Dour   Peissant

Jenlain   Feignies   Sambre

Canche   Scarpe   Bavai

Arras   Maubeuge

Cambrai   Solesmes   Le Foret de Mormal

                            Landrecies

Somme   Le Cateau ✗ 26 August

Venduille   Oisy

Somme   Beaurevoir

Péronne   Estrées   Etreux ✗ 27 August

                            Hirson

Amiens   Guise   Oise

                   St Quentin

Voyennes   Ham   Serre

Roye

Avre   Bussy   La Fère

           Noyon Servais St Gobain

F   Pontoise   Laon   Oise

Compiègne Croutoy Pasly Ailemant   Aisne

           Pierrefonds Attichy

R   Verberie   Soissons

           Néry   Vesle   Rheims

Oise ✗   1 Sept Villers Cotterêts ✗ 1 September

           Baron   Marne

           Nanteuil Betz Marolles   N   C   E

Pontoise   Dammartin   Ourcq

           Lagny   Meaux La Ferté-sous- Jouarre

PARIS   III CORPS II CORPS

           Tournan   I CORPS Coulommiers Grand Morin

           Brie   Retal Rozoy Auberin   Sézanne

                   Chaumes Yéres

Seine   Provins   Aube

Position of British forces, 23 August 1914

British retreat, 23 August – 5 September 1914

✗ British rearguard actions

0   50 kms

0   30 miles

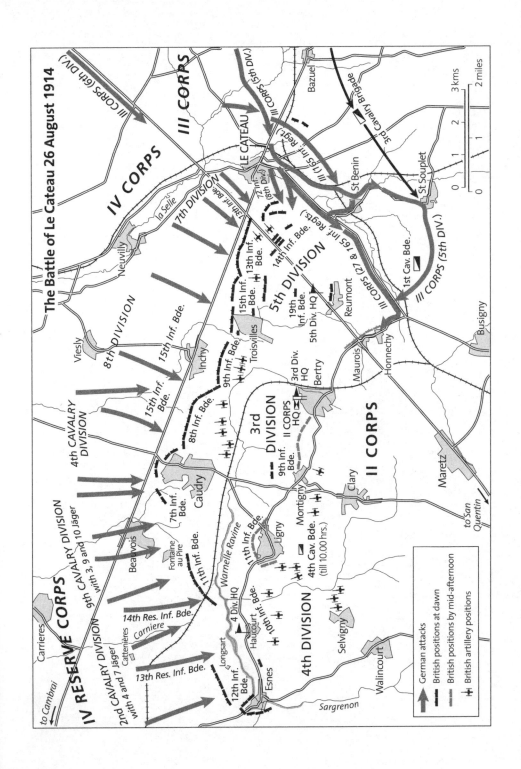

The Battle of Le Cateau 26 August 1914

IV RESERVE CORPS

IV CORPS

III CORPS

II CORPS

to Cambrai

to San Quentin

(III CORPS (6th DIV.))

9th CAVALRY DIVISION
with 3, 9 and 10 Jäger

2nd CAVALRY DIVISION
with 4 and 7 Jäger

4th CAVALRY
DIVISION

la Selle

Neuvilly

Viesly

8th DIVISION

7th DIVISION

LE CATEAU

III CORPS (5th DIV.)

Bazuel

3rd Cavalry Brigade

St Benin

St Souplet

1st Cav. Bde.

III CORPS (5th DIV.)

Busigny

Maretz

Reumont

Honnechy

Maurois

Bertry

Clary

Ligny

Montigny

Selvigny

Walincourt

Sargrenon

Esnes

Beauvois

Inchy

Troisvilles

Caudry

Fontaine
au Pire

Carrières

Cattenières

Carnière

Longsart

Haucourt

5th DIVISION

3rd
DIVISION

4th DIVISION

15th Inf. Bde.

15th Inf.
Bde.

15th Inf.
Bde.

15th Inf.
Bde.

13th Inf.
Bde.

14th Inf. Bde.

19th
Inf. Bde.

5th Div. HQ

72 Inf.
(8th Div.)

II (135) Inf. Regt.

II (113) Inf. Regt. (5th Div.)

165 Inf. Regts.

III CORPS (27 & 165 Inf. Regts.)

23rd Inf. Bde.

9th Inf. Bde.

8th Inf. Bde.

9th Inf.
Bde.

3rd Div.
HQ

II CORPS HQ

7th Inf.
Bde.

11th Inf. Bde.

Warnelle Ravine

11th Inf. Bde.

4 Div. HQ

4th Cav. Bde.
(till 10.00 hrs.)

100th Inf. Bde.

13th Res. Inf. Bde.

14th Res. Inf. Bde.

12th Inf.
Bde.

German attacks

British positions at dawn

British positions by mid-afternoon

British artillery positions

3 kms

2 miles

2

1

0

0

1

2

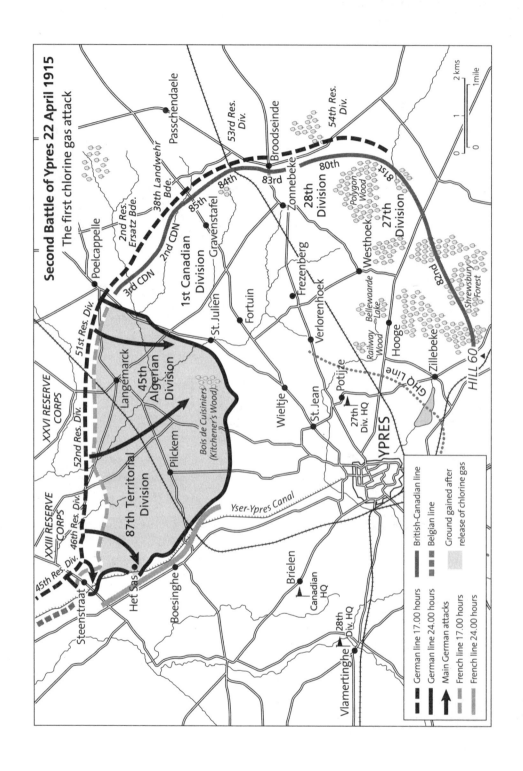

Second Battle of Ypres 22 April 1915
The first chlorine gas attack

Passchendaele

53rd Res. Div.

54th Res. Div.

Broodseinde

XXVI RESERVE CORPS

2nd Res. Ersatz Bde.

38th Landwehr Bde.

Poelcappelle

51st Res. Div.

52nd Res. Div.

3rd CDN

2nd CDN

83rd

80th

81st

28th Division

27th Division

82nd

Polygon Wood

Zonnebeke

84th

85th

Gravenstafel

1st Canadian Division

Westhoek

Railway Wood

Bellewaarde Lake

Shrewsbury Forest

St. Julien

Fortuin

Frezenberg

Verlorenhoek

Hooge

Zillebeke

HILL 60

Langemarck

45th Algerian Division

Pilckem

Bois de Cuisiniers (Kitchener's Wood)

Wieltje

St. Jean

Potijze

27th Div. HQ

87th Territorial Division

XXIII RESERVE CORPS

45th Res. Div.

46th Res. Div.

Steenstraat

Het Sas

Boesinghe

Yser-Ypres Canal

GHQ Line

YPRES

Brielen

Canadian HQ

Vlamertinghe

28th Div. HQ

Legend

German line 17.00 hours	
German line 24.00 hours	
Main German attacks	
French line 17.00 hours	
French line 24.00 hours	
British-Canadian line	
Belgian line	
Ground gained after release of chlorine gas	

2 kms
1 mile
1
0

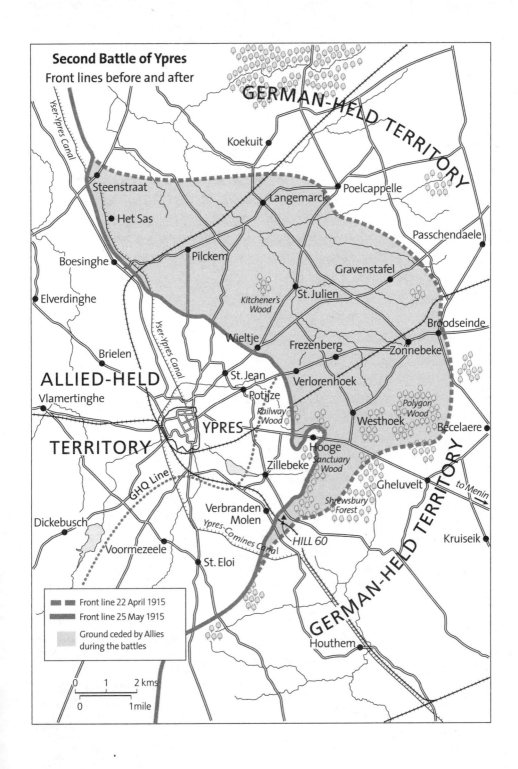

Second Battle of Ypres
Front lines before and after

GERMAN-HELD TERRITORY

Koekuit

Steenstraat

Poelcappelle

Langemarck

Het Sas

Passchendaele

Boesinghe

Pilckem

Gravenstafel

Elverdinghe

Kitchener's Wood

St. Julien

Broodseinde

Wieltje

Frezenberg

Zonnebeke

Brielen

ALLIED-HELD

St. Jean

Verlorenhoek

Vlamertinghe

Potijze

Polygon Wood

Railway Wood

Westhoek

Becelaere

YPRES

TERRITORY

Hooge

Sanctuary Wood

Zillebeke

Gheluvelt

to Menin

GHQ Line

Shrewsbury Forest

Dickebusch

Verbranden Molen

Ypres-Comines Canal

HILL 60

Kruiseik

Voormezeele

St. Eloi

GERMAN-HELD TERRITORY

Yser-Ypres Canal

Houthem

Front line 22 April 1915
Front line 25 May 1915
Ground ceded by Allies
during the battles

0   1   2 kms

0   1 mile

Foreword

Other children had graves to visit. On trips to the Western Front my friends would find great-grandfathers or great-great-uncles; men who had died in their teens – 'all heroes, and all the victims', it was muttered by wise eleven-year-olds schooled by Owen and Blackadder, of 'butchers', 'toffs' and of course the ubiquitous 'donkeys'. As we went off to buy shrapnel and bangers, little did the rest of them know that I had a dark secret, one that only the more observant visitors to the family home in London would have sniffed out. On the wall of our living room was a portrait of a white-haired, square-jawed man, with the prominent Snow nose softened by the obligatory moustache. Below the neck he wears a khaki uniform, left breast packed with ribbons, red tags on his collar. It is Lieutenant General Sir Thomas D'Oyly Snow. He commanded divisions and corps from the first days of the war to nearly its end, at Le Cateau, Ypres, the Somme, Arras and Cambrai. He was my great-grandfather.

He was a very distant figure. My father only briefly overlapped with his grandfather and does not remember him. Sadly, my grandfather died before I was born so Sir Thomas feels even more remote to me. Our family never really discussed him; other relations, such as my maternal grandfather – who had fought in the Second World War – had more compelling stories. We knew Sir Thomas had been to Eton and Cambridge, which led my cousin to joke that our family was a heartening example of downward social mobility. People often find it strange that I am not more interested in 'Family History', yet I have always assumed that a love of history means that one is less likely to need the spur of your ancestor having been involved in an event in order to find it interesting. As I studied history, and eventually came to write it, I became fascinated by the generals, but not with my great-grandfather, particularly since he was not considered a key player by any historians.

Then in 2008 I took part in a documentary for BBC1 in which I was spirited around Northern France and Belgium to learn more about my ancestor. Having spent a good deal of my professional life reading about Rawlinson, Currie, Monash and the other celebrated commanders, it felt strange to know so little about Snow. I learnt a great deal. I rode inexpertly across the fields of Le Cateau, as did he in one of the last battles in British history where generals surveyed the battlefield on horseback, in plain view of both armies. I sat in a room in the comfortable chateau from where, when the wind blew the right way, he could hear the sounds of the Somme bombardment, and where he learnt that his attack against Gommecourt on 1 July 1916 had been among the most futile of that terrible first day's assaults. I was appalled to find out that in the frenzy of buck passing and blame avoidance that followed the catastrophic defeat, Snow set up a subordinate, Major-General E. J. Montagu-Stuart-Wortley, commander of the 46th Division, as a scapegoat. He wrote to Third Army HQ, saying that the men of the 46th Division had demonstrated a 'lack of offensive spirit'. This he ascribed to their commander's failings: '[He] is not of an age, neither has he the constitution, to allow him to be as much among his men in the front lines as is necessary to imbue all ranks with confidence and spirit.'[1]

In fact, the men of the 46th had suffered casualties of up to 85 per cent as they showed extraordinary determination in pushing home badly planned and poorly supported attacks against one of the strongest sections of German line on the Western Front. Bearing this in mind, it was fascinating to discover just how much of Snow's 1914–15 memoirs are devoted to the politics of senior command. He describes the volatility of Kitchener's decision making and the rivalries that poisoned relations at the very top of the BEF. Snow's fury at the

---

1   Letter from T. D'O. Snow to Allenby, 2 July 1916, cited in A. MacDonald, *A Lack of Offensive Spirit: The 46th (North Midland) Division at Gommecourt, 1st July 1916* (Iona, 2008), p. 500.

seemingly arbitrary removal of his brigadiers in 1915 contrasts with his desperate manoeuvring following the Somme debacle. I sat and read his quietly emotional letter to his wife, written after he had been told that he was to be gently moved on from the Western Front, just as all the years of unrelenting toil seemed to be bearing fruit. It is now fairly clear that he was partly blamed for the reverses suffered during the German counterattack at Cambrai at the end of 1917, despite his continual warnings to Third Army HQ that an attack was being prepared in his sector. His advanced age was also an issue, as the average age of general officers was falling towards the end of the war. Like Montagu-Stuart-Wortley, Gough, Smith-Dorrien and many others, Snow eventually discovered that the uncertain and capricious hand of patronage could strip command as suddenly as it was bestowed.

When I dug out his diaries from the Imperial War Museum, there were many other fascinating entries, not least on the very first page, where I was astonished to find that in the first paragraph he makes this remarkable statement: 'If . . . my son or grandson, or whoever is in possession of this story, thinks that its publication would be of interest, let him publish it by all means. The actors will be dead and no one's feelings will be hurt.' It is with great pride therefore that here for the first time we have taken General Snow at his word, and published his memoirs of the retreat from Mons and of 'Second Ypres'. I have been fortunate to have had the opportunity to work with Mark Pottle on this project, and we have both been struck by Snow's remarkably frank and candid recollections of events, and the extent to which my great-grandfather was prepared to acknowledge the limitations of the effectiveness of his command. One of the greatest limitations that he faced was in getting accurate information about what was happening on the battlefield, and so persistent was his frustration in this respect that we have made it the theme of the book. The 'confusion of command' is a phrase used by my great-grandfather quite specifically in connection with the failings of the higher commands at Second Ypres, but it has, we suggest, much broader relevance to the opening campaigns of the war on the Western Front; a theme that we expand upon in the short introduction that follows.

Snow was among the small number of men who held the rank of major-general and above on the Western Front. It would be hard to identify a more maligned group in British history. Yet recent scholarship is providing a fascinating antidote to the prevailing popular view of incompetent generals presiding over senseless slaughter. We are certainly not seeking to resurrect Snow's mediocre reputation; the fact that he was no Alexander does not trouble his descendants. Rather, our edition hopes to tell the story of the first part of the war through the experience of someone who is often, understandably, ignored. It perhaps sheds some light on the thinking of a man who was keenly aware of the challenges emanating from this new kind of warfare. Thomas D'Oyly Snow was frequently exposed to the realities of trench warfare, and he came close to be being killed or injured several times by enemy fire. Nor was he unaware of the shortcomings of himself and of the army that had become his life.

Dan Snow

EDITORIAL NOTE

The two memoirs presented here – 'A story of the doings of the 4th Division BEF from the date of mobilisation to the end of the retreat from Mons' and 'A narrative of the doings of the 27th Division from the date of formation to the end of its tour on the Western Front' – are verbatim reproductions of the originals in the Imperial War Museum (see Bibliography, below).

There are occasional references to both memoirs in histories of the First World War, but neither has been published in its entirety before. In writing them General Snow made use of two particular volumes of the official history of the war, which suggests that he composed them between 1927 and 1933. In his memoir of the 27th Division he refers to *Military Operations, France and Belgium, 1915. Volume I: Winter 1914– 1915: Battle of Neuve Chapelle: Battles of Ypres*, the work of Brigadier General Sir James E. Edmonds and Captain G. C. Wynne, which was published in 1927. And in his memoir of the 4th Division he refers to *Military Operations, France and Belgium, 1914. Volume I: Mons, the Retreat to the Seine, the Marne and the Aisne, August–October 1914*, compiled by Edmonds, which appeared in 1922. However, he does not refer to a revised third edition of the latter work, published in 1933, which he doubtless would have done had it been accessible. It may be that the appearance of the 1927 volume of the official history, covering as it does Second Ypres, was a catalyst, and that both accounts were written close to that date, although one cannot be certain of this.

Edmonds was General Snow's original GSO1 in France in August 1914 and the events relating to the 4th Division at Le Cateau, as well as to the 27th Division at Second Ypres, are especially well covered in the official history (i.e. *Military Operations . . .*), making that work a resource of incomparable value to the editors of the present volume; we would like to take this opportunity to acknowledge a heavy debt to Edmonds and his collaborators. The first of the two 1914 volumes of the official history was the only one in the series to be rewritten, and the passages dealing with events in which the 4th Division was involved were significantly revised. The net effect of the changes is to make that volume subtly but distinctly more critical of the higher commands, which is in keeping with the tenor of General Snow's own account.

In both his memoir of the retreat from Mons, and that of Second Ypres, General Snow's approach is determinedly objective. More is said on this in the Introduction that follows, but it should be noted here that there is a distinct difference between the critical tenor of these two narratives, written many years after the event, and the reassuring tone of the letters that he wrote home to his wife, Charlotte, during his time on the Western Front. The original letters have not survived, but at some stage handwritten excerpts from them were neatly copied in two leather-bound volumes, and these – entitled 'Letters from France' – have been deposited in the Imperial War Museum (see Bibliography).

A stock phrase in the letters is 'all goes well'. Like his old friend Sir Henry Wilson, Snow believed in staying cheerful, and keeping people's spirits up. When applied, however, to the opening days of the battle of the Somme in July 1916, or the German counter-offensive at Cambrai in November 1917, engagements from which Snow does not emerge with great credit, if with credit at all, such blandishments only expose the extent to which he edited his letters to save the feelings of loved ones at home. In this he was of course not exceptional: quite the opposite. It does mean, however, that to have included 'Letters from France' in the present volume would inevitably have detracted from the critical focus of the memoirs, and this we wished to avoid at all cost.

For much the same reason we discounted early on the idea of a biographical study. The book is not about General Snow. Rather, it is about his experiences during the first ten months of a war that defied all expectations. It examines in particular the difficulties that commanders at all levels faced in comprehending what was happening on the battlefield, and in then controlling events. Neither memoir is very long and we are conscious that our notes and appendices take up a substantial part of the book. We have tried, however, not to intrude upon General Snow, and our aim in our editorial commentary has been to develop one of the key themes of his memoirs: this is, as the title of the book suggests, the difficulty that he faced in penetrating the 'fog of war'.

A close comparison of General Snow's memoirs with the official history suggests that in some cases this fog had still not dissipated more than a decade after the events that are described, and readers are advised that these narratives were spontaneously written accounts, recreated largely from memory. Wherever possible the editors have clarified the points arising, but, rather than interrupt the flow of General Snow's short narratives with either footnotes or endnote cues, they have placed their comments in two appendices, one for each memoir: the notes are arranged by page number, but in addition each is prefaced by a short extract of the text to which it refers, allowing the context to be more readily understood. Editorial commentary is also to be found in a series of appendices, in addition to two chronologies, a glossary, and biographical notes – all intended to assist the reader and, wherever possible, illustrate the theme of the 'confusion of command'. Small errors in the text have been silently corrected: for example, the spelling of place names; '9.00 a.m.' for '8.00 a.m.', and so on. General Snow was inconsistent in his use of accents in French place names, and we have standardised this. We have also divided each memoir into several parts, and supplied a heading for each part, in order to make the structure clearer.

Acknowledgements

In addition to our friends and families, we would like to thank: the staff at the Bodleian Library, Oxford; the Imperial War Museum; the National Archives; Wolfson College, Oxford. Rod Suddaby and Simon Offord at the Imperial War Museum greatly assisted us by making the text freely available; a tremendous asset. We should also like to thank Richard Kemp at the Somerset Military Museum, and Paul Reed for their help. Dr Michael Brock and Professor Jon Stallworthy both offered invaluable advice. Finally, we would like to thank our expert publishers at Frontline Books, Michael Leventhal and Deborah Hercun.

Dan Snow and Mark Pottle

INTRODUCTION

Presented here are first-hand accounts of the retreat from Mons and the battles of Second Ypres, written from the perspective of a divisional commander who was at the centre of events.

Lieutenant General Sir Thomas D'Oyly Snow was born in 1858, the eldest son of a Dorset clergyman. He was educated at Eton and St John's College, Cambridge, and joined the army in 1879 when he gained a commission in the Somerset Light Infantry. The regiment was then in South Africa, and he saw action that year as a twenty-one-year-old in the Anglo-Zulu War. In January 1885, when still only twenty-six, he was severely wounded during the Nile Campaign while serving with the camel corps of mounted infantry. After attending Staff College in 1892–3, he became a brigade major at Aldershot, and in 1897 was promoted major in the Royal Inniskilling Fusiliers. The same year he married Charlotte Geraldine Coke, the daughter of a major-general; they had two sons and two daughters. Snow served as a brigade major during the Nile campaign of 1898, and in April 1899 became second in command of the 2nd Battalion, the Northamptonshire Regiment, which was then in India. He thus missed the second South African War (the Boer War), 1899–1902, which proved to be an important learning ground as well as a route to career advancement for many of his peers. He returned to England in March 1903, was promoted colonel and became assistant quartermaster general of the Eastern Command. In 1909 he was given command of the 11th Brigade, which had its headquarters at Colchester, and the next year was promoted major-general. In 1911 he was made commander of the 4th Division, and it was this post that he held at the outbreak of war on 4 August 1914. He was then fifty-six years of age and, by all accounts, a formidable man, standing six feet four inches tall and with a reputation for irascibility.

The 4th Division was one of the six regular divisions – there was also a cavalry division – of the 'Expeditionary Force' that was a product of R. B. Haldane's Edwardian army reforms. In theory this force might be dispatched to any part of the empire in answer to a crisis, but a succession of planners at the War Office – most notably Major-General Henry Wilson, director of military operations, 1910–14 – worked on the basis that it would be deployed on the Continent to defend France against a German invasion. With his French counterparts, Wilson devised a plan for British intervention so detailed that it included timetables for embarkation and the provision of rations en route. Wilson concurred with French thinking that a British Expeditionary Force (BEF) would be ideally deployed in extending the French left wing along the Franco-Belgian border; a strategy that necessitated a concentration of British forces around Maubeuge. But while Wilson's pre-war planning undoubtedly raised French expectations, it did not commit the British government, and considerable uncertainty surrounded the deployment of the BEF immediately after the declaration of war. The decision to send it to France was taken by the cabinet on the morning of 6 August, with 'much less demur' than the prime minister had anticipated, after the wheels had been set in motion at a meeting of the War Council the previous day.[1] Four of the six regular divisions, organised into two corps, were to be dispatched at once, alongside the cavalry division.[2] The decision to retain two divisions at home reflected fears of civil disorder as well as invasion, but these considerations were quickly overshadowed by the scale of the European conflict. The Germans mobilised 1,077 battalions in the west, the French 1,107, and the Belgians 120. The British fielded 48.

---

1   H. H. Asquith to Venetia Stanley, 6 August 1914, Michael Brock Eleanor Brock (eds), *H. H. Asquith: Letters to Venetia Stanley* (Oxford, 1985; hereafter *Asquith–Stanley*), p. 158.

2   The original BEF sent to France consisted of one cavalry division, accompanied by an extra cavalry brigade, and four of the six infantry divisions: the 1st, 2nd, 3rd, and 5th. It was intended that the 4th Division was to follow at a later date, while the 6th would remain at home on garrison duty.

The British Expeditionary Force in August 1914

The BEF has been described, by one who knew it well, and felt great loyalty towards it, as 'incomparably the best trained, best organised, and best equipped British Army which ever went forth to war'.[3] In numerical terms, however, as the author of this assessment himself conceded, it was 'almost negligible' when compared with the continental armies, while in 'heavy guns and howitzers, high-explosive shell, trench mortars, hand-grenades, and much of the subsidiary material required for siege and trench warfare, it was almost wholly deficient'. Its limited capabilities on the eve of war stand in marked contrast to the fighting capacity of the Royal Navy, and, given the potential at least of a continental military commitment in the years before 1914, this betrays an almost catastrophic failure of planning on the part of the greatest industrial power of the age.[4]

The commanders of the BEF did have more combat experience than their German counterparts. The Boer War in particular had seen many of them (although not Snow) enjoy independent command – albeit in a highly mobile context that was the antithesis of most of the fighting in France and Belgium in 1914–18. The tiny army that they led, however, was unused to large-scale operations. The challenges of the 'firepower revolution' had produced a doctrine of the offensive: breeding and indoctrination, it was expected, would see units march through the expected firestorm on the battlefield. As a result, there had been little development of all-arms co-operation, and insufficient thought given to the collaboration of infantry, artillery and machine guns. Gunners were only allowed one week

---

3   The view of Brigadier General J. E. Edmonds, director of the official history of the war, and cited in: *Military Operations France and Belgium, 1914*, 3rd edn (London, 1933; hereafter *MO, 1914*, v. 1), pp. 10–11.

4   'The British general staff had entered on a continental commitment without a continental army. Henry Wilson recognised this point, privately reckoning that six divisions were probably "fifty too few". Wilson was therefore an ardent conscriptionist', Hew Strachan, *The First World War: Volume I: To Arms* (Oxford, 2003), p. 200.

of live firing a year, and exercises, even at brigade level, were all too infrequent. The BEF marched towards contact without a single anti-aircraft gun and far too few shells; what little they had were overwhelmingly of the less effective shrapnel variety rather than high explosive. Worryingly, around half of the BEF were reservists recalled to the colours following the outbreak of war. Many were unfit. The 1st Somerset Light Infantry under General Snow's command spent the period of 10–15 August field training and route marching in a desperate attempt to harden the men up and to reacquaint them with their fieldcraft.[5] One subaltern in the 1st East Lancashires, Lieutenant Hopkinson, doubtless spoke for his colleagues when he said that 'it was a novelty to handle companies and platoons at war strength'.[6] Yet within a few weeks of leaving civilian life to rejoin their regiments these reservists were fighting at Mons, their many hardships during the marathon of the subsequent retreat made worse by the discomfort of boots that had not been worn in.

There were also sharp personality differences in the higher command echelons of the army, which did little to promote cohesion. Sir James Grierson, GOC II. Corps, who was something of a bon viveur, died of a heart attack within days of arriving in France, and the question of his replacement uncovered a major fault line in the BEF. The Commander-in-Chief, Sir John French, wanted the cautious and dependable Herbert Plumer, but Lord Kitchener – who enjoyed a poor relationship with French dating back to the Boer War – sent him Sir Horace Smith-Dorrien instead. Smith-Dorrien and French feuded; a fact well known to Kitchener who, in his interview with Smith-Dorrien prior to his appointment, 'expressed grave doubt as to whether he was wise' to select him.[7] He went ahead nevertheless. Not only did Smith-Dorrien and French have starkly contrasting private lives – the former being a deeply serious,

---

5   Somerset Light Infantry War Diary, August 1914, PRO WO/95/1499, p. 73.

6   E. C. Hopkinson, *Spectamur Agendo* (privately printed, 1926), p. 2.

7   H. Smith-Dorrien, *Memories of Forty-Eight Years' Service* (London, 1925), p. 375.

uxorious man, and the latter a garrulous, charismatic womaniser – but there were also profound professional disagreements. Smith-Dorrien had succeeded French as the commanding officer of the prestigious Aldershot Command, where he proceeded to force unwelcome change on Sir John's beloved cavalry. Where French had clung to a belief in the utility of knee-to-knee massed cavalry charges, pressed home with cold steel, Smith-Dorrien emphasised the cavalrymen's role as mobile infantry, training them to dismount and fight as riflemen.

The commander of I. Corps, Sir Douglas Haig, a dour, religious man so prone to shyness that he came across as rude, shared French's conviction about the continued importance to offensive operations of mounted troops, and was particularly close to the Commander-in-Chief. He had succeeded Smith-Dorrien at Aldershot, and had reversed some of his reforms. Haig had, however, his own concerns about his old friend and superior, Sir John French. He wrote in his diary on 11 August 1914: 'In my own heart, I know that French is quite unfit for this great Command at a time of crisis in our Nation's History. But I thought it sufficient to tell the King that I had "doubts" about the selection.'[8] Within days of being in France Haig had 'unburdened' himself to his aide-de-camp, John Charteris, who observed: 'He is greatly concerned about the composition of British G.H.Q.'[9] In due course Haig 'steadily undermined' his chief, eventually replacing him in December 1915.[10]

The Battle of Mons and the Beginning of the Retreat

The final destination of the BEF was not decided until 12 August, when Asquith ruled against the more rearward position at Amiens in favour of Maubeuge. By this date the embarkation of the original force

8   Quoted in Gary Sheffield and John Bourne (eds), *Douglas Haig: War Diaries and Letters, 1914–1919* (London, 2005), p. 56.

9   John Charteris, *At G.H.Q.* (London, 1931), p. 10.

10   I. F. W. Beckett, 'Sir John French', *Oxford Dictionary of National Biography* (Oxford, 2004).

had already begun. It crossed the Channel on 9–17 August, and by the 20th had virtually completed its concentration around Maubeuge. Thereafter it advanced north, making first contact with the enemy north-east of Mons at dawn on 22 August. Ironically, the massive thrust of the German *First* and *Second armies*[11] through neutral Belgium both guaranteed British involvement in the war and ensured that the BEF would be at the very focal point of their attempt to outflank the French. Although the BEF made up only a fraction of the Allied force, it played a pivotal role in holding the flank of the five French armies to the south, helping to save them from encirclement.

The logic of this situation meant, however, that the BEF was itself exposed on its flanks. Kitchener's prescient fears that 'the Germans are coming north of the Meuse in great force, and will swamp us before we concentrate', were not shared by his colleagues, notably Henry Wilson, who underestimated the strength of the enemy, and consequently encouraged a sense of undue optimism in his chief, Sir John French.[12] Wilson was doubtless influenced by the French staff, which had discounted the possibility of the Germans advancing through Belgium in force. When the British advanced towards Mons, on 22 August, they unwittingly marched towards extreme danger, with '700,000 Germans moving against them through central Belgium, and no French first-line infantry division north of the Sambre'.[13] Luckily, the German *First Army* was ignorant of the location of the BEF, and as late as 20 August the German supreme command believed that the British had not yet arrived in France in any numbers. On the morning of Sunday 23 August the commander of the *First Army*, General von Kluck, was so uncertain as to the BEF's whereabouts that he stopped his army for two hours and prepared to march westwards, in the wrong direction, in search of it. Even as his army paused, its advanced guards ran into the British on the Mons–Condé canal.

---

11 German units are italicised to avoid confusion.
12 Kitchener's fears, as summarised by Wilson, in *Asquith–Stanley*, p. 156.
13 Ibid.

The BEF had taken up positions on an angled front roughly twenty-seven miles long, west and south-east of Mons. On the extreme left, at Condé, was the newly formed 19th Infantry Brigade, in touch with the French 84th Territorial Division on its left. II. Corps entrenched along the canal line from Condé eastwards, covering also a salient where the canal kicked north and then east at Mons. To the south-east of this salient I. Corps took up the line, its defences ending at Grand Reng. There was then a large gap between I. Corp's right and the left of Lanrezac's Fifth Army, while just three French territorial divisions covered the expanse from Condé to coast. Around 9 a.m. on 23 August, German artillery opened fire on II. Corps from the high ground north of the canal, the attack spreading westwards towards Condé. The highest casualties on the British side were sustained by 3rd Division in the salient, and overall II. Corps' losses greatly outnumbered those of I. Corps, which was scarcely involved in the battle. The British were outnumbered by nearly three to one at Mons, and were heavily outgunned, but were not defeated, proving adept at the difficult art of the fighting withdrawal, a tactic much studied before the war. Although forced to retire, the BEF reformed on a defensive line some three miles in the rear, and was ready to fight again the next day – as, indeed, the Commander-in-Chief intended. The continued retirement of General Lanrezac's Fifth Army on his right, however, convinced him of the necessity of withdrawal, and in the early hours of Monday 24 August he began the retreat that ended on the Marne thirteen exhausting days later.

The 4th Division had embarked for France on the 22nd, arriving too late for the battle of Mons on the 23rd, but in time to cover the retreat of Smith-Dorrien's force south towards Le Cateau on the 25th. During that day II. Corps had become separated from I. Corps. The latter were travelling, for logistical reasons, down the eastern side of the extensive Forêt de Mormal, while Smith-Dorrien's force took the Roman road on the west. That night, while the troops of II. Corps either rested at, or were en route to, positions south of the Le Cateau–Cambrai road, those of I. Corps were bivouacked around Landrecies to the east, more than twelve miles away. II. Corps' losses on the previous day, Monday 24th, had been even greater than those at Mons on the 23rd, with the 5th Division this time bearing the brunt. The protective arm extended by the 4th Division, from its positions on the high ground around Solesmes, just north of Le Cateau, was therefore especially welcome. The division, though, was under strength, having been obliged to take the field without its 'divisional cavalry, cyclists, heavy battery, engineers, the greater part of its signal company, train, ammunition column and field ambulances'.[14] As will be seen below, these were important units, especially in the conduct of any rearguard operation.

The three brigades of the 4th Division remained at Solesmes until late in the evening of 25 August, and only when all of the retiring troops had passed through did they move back to Le Cateau. Initially the Commander-in-Chief, Sir John French, had meant to defend this position, with II. Corps on the left and I. Corps on the right – the town of Le Cateau being roughly the junction between them. The further retirement of the French armies on the right and the strength of the enemy forces in front, however, persuaded him otherwise, and at 7.30 p.m. on the 25th he issued orders to all units to continue the retirement. There would be an overnight pause at Le Cateau, but no stand.

The Battle of Le Cateau

At 2 a.m. the following morning, 26 August, this scenario changed dramatically. Smith-Dorrien came to the conclusion that he had no option other than to stand and fight. He later identified seven reasons for this controversial decision, but they can be summarised by an aside to one of his aides just as the battle was breaking: 'he remarked that the enemy was in such strength that he knew that he [the enemy] would force him to fight at daylight, and that he preferred to fight him in position and try to break away after giving him a good hard knock,

---

14 *MO, 1914*, v. 1, pp. 147–8 and notes.

than that he [the enemy] should attack him with his back turned.'[15] Smith-Dorrien asked General Snow to act under him, and the latter assented, as Smith-Dorrien must have known he would. Snow, however, did not receive Smith-Dorrien's request until after 5 a.m., and by the time he warned his brigades of the impending battle some of them were already under attack from the advance guards of the German columns sweeping down from the north-west.

At around the time that General Snow learnt of Smith-Dorrien's decision GHQ also received the news: a written reply was prepared, but was not sent until 11.05 a.m., a telephone connection being established around 6.30 a.m. At one end of this line, representing GHQ, was Henry Wilson, and at the other end was the commander of II. Corps, Smith-Dorrien, who later recalled: '[Wilson] had a message to give me from the Chief to the effect that I should break off the action as soon as possible. I replied that I would endeavour to do so, but that it would be difficult, and that I had hoped to be able to hold on until evening and slip away in the dark.'[16] According to one eye-witness, Smith-Dorrien explained that 'it was impossible to break away now as the action had already begun, and that he could hear the guns firing as he spoke.'[17] Smith-Dorrien was lifted by his comrade's parting words – 'Good luck to you; yours is the first cheerful voice I have heard for three days' – but privately Wilson was pessimistic about II. Corps' chances, remarking to a junior staff officer at GHQ, '"Smith-Doreen" was in the devil of a hole.'[18] That evening the French liaison officer at GHQ gained the impression that II. Corps had been given up as lost – 'Bataille perdue par armée anglaise,' he signalled his headquarters;[19] a telling comment on the mindset of the Commander-in-Chief, as well

---

15 For Smith-Dorrien's reasons see *Forty-Eight Years*, p. 401. The aide was Brigadier General A. Hildebrand, OC II. Corps' Signal Company: see *Army Quarterly*, vol. XXI, no. 1, October 1930, p. 18.

16 Smith-Dorrien, *Forty-Eight Years*, p. 405.

17 *Army Quarterly*, vol. XXI, no. 1, October 1930, p. 17.

18 C. E. Callwell, *Field-Marshal Sir Henry Wilson: His Life and Diaries* (London, 1927), p. 169.

19 The officer was Colonel Huguet: *MO, 1914*, v. 1, p. 201.

as on the quality of staff work at GHQ, which during the day had lost contact with the battlefield.

Smith-Dorrien clearly understood the risks that he was running at Le Cateau and had implored Wilson to dissuade the Commander-in-Chief from coming up to the battle zone because of the danger of encirclement by the enemy. The British line at Le Cateau, as at Mons, hung with its flanks in the air. It stretched from the town westwards towards Caudry, and thence to Esnes, the most westerly point, a distance of about twelve miles. On the extreme right was the 5th Division; in the middle the 3rd Division; and on the left the 4th Division. The 19th Infantry Brigade was in reserve, while the Cavalry Division offered what protection it could to the flanks. For his part, General Snow deployed the 4th Division along an outpost line between Caudry and Wambaix, with the 11th Brigade on the right, the 12th Brigade on the left, and the 10th Brigade in reserve at Haucourt. Even establishing this deployment proved difficult, and the 1st Somerset Light Infantry changed position three times on the eve of the battle, the battalion's commanding officer only being satisfied with its final position at 04.00 hours on the 26th.[20]

Soon after 6 a.m. German artillery opened fire at both ends of the line. On the right the 14th Brigade (5th Division) suffered heavily around Le Cateau, while on the left 12th Brigade was hit particularly hard before Longsart as the enemy tried to find a way around. By mid-morning this flanking movement had been contained, although the 4th Division had been placed under great pressure. The British received a brutal lesson in the use of artillery at Le Cateau. The accuracy of the German counter-battery fire astounded the British troops, who were helpless witnesses to the suffering of their own artillerymen. German aircraft dropped metallic streamers above British batteries, and within seconds a hail of high-explosive shells upended the guns and annihilated the gunners. The battle straddled two different epochs of warfare. Machine guns fired thousands of

---

20 Somerset Light Infantry War Diary August 1914, PRO WO/95/1499, p. 79.

rounds a minute and aircraft circled over the battle, yet there was at least one massed German cavalry charge, and Snow, like the other divisional and brigade commanders, rode across the battlefield in view of the enemy. Of great significance for the future, however, was the decisiveness of the artillery: it was the German gunners rather than the infantry that compelled the British to withdraw.

After midday the position of the 5th Division on the right became untenable and, although General Snow was confident of holding his ground, on the left, Smith-Dorrien took the desperate step of ordering a daylight withdrawal. He later recalled: 'The [5th] Division had stood to the limit of human endurance, and I recognised that the moment had arrived when our retirement should commence.'[21] Although the order for a retirement, beginning with the 5th Division and working west, was thus issued around 2 p.m., it was a considerable time before front-line units received it. The troops on the ground had a deeply confusing day. Orders to retreat were countermanded with instructions to hold ground, while for some units there was just a baffling silence. According to the official history: 'There can be little doubt that the comparative ease with which the first stages of the retreat were accomplished was due to the tenacity of the units which, having received no order to retire, clung with all their strength to the positions they had been ordered to hold.' It is estimated that fewer than a thousand men were involved in these rearguard actions, but they were sufficient to keep the enemy at bay, as evidenced by the German shelling that night of positions that had long been vacated.[22] British losses were 7,812 of all ranks – 40 per cent of those among the 4th Division. A surprise attack on the 1st King's Own soon after dawn contributed to these disproportionately high losses, as did the division's lack of field ambulance units, which meant that it had 'very limited means of attending to wounded, [and] no means of removing them'.[23]

---

21 Smith-Dorrien, *Forty-Eight Years*, p. 406.

22 *MO, 1914*, v. 1, pp. 188, 194.

23 *MO, 1914*, v. 1, p. 148; for British losses at Le Cateau see below, Appendix 5, p. 160.

Much has been made of Smith-Dorrien's decision to fight at Le Cateau, and of the consequences of that action. By delaying the German armies it bought vital time for the French to prepare for their great counterattack later on the Marne, and it may also have saved the BEF from being overtaken by the pursuing German columns, and badly mauled or even annihilated. Smith-Dorrien gave the enemy the 'good hard knock' that he had intended, and the BEF was able to march south to the Marne and regroup. This, however, was not how the battle was seen by either the Germans or GHQ. The former regarded it as a battle lost by the British, who had been forced to retreat from the battlefield mid-afternoon. The Commander-in-Chief, for his part, though at first fulsome in his praise of Smith-Dorrien, later castigated him for an action that, as he alleged, had imperilled the BEF, and been so costly in men and equipment as to severely damage the fighting capacity of II. Corps.[24] And Haig, whose I. Corps had escaped the fighting at Le Cateau after becoming separated from II. Corps on 25 August, agreed. In mid-September his aide-de-camp Charteris observed: 'D.H. is very critical of the 2nd Corps. He still thinks Smith-Dorrien should not have fought at Le Cateau, and believes that the Corps could have disengaged from there without fighting'.[25]

Smith-Dorrien undeniably evinced on the 26th the quality that Napoleon allegedly most sought in his generals: 'He was', it has recently been observed, 'extraordinarily lucky'.[26] After Mons poor German intelligence had led the *First Army* south-west in pursuit of the British instead of south, and at dawn on the 26th von Kluck

---

24 For contradictory first-hand impressions of the effect of Le Cateau on the morale of II. Corps, see Tom Bridges, *Alarms and Excursions: Reminiscences of a Soldier* (London, 1938), p. 80: 'Only soldiers know how long it takes units to efface the memory of such demoralisation and to regain their full fighting value . . .' and C. Ballard, *Smith-Dorrien* (London, 1931), p. 186: 'The next three weeks, however, proved that [II. Corps] was far from being shattered; without a rest it went on for over 200 miles and fought in two big battles.' For the German view see Kuhl, *RUSI*, 66:462, pp. 300–1.

25 Charteris, p. 36.

26 Strachan, p. 223.

only managed to deploy two of the nine infantry divisions that were available to him, though his force grew in strength as the day progressed. After the battle he again lost the scent, tracking south-west while Smith-Dorrien's force marched southwards largely unhindered. At 5.45 a.m. on the 27th Brigadier General Haldane, GOC 10th Brigade, realised that he had fallen as much as seven hours behind the main column of the 4th Division, which had marched through the night while he – uncertain of his orders – had stopped; yet in making up time that day his composite battalion of 1st Royal Irish Fusiliers and 2nd Seaforth Highlanders did not see 'a single German infantryman' in pursuit.[27] One of the reasons that the enemy lost touch was because of the action of the British rearguards, and it was here, perhaps, that Smith-Dorrien had his greatest luck, if such it can be called, given the sacrifice that was involved: the failure to communicate effectively the order to retire to all of the front-line troops at Le Cateau ensured that some of them fought to the finish, enabling their comrades to walk away in daylight.

General Snow was in no doubt about the correctness of Smith-Dorrien's decision to fight on the 26th, and in the memoir presented here he effectively takes issue with Sir John French's interpretation of events. The feud between French and Smith-Dorrien has been extensively reviewed over the years, and the balance of opinion now sits firmly in Smith-Dorrien's favour. Viewed from General Snow's perspective, one can see how limited Smith-Dorrien's options were. According to GHQ, the plan for a retreat from Le Cateau entailed the 4th Division acting as a rearguard, allowing II. Corps to retire in safety.[28] If this was ever GHQ's rationale, it shows how incoherent its planning became during the retreat. In retiring from Solesmes, the 4th Division ceded to the enemy the high ground that it was essential to retain in order to cover a general retirement. And, as General Snow makes clear, the 4th Division was lacking units that were vital to any such rearguard action – notably its signals and divisional cavalry.

---

27 Aylmer Haldane, *A Brigade of the Old Army, 1914* (London, 1920), p. 36.
28 See below, p. 29.

It seems fanciful to imagine that the division, under-strength and isolated, could have held off the weight of the German infantry and artillery for very long. After the war the 4th Division held an annual dinner that Smith-Dorrien attended every year until he died. At Smith-Dorrien's first appearance General Snow 'thanked him on behalf of the members of the division for saving them from death or captivity on the 26th August 1914'.[29] Had the 4th Division been sacrificed for II. Corps, it is far from certain that this would have put an end to von Kluck's close pursuit of the BEF – which, notwithstanding the heavy losses, is what Smith-Dorrien's 'stopping blow' effectively achieved.

General Snow conveys vividly the confusion of the British withdrawal from the battlefield, and the tortuous sleeplessness of the next eleven days, during which Smith-Dorrien's force travelled south towards the Marne, marching on average a minimum of fourteen miles a day. Although its safety was never seriously imperilled, the retreat was anything but uneventful, as the sad episode of the 'Colonels' Surrender' at St Quentin on 27 August illustrates.[30] 'The Retreat' ranks among the great achievements of British armies in the field, and General Snow's account ends with its conclusion at the Marne on 5 September. Such was the fatigue of man and beast by this point, however, that when General Snow's horse fell five days later, he fell with it. He made light of his injuries, but an x-ray revealed a fractured pelvis, and in the middle of October he was sent back to England to recuperate. In the meantime he lost the command of the division that he had prepared for war, and led into battle.

The 27th Division and Second Ypres

At home General Snow was given almost no time to mend. In mid-November he was appointed GOC of the 27th Division, which comprised regular troops from overseas garrisons recalled to Britain after the outbreak of war. Those troops not absorbed into the 27th

---

29 *MO, 1914*, v. 1, p. 192, n. 1.
30 This is described in some detail by General Snow: see below, pp. 44–6.

joined the 28th, the next division to be formed, and both were much needed at the front. In the four-week interval between General Snow returning to England and being given his new command the Germans were repulsed at 'First Ypres', a momentous battle fought by all of the Allies in the west – Belgians and French, as well as British – but which has been described as the 'chief glory' of the original BEF, and the reason why it 'practically ceased to exist'.[31] By the end of 1914 the British army in the field had lost the equivalent of 80 per cent of its original strength. Of the twenty-seven officers of the 1st East Lancashires (11th Brigade), eighteen were casualties by the end of the year, including all of those above the rank of lieutenant.[32]

The British had arrived around Ypres, in Belgium, in the first half of October, when, with French agreement, they had moved north from the Aisne valley, where they had dug in at the end of the Marne offensive. In Flanders the BEF would be closer to the Channel ports that were its means of supply, and it would also be easier to absorb reinforcements as they arrived at the coast. On 7 October the 7th Division and 3rd Cavalry Division disembarked at Ostend and Zeebrugge; by the middle of the month they had moved south-west to Ypres after Antwerp, their original destination, fell to the enemy on 9 October. There was thus a fluid concentration of British forces around Ypres and south to La Bassée by the middle of the month, at the same time as the fall of Antwerp released German forces bent on breaking through towards Calais and the coast. The tremendous battle that was joined around Ypres from mid-October finally ended with the failure of the German attack between Messines and the Menin road on 11 November. The route to the Channel ports had been barred, but at a high cost: the 7th Division had arrived in Belgium with nearly 18,000 men, but was taken out of the line on 5 November with less than a half of this number, and less than one-third of its infantry. In addition, the front line around Ypres now bulged in a pronounced salient that was difficult to defend, supply and reinforce.

---

31 C. R. M. F. Cruttwell, *History of the Great War* (Oxford, 1934), p. 106.
32 Hopkinson, p. 4.

The British losses at Ypres were so great that General Snow and his new division were pressed into service before either was properly ready. They arrived in France on 23 December, and for General Snow the contrast with the battlefield of September could not have been more dramatic. Instead of freshly harvested fields there were water-logged trenches, and where armies had marched and counter-marched he now beheld siege warfare on an industrial scale. In his absence the BEF had expanded to eleven infantry and five cavalry divisions, and on Boxing Day it was reorganised into two armies: First Army under Haig, and Second Army under Smith-Dorrien. The 27th Division was assigned to the latter, and, with the 28th Division, and later the Canadian Division, formed V. Corps under General Plumer. In April this corps took over around three-quarters of the Ypres salient in a further extension of the British line northwards.

Plumer's corps came into the salient just before the Second Battle of Ypres, which began on 22 April. It is, by common consent, a complex affair, as is indicated by the official nomenclature, which treats it not as a single engagement, but rather as four, collectively known as the 'Battles of Ypres 1915'.[33] For the purposes of abbreviation and simplicity these four battles are here referred to collectively as 'Second Ypres', and viewed in three distinct phases. In the first, from 22 to 28 April, the British and French unsuccessfully tried to restore the four and a half miles of front in the north of the salient that had collapsed when French troops fled following the gas attack of 22 April. The second phase, from 28 April to 3 May, covers the period when the British troops in the salient, now under the overall command of General Plumer, prepared and executed, after several delays, a retirement to a much-shortened line, which had been advocated by Plumer's predecessor, Smith-Dorrien. The third and final phase, from 4 to 25 May, saw the British attempt to defend their now shortened line against the continued assaults of the enemy.[34]

---

33 They are Gravenstafel Ridge, 22–23 April; St Julien, 24 April–4 May; Frezenberg Ridge, 8–13 May; and Bellewaarde Ridge, 24–25 May.

34 The tripartite division is Cruttwell's, pp. 156–7.

General Snow's account of the battle treats the period 22 April to 3 May, i.e. the first and second of these phases, in great depth, but the third hardly at all. The reason perhaps is that with the shortening of the line on 3 May his headquarters moved out of the salient to a position west of Ypres, and from that point onwards he was less in touch with events. His account begins with a description of the gas attack of 22 April, the first occasion on which gas was used in the west, and the disturbing effects of which he witnessed from his headquarters at Potijze directly to the south. Many pages of his narrative are devoted to the events of the next forty-eight hours, when frantic efforts were made by the British and Canadians to seal the large gap that had opened up in the line held by the French. Among the ironies of Second Ypres are the facts that the Allies had some foreknowledge that a gas attack was planned by the enemy, but took no real steps to guard against it, while the Germans had what they hoped would be a war-winning weapon, and yet were not in a position to exploit it.[35] For several hours after the gas attack, while there was still daylight, Ypres lay exposed, but the German infantry did not take advantage of this opportunity, allowing the Canadians and British to improvise a precarious defensive line under cover of darkness. By the following night, 23/24 April, all available reserves had been thrown forward in an effort to defend this line, although the original front was not to be restored.

General Snow was convinced early on of the logic of shortening the line at Ypres after the events of the 22nd. He regarded as futile the many counterattacks that were launched, particularly those planned in co-operation with the French, who protested their determination to recover their line, but never made a really effective attempt to do so. In his opinion the inability of the British to provide artillery cover for their attacks, because of a shortage of guns as well as ammunition, should have precluded many of the operations that took place. That they were not prevented from happening was due both to

---

35 For an explanation of these ironies see Notes to Part Two below, p. 123 (gas warnings), and p. 125 (exploitation).

the Commander-in-Chief's susceptibility to pressure from General Foch, and his own misplaced sense of optimism. In this context Smith-Dorrien's pragmatic advocacy of a tactical withdrawal was an unwelcome intrusion, and gave Sir John French the grounds that he sought to bring his feud against the commander of Second Army to its bitter conclusion. On 27 April Smith-Dorrien wrote to his chief that, unless the French were going to make a 'big push' to recover their line, the British should reduce theirs, falling back to a front drawn closer to Ypres. Sir John French's Chief of Staff responded on his behalf: 'Chief does not regard situation nearly so unfavourable as your letter represents. He thinks you have abundance of troops and especially notes the large reserves you have. He wishes you to act vigorously with the full means available in co-operating with and assisting the French attack . . .'[36] Later that day the Commander-in-Chief instructed Smith-Dorrien to hand command of all troops engaged in the defence of Ypres to his subordinate, General Plumer. This effectively reduced Smith-Dorrien to the status of a corps commander, and on the evening of 6 May he was ordered to hand over command of the Second Army to Plumer and return to England the next day.

These events are the subtext of General Snow's account of Second Ypres, which reaches its effective conclusion with the retirement of the British and Canadian forces to a reduced line on 3 May: a strategy that Smith-Dorrien had advocated, but which Plumer executed, and to which the Commander-in-Chief shamelessly assented. Snow offers no comment on Sir John French's treatment of Smith-Dorrien, and throughout this account, and that of the retreat, he mostly eschews direct criticism of individuals – although in his frustration with the course of events he sometimes implied as much. The Germans demonstrated at Second Ypres their mastery of siege warfare, and their foresight in harnessing modern technology to military ends. It was, as one British commander described it, a case of 'rifles against heavy

---

36 *Military Operations, France and Belgium, 1915. Volume I: Winter 1914–1915: Battle of Neuve Chapelle: Battles of Ypres*, (London, 1927; hereafter *MO, 1915*, v. 1), pp. 400–2.

guns'. General Snow's account amply illustrates this. It also reaffirms, however, the supreme importance of the human spirit in war, which alone explains the doggedness and ultimately the success of the British resistance at Second Ypres.[37] For his handling of the 27th Division in the salient, General Snow was appointed KCB, gazetted on 23 June, and given command of VII. Corps, which he led for the remainder of his time on the Western Front. Controversy surrounds his role in the Somme offensive, and in the German counter-offensive at Cambrai in November 1917, after which he requested to be relieved of his command. He returned to England on 4 January 1918, becoming GOC of the Western Command, and finally retired from the army in September 1919, by which time he was increasingly lame.

The 'Confusion of Command'

Sitting in his headquarters at Potijze in the heart of the salient during a particularly heavy bombardment at the height of Second Ypres, his dug-out rocking 'like a ship in a storm', General Snow experienced at first hand the devastating fire power of the German artillery. Against this the British had no answer, and General Snow's account is entirely candid about such failings. He even drew up a list of 'certain points which are to be regretted' – the understatement is characteristic of him – at the top of which he placed: 'The confusion of command'. This can be briefly summarised as a breakdown in the chain of command. Throughout Second Ypres the headquarters of two of the three divisions fighting in the salient were located some way west of the town. Because telephone wires and signals cables were constantly being cut by enemy artillery, these two headquarters were frequently out of touch with the front. General Snow, by contrast, kept his headquarters in the salient and close to the front lines, and because he was the senior officer on the spot, brigades and battalions that were

---

37 When the term 'British' is used here in respect of Second Ypres, 'Canadian' is also generally implied, for the troops of that country were in the thick of the fighting from the start to the finish.

not his frequently looked to him for command. He had in fact been authorised by General Plumer to assume such a role, but this did not prevent the divisional commanders west of Ypres from issuing their own instructions. Wires inevitably became crossed.

This straightforward breakdown in the chain of command was further complicated by the extreme measures that had to be taken by the British and Canadians to bridge the large gap in the line north of Ypres after 22 April. Battalions were thrown into the breach as they became available, irrespective of where their own divisional and brigade headquarters might be. To provide some semblance of order, ad hoc commands were created, but often without the staffs necessary to function properly. In General Snow's opinion this multiplicity of commands was not conducive to co-ordinated action. In the operation known as 'Hull's Attack' on 25 April, fifteen battalions (from six divisions) were assigned to Brigadier General C. P. A. Hull, commander of the 10th Infantry Brigade. Hull thus had the combined strength of more than a division, but only the staff of a brigade, and neither a signals company nor divisional troops. Tellingly, at zero hour only five of his fifteen battalions were ready to advance, and these were all from his own brigade. His 'magnificent but hopeless attempt' on the German lines went ahead with one-third of its planned strength.[38]

'The confusion of command' was thus used narrowly by General Snow in the specific senses outlined above: the chain of command broke, either because commanders were not on the spot, or because ad hoc commands were created alongside existing ones. Interpreted more broadly, however, in the sense of a breakdown in *communication*, it is a theme that runs through the pages of both of the memoirs presented here. Each illustrates the difficulty that commanders at all levels faced in influencing events positively, owing to a lack of accurate and up-to-date information coming from the battlefield, as well as a difficulty in getting orders to the relevant parties in time to have the desired effect. At Ypres, one of the principal reasons for this was the power

---

38 *MO, 1915*, v. 1, pp. 242–3

and persistence of the German shelling, which cut communications cables and killed or wounded the runners. In consequence, the flow of information to headquarters and of instructions to the battlefield was very frequently impeded.

During the retreat from Mons this same difficulty — of confusion arising from breaks in the reciprocal flow of information — was encountered, but largely for different reasons. Here the distances between units, and the fact that they were frequently moving, clouded the picture. The total loss of contact between I. and II. Corps on 25 August as they travelled south along opposite sides of the Forêt de Mormal offers an example. Smith-Dorrien appears to have believed, as a result, that I. Corps was in more danger than was actually the case, and that he must protect its flank; while Haig marched south early on the 26th not having been informed by GHQ of the grave danger that II. Corps faced. At Le Cateau General Snow had cause to complain about the lack of information given to him by II. Corps headquarters and GHQ, but the lines of communication between these two centres were poor, and between the two corps headquarters they were virtually non-existent.

Sir Horace Smith-Dorrien later recalled the confused picture before him on the eve of Le Cateau:

> It will be difficult for any reader to realise the fog of war which surrounded us that night. Communication was most difficult, and although the Corps signallers . . . performed miracles with their wires and cables, it was impossible to find out the positions of units until hours after they reached them. Then it was not as if I only had the II. Corps to deal with, for mixed up with them, fighting and retiring together, were the Cavalry Division, the 19th Infantry Brigade, and the 4th Division, none of which were under me, but were reporting their movements to and getting their orders from General Headquarters, twenty-six miles to the rear. It is true that General Headquarters issued an order timed 1 p.m. 25th August, placing the 19th Brigade under the II. Corps, but it was then with the Cavalry Division, miles away, and Heaven knows when it got the order.[39]

---

39 Smith-Dorrien, *Forty-Eight Years*, p. 398.

Smith-Dorrien reached his decision to stand and fight at around 2 a.m., but there was a substantial delay before he could inform GHQ. He had first to draft a detailed explanation of his position. At 3.30 a.m. this was sent by motor car to GHQ at St Quentin, but it took an hour and a half to get there. Shortly after it was dispatched, GHQ sent Smith-Dorrien a message, timed 3.45 a.m., confirming the existing orders to continue the retreat, and these messages crossed. When, at 5 a.m. the Commander-in-Chief was confronted with the contents of Smith-Dorrien's message, he 'did not quite grasp what it involved'.[40] He declined to wake up his CGS, Archibald Murray, to consult him, and the situation was not properly clarified until the telephone conversation between Wilson and Smith-Dorrien at around 6.30 a.m. By this time the battle had already begun. It is worth remembering, too, that this important telephone conversation was only enabled because signals officers discovered the existence of a fixed line between the railway stations close to the respective headquarters.

Although wireless was available, and played a part in the Anglo-French victory on the Marne in September, General Snow never once refers to it, and there is scant evidence in the official history of its use by the British during the retreat.[41] The battlefield had become a larger and more complex place, with the increased range of weapons and the number of armies deployed, yet the means of communication readily available to commanders had not kept pace. There was a heavy reliance on runners and riders, methods that Wellington would have recognised, but which, with the effectiveness of modern artillery, had become infinitely more dangerous and therefore less reliable. In addition there were telegraph, heliograph, telephone, and, very exceptionally, aeroplane: it is significant that it was during the battle of Le Cateau that British airmen were used for liaison work for the first time. Where messengers were employed, however, there was always

---

40 Callwell, p. 168.

41 For the role of radio in the victory on the Marne see John Ferris, *The British Army and Signals Intelligence During the First World War* (Stroud, 1992), p. 5.

the possibility that either their outward or return destination would change en route, leading to delays in the transmission of information. When Smith-Dorrien went to report to the Commander-in-Chief on the evening of the 26th he found, on arrival at St Quentin, that GHQ had moved to Noyon that afternoon, more than twenty miles to the south. He had no option but to follow it there.

For his part, General Snow was placed in a particularly difficult position at Le Cateau because he was lacking his divisional cavalry and the greater part of his signal company. He had:

> . . . no means of controlling from divisional headquarters the general movements of some fifteen thousand men extended along a front of five miles, except by the use of mounted officers and orderlies. The ground on which the 4th Division lay, on the left of the British line, was . . . soaked by the rain of the previous night, and in many places churned into deep mud by the passage of men, horses, guns and vehicles; over such a surface horses, already none too fresh were soon exhausted by a few hard gallops.[42]

Unsurprisingly, he lost contact with his brigades, and similar difficulties were experienced by his brigadiers. Throughout the battle Brigadier General Haldane had no contact whatsoever with two of his battalions, the 1st Warwickshires and 2nd Royal Dublin Fusiliers. Haldane had lost most of his brigade signals section at the very start of the battle, when it had been unwisely thrown – in his absence – into the abortive attempt to rescue the 1st King's Own before Longsart, and his communications were similarly affected by the muddy ground: 'the horses of my staff and orderlies were too exhausted to move beyond a walk. The result was that practically all means of maintaining communication between headquarters of the brigade and its several battalions were at an end . . .'[43] When the order came to retire in the middle of the afternoon he could only hope that the 1st Warwickshires and the 2nd Fusiliers had received it. In fact substantial numbers of both battalions *did not*, and dutifully remained

---

42 *MO, 1914*, v. 1, p. 148.
43 Haldane, p. 21.

in position until a late hour, fighting a rearguard action. This situation was repeated all along the line at Le Cateau. That Smith-Dorrien's force was able to march away from an enemy numerically stronger, with greater fire power, and while there were still several hours of daylight left, is of course testimony to the magnificent courage and resolve of the troops who stayed behind. But that they were there at all reflects the difficulties that Smith-Dorrien and his divisional and brigade commanders had in getting information in, and orders out. Without the means of communication, they did not have the means of command: a reality that was to be confronted time and again by the higher ranks of the BEF in the years ahead.

That breakdowns in the chain of command and in communications led to confusion on the battlefield is not a new idea, and there is of course nothing original in the notion of the 'fog of war'. What is perhaps fresh about General Snow's approach, however, is the determined candour with which he addressed the problem, and his unwillingness to gloss over the consequences, even where they reflected badly upon himself. If the overall effect of his memoirs is to diminish the perceived significance of his own command, then it must also be to enhance the role of those beneath him; what he wrote of the retreat from Mons might be said of many of the battles in the four years of war that followed: '[It] was a badly bungled affair only prevented from being a disaster of the first magnitude by the grit displayed by the officers and men.'

PART ONE

THE 4TH DIVISION FROM MOBILISATION TO THE END OF THE RETREAT FROM MONS

Who that heard 'Tipperary' sung by careless men marching in France in a summer which seems a century gone will hear that foolish tune again without a sudden fear that he will be unable to control his emotion? And those Nobodies of Mons, the Marne, and the Aisne, what were they? The 'hungry squad', the men shut outside the factory gates, the useless surplus of the labour market so necessary for a great nation's commercial prosperity . . . Yet the Nobodies stood to it at Mons. They bore us no resentment.

H. M. Tomlinson,
Waiting for Daylight (London, 1929), pp. 136–7

5 September 1914: Early on this morning reinforcements from England joined us, and the difference in their appearance and ours was amazing. They looked plump, clean, tidy and very wide-awake. Whereas we were filthy, thin, and haggard. Most of us had beards; what equipment was left was torn; instead of boots we had puttees, rags, old shoes, field boots – anything and everything wrapped round our feet. Our hats were the same, women's hats, peasants' hats, caps, any old covering, while our trousers were mostly ribbons. The officers were in a similar condition.'

Corporal Bernard John Denore,
'The Retreat from Mons', in C. B. Purdom (ed.), *Everyman at War:
Sixty Personal Narratives of the War* (London, 1930), p. 8

A story of the doings of the 4th Division BEF from the date of mobilisation to the end of the retreat from Mons

This story is for private circulation only and is not to be published during the lifetime of any of the actors mentioned, if at all. I do not say that it is never to be published as I feel sure that the day will come when the student of Military History discovers that the retreat of 1914 was not, as is now imagined, a great military achievement, but was a badly bungled affair only prevented from being a disaster of the first magnitude by the grit displayed by the officers and men. If, when that time arrives, my son, or grandson, or whoever is in possession of this story, thinks that its publication would be of interest, let him publish it by all means. The actors will be dead and no one's feelings will be hurt.

Large issues of which I, in my position as a divisional commander, could not be aware may no doubt have caused orders to be issued and things to be done which appear indefensible, but, after making all allowances, it must be admitted that things took place during the retreat which never ought to have taken place in an army supposed to be trained, things which cannot survive the impartial searchlight turned on them by the historian.

I blame no particular General nor his Staff, each one was as bad, or I should say as ignorant, as the other. We were dealing with much larger bodies than we had ever dealt with except on paper, the higher staffs had had no practice in command, and although they had been well trained in the theory of the writing and issue of orders, they failed in the practice. The restrictions placed on manoeuvres in England so far as the use of ground was concerned prevented the study of the use of ground in peace time on any large scale and had even taught us false lessons. Added to this we all suffered from the fault common to all Englishmen, a fault we did not know we suffered from till war revealed it, a total lack of imagination.

I. Mobilisation and Arrival in France

In 1911 I was given command of the 4th Division. Its Headquarters, two brigades of Artillery (one field, one howitzer) and a heavy battery of 60-pounders were at Woolwich, one brigade of Artillery and the 10th Infantry Brigade were at Shorncliffe, a brigade of Artillery and the 11th Infantry Brigade were at Colchester, while the 12th Infantry Brigade was distributed between Dover, Gravesend and Chatham. Of the two Field Engineer Companies, one was at Woolwich, the other at Shorncliffe. In those days the peace establishment of a division only included Artillery, Engineers and Infantry; all other units joining the division on mobilisation. The peace staff consisted of a General Staff Officer – Colonel J. E. Edmonds; a D.A.A.G. – Captain B. Burnett Hitchcock; a C.R.A. – Brig.-General G. F. Milne and a C.R.E. – Colonel H. B. Jones.

I was lucky in my staff. Colonel Edmonds was a man with a brain and an education not often met with in a soldier and he had a memory for history which was unique. I cannot imagine a better staff officer or at any rate one who suited me better. He was not, however, over robust. Captain Burnett Hitchcock I need not remark on. His wonderful organising power, especially as regards mobilisation, brought him lasting fame. Brig.-General Milne also rose to the top of his profession. I owe all these officers, together with those who came to me on mobilisation, a debt of gratitude for the way they helped me through the anxious days of the retreat. My A.D.C., Captain H. I. R. Allfrey, Somerset Light Infantry, beside being a great friend, was an ideal A.D.C.

It used to be imagined that the 4th Division was much handicapped as regards training in comparison with the Aldershot and Salisbury Plain divisions because it was so split up. No greater mistake was ever made. I was constantly about supervising the training, and any brilliant idea which I gleaned from one Commander I introduced as my own to the other two. They adopted it readily thinking it was mine, while, had they known it was the creation of a brother brigadier, which they would have done had they been in the same station, they might have resented it. We concentrated every summer for training and manoeuvres and so we were a very level lot, all trained on the same lines. I had always made a hobby of route-marching and we arrived at such a pitch of excellence in this respect that we were held up as an example to others by two C.I.G.S.'s in succession, Sir John French and Sir Charles Douglas.

The officers who were to form my Staff in war had been allotted, though in peace they were otherwise employed. The most noticeable was Major A. A. Montgomery, who was our second G.S. Officer. He afterwards rose to high estate.

In our staff tour in the Spring of 1914 we were fortunate enough to get all our war staff out. This staff tour was so prophetic that it is worth mentioning. Sir Charles Douglas, who was first Inspector General and afterwards C.I.G.S., would not allow troops to be exercised in anything to do with a retreat or a retirement as he said it had a bad effect on their morale. This did not prevent him in the interdivisional manoeuvres of 1913 setting a scheme which caused my Division to retreat hastily for 24 hours, pursued by the 3rd Division commanded by Sir Henry Rawlinson. The mess we got into and the number of unexpected difficulties that presented themselves made me determined to practise that particular manoeuvre. I therefore made a scheme for this staff tour which brought about a hasty retirement for 2½ days after an unsuccessful action. We had out at this tour our complete war staff, Brigadiers of Infantry with their staff, Artillery Brigade Commanders and their staffs, Battery Commanders, Infantry Commanders with their Adjutants and Quarter-masters, R.E. Company Commanders, Signal Company and an improvised Q. Staff under Captain Taylor, A.S.C., my D.A.Q.M.G.

We learned a great deal and found out what the difficulties were which we should encounter in a retreat, how to overcome those difficulties, and the duties of every member of the staff in a retreat. I shall always be thankful we selected this particular exercise and what it must have saved us both in lives and work when we took part in the real thing it is impossible to say.

Thus in August 1914 the Division may be put down as having arrived at as high a state of efficiency as is possible in peace, but we were terribly short in numbers, and the restrictions as to training ground cramped the important study of ground. Still the training of the officers had reached a high level and there were sufficient N.C.O.s and men trained to leaven the reservists when they arrived. My three Brigadiers, J. A. L. Haldane, 10th Brigade, A. G. Hunter-Weston, 11th Brigade and H. F. M. Wilson, 12th Brigade, were far and away better than the Brigadiers of other Divisions and all became eventually Corps Commanders. I knew their ways and they knew mine. Colonel Edmonds and Captain Burnett Hitchcock had just completed our war standing orders, a most complete volume which was of great value. These orders had been published in the previous winter and were so good that the 3rd, 5th and 6th Divisions adopted them at once, and later, most of the Service and Territorial Divisional standing orders were taken from them.

Although ever since the murder of the Heir Apparent to the Austrian Throne the papers had hinted at the grave condition of Europe, it was not until about the 29th of July that soldiers realised that the time had come when they would have to give an account of themselves. I and my Staff had been busy preparing for our training and manoeuvres and on the 28th we had gone down to Shorncliffe on one of my usual visits. There was little or no news on the 28th and after seeing the troops at training we spent the afternoon completing schemes for Brigade and Divisional training.

On the 29th Sir James Grierson commanding the Eastern Command, came down and saw the troops at their ordinary work but about noon he received a telegram ordering him to return to Town. Even then we hardly realised the serious nature of things, but about 5 p.m. we received news from our Headquarters which made us return to Woolwich by the next train. This news was that the Precautionary Period, a term used to denote the possibility of attack, was to come into force at once. Coast defences were manned and garrisons sent to vulnerable points. For the 4th Division this meant manning the Dover, Sheerness, and Harwich defences by regulars until the Territorials could relieve them, and many other duties of a similar nature.

The next few days were spent wondering what the Government would do and in hoping for the declaration of war.

At 6 p.m. on 4th August the order of mobilisation arrived. Although the troops were mostly away from their peace stations, mobilisation proceeded regularly and up to time thanks to the care that Captain Burnett Hitchcock had taken over the mobilisation instructions and the clear way that he had explained these instructions to all concerned.

On August 9th we received orders for Headquarters of the Division to move to Bury St. Edmunds and the Division to move to various places on the east coast, which moves were carried out on the morning of the 10th.

Some years previously I had been General Staff Officer to the Commander-in-Chief, Eastern Command, and during that time it had fallen to my lot to write the Eastern Command Defence Scheme, on which very flattering remarks were recorded at the War Office. Thus I was quite aware of what was required of me and my troops. I found that very few people knew, or cared, that such a scheme existed and the chaos on the East Coast was appalling. Both the Naval and Military Authorities were in a state of panic. The Admiralty said they could not be responsible in any way for preventing a landing, though they hoped to be able to give some warning if one was imminent. The War Office knew little of what was required, the entire General Staff having vanished on mobilisation, the exact moment when they were most required.

Gradually we got things into some order but the greatest difficulty was to persuade people that we were at war. Peace and War were curiously mixed. One day on the coast I saw two companies of Territorials throwing up an earthwork, the purpose of which neither they nor I could understand, neither did they know who ordered it. Close by were masses of children digging on the beach in front of rows and rows of bathing tents. A mile out to sea were six mine sweepers, sweeping the inner channel, while through the middle of them paddled a Clacton pleasure steamer, crowded with trippers with a band thumping out the latest popular air.

No one had thought of ordering pier lights to be extinguished and all piers were all fully illuminated each night. I had no power whatever and had I suggested the lowering of lights I should have been written down as mad. One night, when an extra special entertainment was being held on Lowestoft pier and some hundreds of people were dancing to the strains of the Municipal band I received a telegram saying that German war vessels had been sighted some 10 to 12 miles off Lowestoft and I was to be prepared for attack. Fortunately for the ball dancers the raid mis-fired. One other incident I must record, though I might devote pages to similar incidents. There is an important railway bridge which connects the Yarmouth–Lowestoft Island with the mainland. Fearing a landing on this Island, it being admitted that this was one of the most favourable landing places from the enemy point of view, I prepared this bridge, with others, for demolition so that I could blow it up if necessary. The manager of the Great Eastern Railway was furious and I got a wire from the War Office asking me if I was aware that if the bridge was injured the traffic with Lowestoft would be seriously interfered with in the middle of the tourist season, etc., etc., and that I was at once to withdraw the charge. As a matter of fact I disobeyed the order.

The Spy mania was in full swing. No doubt there were many spies about, but the energies of the police always seemed to be in the wrong direction and they would have nothing to do with what I considered the really dangerous suspects. In the case of a so-called Swiss, whom I suspected, the police tried to persuade me that I was mistaken and as a proof of this man's honesty they told me he was going over to the Continent that night. Needless to say my friend did not go to the Continent that night, but it was no thanks to the police.

Early in the evening of my first evening at Bury St Edmunds I got a wire from the War Office worded in a curious manner, thus: 'Invasion imminent be prepared to receive and issue orders at a moment's notice'. Altering the wording into a more business-like form I sent it round to all concerned. It did not cause me much anxiety as I had served on Lord Kitchener's Staff and I detected the 'pencil and telegraph pad' ring about the wording to which I had been accustomed in the Sudan. The second night at Bury a similarly worded telegram was again received, amended and passed round. On the third night, however, when much the same sort of telegram was received we remembered the old story of 'Wolf! Wolf!' and decided not to pass on any more such alarming telegrams. Whether, had the Germans invaded during this fortnight, we could have done much to stop them I cannot say, though I rather doubt it. It would have depended on numbers, to a certain extent on luck, and to a great extent on how little the War Office interfered. If the 4th Division could not stop them, all would have been over as, except for the Division, chaos ruled supreme, although a certain number of Territorial units were mobilising in various places.

While I was on the East Coast, with my troops located at the spots which, I was convinced, were the most suitable, I received a wire from the War Office ordering me to despatch a Brigade to Cromer. Now Cromer is the one place of all others where troops should not be placed as it is more or less on a promontory and troops there would be cut off if the enemy landed at the far more suitable places which exist on either side. I believe the reason for the telegram was that Mrs. Winston Churchill was playing golf at Sheringham, a few miles from Cromer, where she was joined by her husband. The First Lord of the Admiralty, seeing no troops about, thought that such an important place as Cromer should be protected and knowing nothing at all of the situation, and very little on military matters generally, telegraphed for a Brigade. How we managed to muddle through those first few weeks whilst such chaos was ruling I cannot imagine, but it was mostly owing to the want of initiative on the part of the enemy.

On the 16th we had completed mobilisation and I reported to the War Office. I was sent for by Sir Charles Douglas, the C.I.G.S., who was not communicative but from whom I gathered that the Cavalry Division, the 1st, 2nd, 3rd and 5th Divisions were in France and that the 6th Division, which was the next Division due to start, had not yet finished mobilising.[1] The 4th Division was therefore to assemble at Harrow and the 6th was to relieve us on the East Coast.

We moved to Harrow on 17th and remained there till the 22nd. We spent the time route-marching, and before we left, the reservists really began to get into shape, and I was very thankful that we had had those few days to get feet and boots in order instead of being rushed overseas like the other four Divisions had been. It made all the difference to us later. We left Harrow early on the morning of the 22nd, the whole Division entraining between midnight 21st/22nd and midnight 22nd/23rd. Nothing could have been better done than the arrangements for entraining and embarkation and the whole thing was a great triumph for the Quartermaster-General. The only hitch was that the vessel allotted to the H.Q. Staff of the Division was so light, and therefore so high out of the water, that the cranes on the jetties were not high enough, or the chains long enough, to be able to load her. The stores earmarked for that ship had to go on another which caused some confusion. Whether ours was the only ship so affected I do not know.

We got out of Southampton Dock about 3 p.m. and proceeded to the examination area off Shanklin, where we anchored for some time. The reason for our reporting on the examination area was not clear and no one could explain it to us. We came out of harbour, therefore could not be an enemy ship; we were not formed into convoys, neither had we any escort. After anchoring for an hour or so, we proceeded independently, half the Division to Havre and half to Rouen. Headquarters proceeded to Havre.

We arrived at Havre about 11 p.m. [on 22 August] and made an hotel our headquarters, while the troops proceeded to one or other of the rest camps. These camps were, in some cases, 6 miles distant, with a very stiff climb to get to them. Whether this could have been avoided I do not know, but it took a lot out of men and horses, and as all the troops were off again in 24 hours one would have thought some other arrangements could have been made, at any rate for the infantry.

---

1   In fact the cabinet had agreed on 6 August that the 4th Division, not the 6th, would be the next to go: see Notes to Part One, below, p. 52.

It was while we were at Havre that I first realised how easily discipline could be undermined when the inhabitants began buying and begging souvenirs from the men. Cap badges and buttons began to disappear rapidly, and altogether the stay at Havre, short though it was, did the morale of the troops great harm. Such a possibility ought to have been foreseen and guarded against and was gross carelessness on someone's part, that of myself and Staff included. The day of the 23rd I spent visiting rest camps. In the morning I went with Colonel Sandbach, the Commandant, to the Cathedral to a Ceremonial gathering. The Bishop who preached enlarged on the fact that not a German was on French soil. He might have been right at that exact hour, but it must have been a near thing.

We got orders to move to the front and the Division entrained throughout the evening and night of the 23rd/24th. The French order that troops have to be at the station some hours before entrainment was very inconvenient. I and my Headquarters left Havre at 11 p.m. We arrived at Rouen in the early dawn, and at Amiens later.

At these places we saw a large number of chaplains. It appears that the Chaplain General thought that the place for chaplains was with the base hospitals, and so forbade any being allowed to go to the front. This state of affairs continued until the Rev. Simms, a more broad minded man, took charge, and after that the chaplains were oftener to be found in the firing line than elsewhere and did much good.

At Amiens I saw General Robb, the G.O.C., Lines of Communication and Base. He had at that time received no bad news from the front, though the troops had been retreating for 24 hours and every mile they retreated made Amiens, as a Base, more dangerous. One would have thought that the chief person to be kept informed of any retrograde movement was the G.O.C., Lines of Communication, especially when those lines of communication were to a flank.

During the day we received orders that

> Divisional Headquarters were to detrain at Busigny.
> 10th Infantry Brigade to detrain at Le Cateau thence by road to Beaumont.

11th Infantry Brigade to detrain at Le Cateau then march to Troisville.

12th Infantry Brigade to detrain at Bertry thence by road to Montigny and Ligny.

Divisional Artillery to detrain at Busigny and Bohain.

I have often heard it said that the 4th Division arrived [during night of 24/25 August] exactly at the right moment to prevent the retreat of the II Corps becoming a rout. Without going so far as that I will say that it was very lucky it arrived when it did and it was pure luck. No pressure was brought to bear from G.H.Q., France, on the War Office to hurry up the Division, neither, when the Division embarked, was there any reason to believe that its presence was so urgently required. Had we arrived 24 hours later we certainly could have taken no part in covering the retirement of the 3rd and 5th Divisions on to the Le Cateau position, though I don't think that would have mattered much. We might have been in time to take some part in the battle of Le Cateau without our guns, but even that is doubtful as the authorities would have hardly detrained us so far forward as Le Cateau and Busigny in the conditions that existed on the evening of the 25th August.

II. The Battle of Le Cateau

On our way to Busigny, after we left St. Quentin, I noticed from the train window large and heavily laden convoys making their way south. This filled me with uneasiness as, though I might have expected to see convoys on the move, those moving south would, if all had been going well, have been empty.

On arriving at Busigny, about 4 p.m. [24 August], a G.H.Q. car met me to take me at once to Le Cateau. I gleaned something of the situation from the officer who accompanied the car. It is just as well that I did, or the news I received on arrival at Le Cateau might have overwhelmed me.

The situation was explained to me by my dear old friend Henry Wilson, who was Deputy Chief of the Staff, in that half chaffing, half serious way, which was peculiar to him. Coming in that way and from a man who was the greatest optimist I have ever met, it was not quite so overwhelming as it might have been if unfolded by others, but in all conscience it was bad enough. I gleaned that the 3rd and 5th Divisions had been retreating and fighting for 36 hours, and that they had had about as much as any troops could stand, and G.H.Q. feared that one little push more and they might be over the brink and the retreat would become a rout. I also gathered that the I Corps had had little or no fighting, but were tired out with marching and were separated from the II Corps by the Foret de Mormal, a huge forest about 10 miles through from east to west, and so no hope could be expected from that quarter. I also gathered that I was, as soon as I could collect enough troops, to push north and intervene between the enemy and the hard-pressed 3rd and 5th Divisions and cover their retreat even if my Division got decimated in doing so.

I was also told that the idea was to fall back on the Le Cateau–Cambrai position and there accept battle, and that the position was being prepared by impressed labour, and that the position of my Division would be about Beaurevoir and Cattenières.

About this time a great friend of mine, Colonel Bowes, who was liaison officer between G.H.Q. and the French, turned up and, having nothing to do pending the arrival of the troops, I went with him to inspect the Le Cateau–Cambrai position. I found it quite a fair position, and from the left, where the left of my Division rested two days later, there was a good view towards Cambrai. We saw nothing of any prepared trenches or requisitioned villagers, and I feel sure the idea was a myth, or if started it never materialised. We then returned to Inchy, where my Headquarters had been established, and then motored down to Neuvilly. Except for a certain amount of excitement among the villagers all was quiet.

On my return to Headquarters we modified the orders slightly and ordered:

> 10th Brigade to move to St. Python by 4.30 a.m. next day [25 August].

11th Brigade to move to Briastre by 4.30 a.m.

12th Brigade to arrive Viesly by 4 a.m.

Divisional Headquarters to open at Briastre Church at 4.30 a.m.

Two squadrons of Irish Horse, which were to be attached to the
    Division, were at Solesmes.

2nd Line Transport to park at Ligny, escorted by Inniskilling
    Fusiliers.

During the early part of the night I was again sent for to G.H.Q.
Why, I don't know, unless it eased their anxiety to talk to somebody.
There I was again informed of the position of affairs but not by
Henry Wilson, and the impression left on my mind was one of
extreme pessimism, so that on my return to my Headquarters I
could not sleep. About midnight there was a most appalling tumult
in Viesly or Neuvilly and I sent Captain Burnett Hitchcock to rouse
the French liaison officer and to go down with him to find out what
was the matter. Captain Burnett Hitchcock found the liaison officer
undressed and very drunk and it was only after copious applications
of cold water that he could be got in a fit state to dress and get
into the car. Captain Burnett Hitchcock reported on his return that
the noise was occasioned by a panic among the inhabitants as they
imagined that the Germans were entering the town. When this news
was found to be false things quietened down.

We were off betimes the next morning [25 August]. All the
infantry, except one battalion of the 11th Brigade and one of the
12th, had got to their allotted places and one brigade of Artillery
had detrained and joined us. The Division took up a position on the
high ground south-west of Solesmes and St. Python, 11th Brigade
on the right and the 10th on the left, with the 12th Brigade at Viesly.
Headquarters were established on some high ground just south-west
of Viesly. We had information that a strong force was advancing on
us from Saulzoir.

The reason of our being sent forward was to help the retirement
of the 19th Brigade, 3rd Division, and Cavalry Division. Whether we
were much more than a moral support I am not sure. We certainly

should have prevented any turning movement from the north-west, but whether any German troops were near enough to try such a movement I doubt. It was very unlikely that such a movement could have been attempted by any other arm than Cavalry, and this could have been secured against by employing one of my brigades, leaving two brigades free to continue the preparation of the Le Cateau–Cambrai position. We may have accomplished our purpose but it was a waste of force.

We were handicapped by the absence of our signal company and Divisional cavalry, and found it hard to get in touch with the 19th Brigade and 3rd Division. We somehow managed to do so.

During the morning [of the 25th] I ordered up a part of the 12th Brigade to extend my left towards Quievy. I was much horrified when I went to visit them to find that they had piled arms in an open space on a slope facing the direction of the enemy and had taken off their accoutrements and hung them up on the piles of rifles. Had artillery fire been opened there would have been a disaster. I was very angry and such a thing never happened again: but I quote it to uphold the statement I made earlier, namely that an Englishman has very little imagination.

I rode round the troops who were supposed to be entrenched. In spite of what troops had learned in the Boer War, in spite of what they had been taught, all they had done was to make a few scratchings of the nature of what was called, fifty years ago, a shelter pit, of no use whatever against any sort of fire. I came to the conclusion then, and never altered it during the war, that unless driven to it by his officers, the British soldier would sooner die than dig, but whether the reason for this was stupidity, lack of imagination or laziness I don't know, but probably it was a little of all three.

Sir John French and his Chief of the Staff, General Murray, came to visit me. He was just late enough to miss the piled arms episode. He was somewhat surprised at the good spirits I was in, but I was quite sure the Division would give a good account of itself and from some kink in my character I always cheer up when other people are downhearted, and the reverse.

While I was talking to them, Sir John asked Murray whether anything more had been heard of a large force which had been reported as entering the northern edge of the Forêt de Mormal in the early dawn. Murray told him the Intelligence Dept. thought it was a false report, but in view of what happened at Landrecies that night I have often wondered whether that was the case.

Nothing of any importance occurred during the day. Our outposts kept on reporting parties of the enemy trying to get round their left flank, but these parties must have been very few if they existed at all. However, I did prolong the left to insure against accidents.

Hearing that the remaining battalion of the 12th Brigade, the Inniskilling Fusiliers, had detrained, and considering it too long a march to bring them up to where we were I ordered them to remain with the guns but to send a detachment to block the Cambrai–Le Cateau Road, near Beauvois[-en-Cambrésis]. I gave this order more to employ the troops than because I really thought it necessary to block the road. It is lucky I did so as will be seen later.

The difficulty was to find out what was going on. We got no news from G.H.Q. or from any other troops we were trying to get touch with. G.H.Q. must have been getting information, but certainly they sent none on to us. We had no way of getting information ourselves, except by sending out staff officers in motor cars.

Late in the afternoon we got touch with the 3rd Division and also got a report that the G.O.C., 19th Brigade, was in Haussy and intended retiring to Le Cateau moving off at 2 p.m., but we got no information at all as regards the Cavalry.

We took the view that we must any way remain where we were till all the troops of the 3rd Division and the 19th Brigade had passed through, and we reported this intention to G.H.Q.

This view was confirmed by a private letter from General [Henry] Wilson. This letter, later confirmed by Operation Order No. 8 of 25th, added that it was the intention of G.H.Q. that the Army should retire to the line Le Catelet–[Busigny], about 9 miles south of the Le Cateau–Cambrai position, the 4th Division to begin the retirement at 7 a.m. 26th August from approximately the line Caudry–Wambaix.

The rest of the force was to conform. When we received this message we were in position seven or eight miles north of the latter line.

Orders were therefore issued at 5 p.m. on the 25th for the 4th Division to take up a position for the night on the line Caudry (exclusive)–Fontaine au Pire–Wambaix–Knoll just south[-west of] Séranvillers, but that no movement from the present position was to take place till ordered.

About this time I saw Hubert Hamilton, G.O.C., 3rd Division, and his Staff. I was much struck with the drawn and tired look on all their faces. They were all, however, cheery.

About 5.30 p.m. it came on to rain heavily, and about the same time the enemy commenced some indiscriminate shelling. Where the shells came from puzzled our gunners who knew they ought to try and silence the enemy's guns but had not the least idea where to locate them. This is bound to happen at the beginning of any war as it is impossible in peace time to acquire much training in this matter. Aeroplanes, of course, are the best method to discover the hostile guns, but at the time I am writing of we had very few aeroplanes and none of them had had any practice in picking up targets.

About 6 p.m. the 3rd Division had all passed through, and we definitely located the 19th Brigade. Orders were slightly modified and the 11th Infantry Brigade ordered to occupy from Fontaine au Pire to the railway station at Cattenieres, 12th Brigade to continue the line to Wambaix, 10th to go into reserve at Haucourt.

This movement was eventually carried out, but owing to delay caused by the transport of Cavalry Division and 3rd Division in Viesly the movement could not begin till after nine p.m., and the last units moved off after midnight.

The night was very dark and the whole sky to the northward was lit up by what we thought were burning villages. As a matter of fact they were probably only big fires lighted to dry the men's clothes after the soaking rain.

Just before daylight [on the 26th] I met generals Haldane and Hunter-Weston about Fontaine au Pire and we decided it would be best if the troops were to lie down and get an hour's rest where they were, and wait for daylight before taking up the positions assigned to them. I then rode on to Haucourt.

It will be remembered that, during the day, I had ordered a detachment of the Inniskilling Fusiliers to take up a position on the main road near Beauvois. Soon after I had done so we got news of several motor cars moving from Valenciennes on Cambrai. I cannot say I took much notice of this but at about 11 p.m. [25 August], before the 4th Division had begun to cross the Le Cateau–Cambrai road on its movement south, several cars filled with men whom the O.C., Detachment, Inniskilling Fusiliers, declared were in French uniform, or any way were wearing French caps, drove up from the west. When challenged the cars were turned round and made off before the O.C., Detachment had determined how to act. Had these motor cars got through they would have done a deal of harm as they probably carried machine-gun detachments, and German machine-gunners were exceedingly determined men as we found out afterwards to our cost.

So ended a rather unsatisfactory day. The 4th Division was supposed to have done a great deal of good by their intervention and was supposed to have been well handled. As a matter of fact there was very little intervention and still less handling. Our losses for the day were trivial – 60 in all. Had we been properly dug in, the casualties would probably have been nil.

I have often wondered since how I could have left the troops and ridden on to Haucourt in such a careless frame of mind. Although I quite realised we might have to fight on the morrow [26 August], I knew the troops were practically in the position assigned to them, and that the Brigadiers would see that the positions were taken up as soon as it was light enough to see what they were about and I knew the troops were covered by outposts. What I did not realise, and what I ought to have known, was that the Germans were so close on my heels; another instance of want of imagination.

For the last eight hours I had had no information of any sort from anyone, and in going to Haucourt I intended to snatch an hour's sleep, while the Staff got out orders for the continuation of the retirement, or for accepting battle, according to which of these two alternatives G.H.Q inclined.[2]

I don't think that I could have been asleep for more than ten minutes when Colonel Edmonds came and woke me and told me that a message had been received from General Smith-Dorrien, commanding II Corps, saying he intended to accept battle on the position the troops were then on and would I do the same. I told Colonel Edmonds to say 'Yes' and we agreed there was no necessity to issue further orders as the orders of the night before would now hold good. I felt, however, I should like to see what was going on in the front line before the battle commenced. I snatched a cup of tea and an egg and ran out into the courtyard but found my car was not ready. Colonel Bowes had just driven up, and I jumped into his car and started off for Cattenieres. In getting out of the village we overshot the turning and found ourselves on the road to Esnes. As we were turning to retrace our steps the road we had intended to take was swept by an outburst of shrapnel, and at the same time I saw shells bursting all along the position, and soon afterwards a good many stragglers began coming back from the ridge. Haucourt village was also being shelled; so we left the car and walked across the field to a grove of trees, west of Haucourt. There we met Captain Allfrey, who told me that the rumour was that I had been killed and that General Milne had taken command. Gradually the staff rejoined me, and I was told that all the transport had been got away safely and that Captain Burnett Hitchcock had done a very gallant act in rallying the stragglers whom I had noticed, and on horseback leading them back to the firing line.

About this time we got an order placing the Division under command of General Smith-Dorrien, commanding II Corps.

We got the guns into position, but they were a long time in opening fire as they could not locate any targets and were uncertain who was enemy and who were friends. This difficulty was caused by the total

---

2 General Snow appears to have forgotten that at midnight he had received Operation Order No. 8 continuing the retreat: see Appendix 2 below, pp. 149–50, 153–4.

neglect in peace time of using forward observing officers, the old idea being that the battery commander observed and directed the fire from a point close to the guns. One of the reasons why we had never made use of forward observing officers was that batteries had very little telephone wire; another was that, in peace time, forward observing officers could not be used without danger to themselves.

To return to the infantry whom we left snatching a little rest before taking up their position. The decision the Brigadiers and I arrived at, namely, to delay taking up the position till daylight, was unfortunate. The Germans brought up a large number of machine guns, and the King's Own and, immediately afterwards, the Lancashire Fusiliers came under a heavy fire from machine guns as they were forming up to entrench. Both these battalions, together with two companies of Inniskilling Fusiliers, who came to their help, lost heavily before getting into fighting formation.

When things had settled down and I could take stock of the position, I was fairly happy in my mind. I was convinced that there was nothing at present up against me except artillery and machine guns, and this I reported to H.Q. II Corps. I had not been told anything about overwhelming forces being in the neighbourhood, or that there was any chance of an encircling movement from the north-west, all of which was known at G.H.Q. and probably at H.Q. II Corps. Why this information was not passed down I do not know, but I presume it was bad staff work, everyone being strange to the job.

I was certainly very nervous of my left flank, not because I was led to expect a turning movement but because my flank was in the air, and I imagined it much more in the air than it really was.

I had no Divisional Cavalry or Cyclists with which I could guard my flank, and our eyes from where we stood were our only means of piercing the fog of war. I had no notion that Cambrai with some of its surrounding hamlets was occupied by French Territorials, and although Colonel Bowes had told me of the existence of General Sordet's cavalry I knew little about it and no one thought fit to enlighten me. All I could do was to tell General Haldane to detach a company or so from the reserve to watch as far as possible my left flank.

The next move was to try and get more to the rear, as the place where we found ourselves was hardly the right place for Divisional Headquarters. It was not easy to get further back as I did not want the troops to see the G.O.C. making his way among the stragglers to the rear. However, by moving first towards one flank and then towards the other I gradually got back to the place west of Caullery, which did very well; but owing to the absence of my signal company every message had to be carried by one of my staff, who already had their hands full.

The men, on the whole, were behaving well. There was the usual tendency for unwounded men to help the wounded men to the rear, and I saw many machine gunners wandering about in rear of the reserves saying that they were looking about for positions for their guns. This was our own fault as we had always taught the machine gunners to take up a position well in rear, very different to what the Germans had been taught, namely that the place for the machine gun was in, or in front of, the firing line.

By about 8 a.m. the 11th Brigade was more or less extended from Caudry to the 'Quarry', south-west of Fontaine au Pire, with the 12th Brigade and two battalions of the 10th continuing the line to Wambaix. The remaining battalions of the 10th were in reserve at Haucourt. The XIV. Brigade, R.F.A. was in action south-west of Haucourt, supporting the 12th Brigade; the XXIX. Brigade, R.F.A. was in action east of Haucourt, supporting the 11th and 12th Brigades. The XXXII. R.F.A. were in action south-west of Ligny. The XXXVII. R.F.A. were in action west of Caullery.

The left part of the position was given up about 9 a.m. and the 12th Brigade fell back on Haucourt with its left about Esnes. I never quite understood the necessity of this retirement, except that the Brigade had been shaken at the outset. The German account implied that no pressure was brought to bear in this area till about 2 p.m. The 11th Brigade still held on north of the railway.

The thing that struck me most was the rapidity with which the German artillery got on to their target. It appeared to me as if they always got the bracket in two rounds and then the next round was plumb on the target. At one time I and a good many of my staff were dismounted in the open and our horses were being led about near by. We were spotted and had fire opened on us very quickly. No damage resulted though the shells were all around us. We galloped away as quick as possible and were followed by shrapnel till we took refuge in a fold of the ground. Even then the hollow we had disappeared into was searched up and down. The way the Germans picked up targets seemed to me at the time almost uncanny, but it really was because they made use of aeroplanes.

Soon after midday it became clear that Ligny was going to play a great part in the battle and the 12th Brigade was ordered to put Selvigny in a state of defence.

About 1 p.m. I felt that the enemy might break through between my right and the 3rd Division's left and I appealed to II Corps Headquarters. I got a reply saying that two battalions were being sent, but they never arrived as they were taken to support the 3rd Division which had fallen back from Caudry with its left on Montigny.

About this time – 2 p.m. – we were, in our part of the field, more than holding our own and the 12th Brigade advanced on Longsart towards our original position in order to withdraw as many wounded as possible, and was successful in moving a considerable number.

Being without my field ambulances, there was nothing behind the regimental aid posts, but my D.A.D.M.S., Major Ensor, in some wonderful way managed to collect a number of country carts, and during the day got away some seven hundred wounded and entrained them. Had it not been for this wonderful bit of initiative these men would have fallen into the hands of the enemy.

About 3 p.m. the advanced posts of the 11th Brigade had to retire as their right was exposed owing to the retirement of the 3rd Division.

I was watching one of our batteries near Caullery. It was under fire from some 12 guns. The enemy were firing salvoes and each salvo looked as if it must have annihilated our battery. Directly, however, the last shell of the salvo burst, Bang! Bang! Bang! Bang! Bang! Bang! went the guns of the battery, and you could see lanes being driven through the dense masses advancing on Ligny. Nothing could shake the defence of Ligny, whose garrison obviously mowed down the attacking Germans in large numbers.

I had received the order for the retirement about 2 p.m. and issued orders accordingly.

The line of retirement being at an angle of 45 degrees to the line of battle made an orderly retirement very difficult. If a retirement is directly to the rear, it is not of great consequence that everyone should know the exact line of retreat, as those who do not know it conform to the movements of others and gradually units are got in hand. But in a retreat to a flank it is vital that everyone should know the exact line of retreat, otherwise units retire straight to their rear and so get out of touch. It is always difficult to get orders to everyone in the front line, but ten times more so when you have no machinery to help you as was the case in this instance.

The line of retreat given was Walincourt–Malincourt–Aubencheul to Vendhuile. Bodies of men, not getting this order, retired on to Clary and Serain and so got mixed up with the 3rd and even the 5th Divisions. I do not think it an exaggeration to say that a quarter of my infantry thus went wrong, and the Division was not again concentrated till the morning of the 28th behind the Somme.

In the first instance the guns were sent back to the high ground east of Liheries, from which place theoretically they should have been able to cover the retirement of the infantry across the Esnes brook.

There were some gallant, and what appeared to be impossible, deeds done in getting out the guns. Orders had been sent round to say that guns which could not be pulled out should be abandoned, but the gunners true to their traditions would not have it so. To quote two instances out of many.

The 135th Battery XXXII. Bde., R.F.A. was in close support of the infantry near Ligny and under a terrible fire from at least a brigade of hostile artillery; but the battery commander – Major [C. H.] Liveing – decided to try and save his guns and, withdrawing them and their wagons by hand, brought all of them, except one wagon, safely away.

To the west of Ligny the position of the 27th Battery XXXII. Bde., R.F.A. was even worse; nevertheless the gunners, taking advantage of every lull, succeeded in running back four guns and limbers to the sunken road in rear, where increases in the hostile artillery fire compelled them to abandon the other two. The Battery then formed up and awaited its opportunity. It eventually made a dash to the south-west and, though pursued by German shells, got its four guns safely away. Its commander, Major H. E. Vallentin, and also Major Liveing of the 135th Battery, received distinguished service orders.

The two guns of the 27th Battery and the wagon of the 135th Battery were the only artillery material which the Division lost at Le Cateau, and as we salved one howitzer belonging to some other division we did not come out badly.

In sending orders to General Haldane re his retirement from Haucourt, I remembered a sunken road or gully which I had ridden along in the morning, and I told him to retire by this gully. He complained bitterly of the order afterwards as he said the gully was being heavily shelled. Of course it was within his power to act up to the spirit and not the letter of the order, but I quote the incident to show how careful one should be in framing orders. I ought to have told him to retire on Selvigny and not given him a route. If I thought it expedient to call his attention to the sunken road I should have made it the substance of a message nothing to do with orders.

The retirement was much mixed up. Apparently part of the 12th Brigade, the Essex and two companies of the Inniskilling, moved off soon after 5 p.m. The Lancashire fusiliers (12th Brigade) and half the Dublin Fusiliers (10th Infantry Brigade) and part of the King's Own (12th Brigade) started later, though half of the King's Own, receiving no warning to retire, remained in position at Haucourt. The rest of the Inniskillings slipped away in small parties from Esnes.

The 11th Infantry Brigade and the remainder of the 12th held their positions until 6 p.m. and even later. Colonel Swayne, Somerset L.I. (11th Brigade) brought away half the Battalion which rejoined the column early next morning. The remainder of the Battalion under Major [C. B.] Prowse, fought on at Ligny till a late hour. The larger portion of the 1st Rifle Brigade found their way to Selvigny, though the Colonel and about 40 men, who thought they were the sole survivors, retired to Malincourt with the Headquarters of the Division. The Hampshires retired about 7 p.m. and overtook the portion of the Brigade, which was with the Brigadier at Serain. This portion of the Brigade rejoined the Division on the Somme on the 28th.

Of the 10th Infantry Brigade only the Seaforth Highlanders and the greater part of the Irish Fusiliers were under their Brigadier's hand. Half of the Warwickshires and a good number of the Dublin Fusiliers were in Haucourt to a late hour and finally retired to St. Quentin.

I myself with my staff got on to the high ground east of Liheries and as long as the light lasted we managed, with the help of some gallopers from the artillery, to retrieve many wanderers. Unfortunately it got dark very suddenly owing to heavy rain commencing.

It seems that the 3rd Division was given a route which took it through the east portion of Malincourt, while the 4th Division was given a route which took it through the west portion.

This is never a safe proceeding with anything as small as a one inch map or smaller scale to work with, and the mix up in Malincourt, not only of the 4th and 3rd but also of the 5th was appalling. Staff officers stood at the cross roads and asked each body of men or each vehicle what they were and directed them accordingly.

By degrees the transport, the artillery, and that part of the infantry above described was got into a column and set out for Vendhuile. The gun fire on the battle field increased and there is little doubt that those parties who had received no orders fought it out to the end and certainly saved us from pursuit which, in the mixed up state of affairs, would have been fatal. It spoke volumes for our discipline that a column was formed at all.

About midnight we arrived at Vendhuile. I felt quite sure that we had escaped unnoticed and I was anxious to keep our whereabouts secret. It was with some horror therefore that I saw the gunners setting fire to the stocks of oats, I suppose with a view to drying their clothes. The whole countryside was illuminated and it only shows the supineness of the Germans in not taking advantage of such a give away of our whereabouts.

We got some food and afterwards slept in a small front room of a cottage. It was a very hot, stuffy night, but the good old couple who slept in the adjoining room refused to let the windows of their room be opened as they complained of the draught. However, we were too tired to be kept awake by anything.

III. The Decision to Fight at Le Cateau

I have said nothing of the controversy as to whether Sir Horace Smith-Dorrien should or should not have decided to fight on the Le Cateau position.

Whether the 3rd and 5th Divisions were fit enough to continue the march before dawn on 26th I cannot say. Sir John French, in his book '1914' has fully explained the condition of these troops and named their billets, though he takes a somewhat optimistic view of the hours they arrived at those billets.

He dismisses the 4th Division with the remark that 'the 4th Division was comparatively fresh', which is true, but he rather leaves it to be inferred that the troops of the 4th Division were in or near their billets by 6 p.m. on the 25th. As a matter of fact the 12th Brigade, the first Brigade to move, left the high ground south-west of Solesmes at 9 p.m. on 25th, the 11th at 10 p.m. and the 10th at midnight, having an average march of 8 or 9 miles to reach those billets.

By 2.45 a.m. on 26th the greater part of the infantry had not reached the position they were to take up but were in and around Fontaine au Pire. It was very dark, and it was very difficult to identify the exact spot we had arrived at. I have already described how I saw General Haldane and General Hunter-Weston and how we agreed that the men had better bivouac where they were till there was sufficient light to see what we were doing. The troops started again before daylight, but as they arrived on the positions they were to occupy they were involved in practically what was a battle of encounter.

Now I am not one of these people who think that troops can be pinned to a position as I feel convinced that in these days of long range weapons troops can always slip away, but I think retiring troops may be forced to halt by a vigorous attack made on them and that it may be two or three hours before they can make such arrangements as to enable them gradually to retire under cover of a rear-guard. Therefore, considering that the Division had to deploy or was partially deployed when it was attacked at about 5.30 a.m. I do not think it could have continued its retirement till say 8.30 a.m. at the earliest.

Had therefore the 3rd and 5th Divisions continued their retirement before dawn, as Sir John French thinks they should have done, say about 4.30 a.m., they would certainly have got some seven or eight miles on their way at the very least, while the 4th Division was still engaged on the Fontaine au Pire–Wambaix position. The enemy would then have been able to pour down on the 4th Division's right flank and the Division would, in all probability, have been surrounded or forced back on to Cambrai.

When this proposition was suggested to General Sir Archibald Murray some years after 1914, that officer said that the G.H.Q. idea was that the 3rd and 5th Divisions should have continued the retirement before dawn on the 26th under cover of a strong rear-guard composed of the 4th Division and the guns of the three divisions. This suggestion seems to show that G.H.Q. was not aware of the position of the 4th Division at dawn on 26th and that G.H.Q. imagined the 4th Division to be complete whereas it was deficient of its Divisional Cavalry, Signal Companies, Field Companies, R.E., Heavy Artillery and Field Ambulances. All very important units in connection with a strong rear-guard.

There has been a good deal said at various times as to why the left flank of the 4th Division was not turned at Le Cateau. Lord French, in his book '1914', gives the credit to General Sordet although in his original despatch he said General Sordet gave no help and he severely blamed him for withholding that help. Sir Horace Smith-Dorrien also seems to imply that General Sordet saved the left as he describes how he, hearing guns to the westward about 6 p.m. rode to see what they were, and on reaching some high ground he found they were General Sordet's guns.

As a matter of fact General Sordet had nothing to do with the matter whatever. The real reason was that there were not sufficient Germans on the ground to attempt a turning movement till about 3 p.m., by which hour the 4th Division was beginning its retirement.

The German 7th Reserve Division reached the Cambrai–Le Cateau road, north of Cattenières about 2 p.m., the guns having been sent forward and being in action, the cavalry having been thrown on the defensive. (Note 1 p. 174, British Official History of the War.)[3] At the same time the 22nd German Reserve Division, belonging to same Corps, advanced on the right wing of the Corps and deployed about 2 p.m. north of the Le Cateau–Cambrai road about Carnières and Cauroi and advanced in the first instance against French Cuirassiers and then against French infantry at Séranvillers. The Division met with considerable opposition and was shelled by French and British artillery. (British Official account p. 201 note.)

I admit that these Cuirassiers and these guns may have belonged to General Sordet though there is no evidence to show they did, and the guns are more likely to have belonged to the garrison of Cambrai, which was under the command of General D'Amade. At any rate the infantry encountered at Séranvillers belonged to General D'Amade, which shows that the outposts of the Cambrai garrison were in the adjoining villages where possibly they may have absorbed some of General Sordet's patrols.

Thus at 2 p.m. there was only a gap of some 3 miles between the 4th Division's left and the Cambrai garrison and this gap would have appeared even narrower to an attack from the north as the 4th Division's left was due south of the easternmost of the French troops.

The garrison of Cambrai was certainly a support to the 4th Division as the Germans, even if they detected the gap, which is very doubtful,

---

3   Here and elsewhere in this narrative General Snow refers to the 1922 edition of *Military Operations, France and Belgium, 1914. Volume I: Mons, the Retreat to the Seine, the Marne and the Aisne, August–October 1914*.

would have hesitated to push through it with a hostile force of unknown strength in Cambrai unless they were strong enough to contain that force. Nothing in any German account that I know of speaks of any attempt to turn the 4th Division's left, but some accounts do treat the whole position from Le Cateau to Cambrai as one continuous position. Therefore until the French Territorials could be driven back no attempt could be made to turn the 4th Division's left. In the end the garrison of Cambrai and the 4th Division began their retirement about the same time, that is 3 p.m. and this retiring together was a matter of luck not of arrangement.

But to return to General Sordet's Corps. Even admitting that the Cuirassiers which the Germans encountered at Carnières belonged to his troops, it is impossible from his general movements that day to believe that he ever had any intention of doing more than demonstrate during the battle. We hear of his Corps bivouacking about Walincourt and Esnes on the night of the 25th/26th, wet through and the horses dead beat. We know that two days before he had told Lord French that his horses were too tired to move and we know he had covered a long distance since then. We also know that he moved off at a very early hour on the 26th August in a southerly direction as Colonel Bowes, the liaison officer, came across the tail of his column very early in the morning and appreciated that the corps must be too far away to give assistance that day. We know that the destination of one of Sordet's Divisions, namely the 1st, was Villers Guislain, 14 miles south of Cambrai and about the same distance from the 4th Division's left. We are told that about 2 p.m. on the 26th the 1st Division moved forward from Villers Guislain to within a short distance of Cambrai, where its guns engaged hostile infantry (*II. Corps*) coming out of the town about 6.30 p.m., by which time the 4th Division was beyond all need of support.[4] It then retired with the 5th Cavalry Division, whose previous movements are unknown, to Gouzeaucourt, 12 miles south of Cambrai.

---

4   General Snow appears to be mistaken about the time at which General Sordet's guns opened: see Notes to Part One below, p. 61.

In the preface of the Official History we are told that information re General Sordet's Corps was furnished very courteously by the French General Staff. As the French General Staff must have known from Lord French's original despatch that the English viewed General Sordet's support with some suspicion, they would naturally have brought forward all the evidence they could to prove he did support the British troops, but they have been unable to bring forward anything very convincing. If General Sordet had really intended to do all he could to help us he would not have hurried his troops away from Esnes and Walincourt in the early morning, when he was in the exact spot to give us efficient support if we stood and fought. Neither would he have gone for a gratuitous route march of some 20 miles, with his horses already tired, before appearing late in the afternoon south of Cambrai.

It may be urged that he thought we were going on with the retreat on the 26th. If he did think so he ought to have conformed to our movements and kept within supporting distance of our left. But it is difficult to believe that he really thought we were going on with the retirement as he should have heard of the proposed stand during the night, and even if he did not, his ears would have told him what was happening by 5.30 a.m. on the 26th.

When Colonel Bowes told me of the existence of this cavalry very early in the battle, I asked him to try and get to General Sordet and ask him to do something to cover my left flank. Colonel Bowes got so hung up in the rear of General Sordet's cavalry at about 7 a.m. that he gave my message to a French Cyclist and also to a French Mounted officer to deliver. Probably therefore General Sordet got my message about 8.30 a.m., and so must have known by then of the battle if he did not know earlier.

Why Lord French suddenly altered his opinion and was so profuse in his thanks to General Sordet I do not know, but I feel certain that no action on the part of the latter had any effect on the battle of Le Cateau and I do not believe that General Sordet, at any time of the day, tried even to persuade himself that he was trying to help us.

I believe that he deliberately left us to our fate.

Looking back on the battle of Le Cateau I have little to reproach myself with, but only one thing to congratulate myself about, and that one thing was the splendid behaviour of the men and the efficiency of the Brigadiers, commanding officers and regimental officers. I feel I can legitimately claim credit for some small portion of this as I had always during peace training worked with a view to such a result. But when I have said that I have said all. Very little, if anything, of what I did during the day had any effect on the result of the battle. I was heavily handicapped by the absence of my signal company, as I was unable to get messages to the Brigadiers, except by sending off my staff to carry such messages. The Brigadiers were even worse off than I was, as, having a smaller staff, it was as much as they could do to get their orders to the troops without worrying about sending back information, the consequence being that I was very much in the dark as to what was going on in the Front line. I had never been told, not even during that depressing interview at G.H.Q. on the 24th, that the enemy were in overwhelming numbers, and I was never made to understand that, whatever the result of the battle, retreat was inevitable. This omission might have had a serious effect as at about 1 p.m. I was convinced that I was fighting a winning action and indeed my left was advancing. Had I not stopped this advance, and I did so because I heard that the whole front was to retire, my left would have been advancing at the very moment the enemy were in position to turn it and I should have been making his task easier.

As I have already said I was never told that Cambrai was defended or that there was, or ought to have been, a large force of French cavalry in rear of my left. I did find out about the cavalry early in the battle from Colonel Bowes, but almost by accident.

The worst mistake was not telling me that retreat was inevitable. Had I known that fact earlier I should have been able to have had the line of retreat reconnoitred, and been able to give more thought as to how the retirement was to be carried out.

Whether it was necessary to give me a line of retirement at such an angle with the battle front I cannot say; probably it was, but it had disastrous consequences which I again repeat. Large portions of units never got any orders to retire and only conformed when they saw what was going on. When it got dark, and it got dark very early and suddenly that night, touch was lost and those portions which had received no orders as to the line of retirement continued their movement direct to the rear, thus getting mixed up with units of the 3rd and 5th Division and so retiring on their roads. A very large portion of my Division, including two Brigadiers, was separated from the Division and rejoined me by driblets during the next two or three days.

Owing to the absence of my field ambulances I only could bring away the walking wounded, in addition to the six or seven hundred Major Ensor, as before described, got away in country carts.

I can only say that whoever was responsible for not rushing up my signal company and field ambulances, when it became evident that a battle was imminent, made a very great and serious error, and whoever was responsible for leaving me with so little information was still more to blame. My Brigadiers, no doubt, laid the same charge at my door, but I have tried to explain in the above passage the reason for my action or rather lack of action.

IV. The Retreat – From Le Cateau to the Marne

How it was I felt so happy in my mind on the evening of Le Cateau, after we had arrived at Vendhuile, and how I managed to sleep so peacefully has always been a wonder to me. It is true we had fought more or less a winning action and had, as I knew, inflicted heavy losses on the enemy. I did not realise that I was only forming part of a beaten and retreating army, as nobody told me so and there was nothing in my surroundings to show me that was the case. I also knew that I was not being followed at the moment, that I had come 10 miles from the battlefield, and that we should be off again in a few hours. But even then I cannot understand how I took things so easily. I ought to have realised that my outposts were, to say the least of it, sketchy and the men furnishing them dead tired. I ought to have realised that even if the enemy had lost touch for the moment he would make every effort to regain it and would follow me up for all he was worth. I can conscientiously say that it was the last time during the campaign that I took things easily and that ever after I always prepared for the worst. Thank goodness that night the enemy acted in an inconceivable manner and so our sins of omission were not visited on us, but I can never contemplate that night without a cold shiver running down my back, and if there are such things as lucky stars mine was functioning exceedingly well on my behalf on that night.

We were off again by 5.30 a.m. on 27th with orders to halt on the high ground north of Lempier. This was a sound order as the position was a very strong one as the enemy found to his cost in 1917 and 1918. I was very glad when we reached that position as the road from Vendhuile to Lempier was a steep and long ascent and in full view from the high ground about Le Cetelet. I sent a message to General Allenby, commanding the Cavalry Division, saying that unless I received other orders I should retire through Roisel and Hancourt.

Leaving the 12th Brigade as a rear-guard on the Ronssoy position we reached Roisel about 9 a.m. and halted to water horses and have breakfast. An indecisive action between German and French cavalry took place at Villers Faucon near by, but as far as I could make out it only consisted of mutual shelling. Roisel was also lightly shelled.

It was while we were here that I caught my first glimpse of General Sordet's Cavalry. I was on some high ground and could see several squadrons of French cavalry drawn up behind a wood about 2 miles on my left. This was a very comforting sight. I told Colonel Edmonds to send them a stirring message to the effect that we would stand by them to death or something equally absurd and got a suitable response. Hardly had I received it than I saw shrapnel bursting one, two, three, high above the squadrons. The squadrons wheeled about, moved off at a walk, which increased to a trot, then to a gallop, and that is the last I saw or heard of the great Sordet and his cavalry during the retreat.

Horses having been watered we retired to the Hancourt plateau, a very strong position, where several of our wandering parties joined us, noticeably General Haldane and his party.

We dug, or rather I should say scratched, ourselves in in a retired position, our right on the village of Bernes, left on Nobescourt

Farm. We got no information but many rumours, one being that a huge force of German infantry was well behind our left flank, but this particular report was impossible to credit and like most other reports turned out to be false. However, the cavalry, who were by way of covering me, sent me back no information and I did not even know whether they were between me and the enemy or not. The 12th Brigade joined in about 6 p.m.

The rest here did the Division much good, although the staff and the regimental officers were too busy to take advantage of it.

Orders were received to retire to Voyennes and then cover the crossing of the Somme. We marched off at 7 p.m., 10th Brigade leading, 12th as rear-guard, and were clear of Hancourt by 9 p.m. My staff managed the march wonderfully well. Captain Burnett Hitchcock had ready a large number of country carts to act as ambulances in every big village through which we passed and he also placed light obstructions on every branch road so that even if touch was lost, the road we were following was clearly indicated. The march discipline was wonderfully good, though the men were very tired. No doubt, however, many men who were quite fit to march took advantage of getting a lift in the country carts. These carts constantly broke down and had to be turned into the ditch to clear the road. When this had to be done it was very difficult to get the men out of the carts and physical force was often necessary. There were long halts and every time a halt came from the front it was impossible to be quite sure it was not that the head of some unit had gone to sleep. However, sticking to the good old rule that each unit was responsible that the one in rear was following, we kept going.

We arrived at Voyennes at about 4 a.m. 28th August.

The position was a difficult one to know what to do with. All these French rivers are very difficult to defend from behind the river as there is no field of fire. At this time in the campaign we had not learned to use our artillery, neither had we the ammunition to leave the defence to that arm as we should have done later. I took up the best position I could and then walked along the north side of the river with General Milne so as to see the position from the enemy's point of view. I have often laughed since at this idiotic proceeding. We might very easily have been taken prisoner and it would have served us right but I don't believe such a thought ever crossed the minds of either of us at the time. We did not find the car and it was past 10 a.m. before we got back to Headquarters.

There Colonel Edmonds showed me two orders which had been received in my absence. One was that a large force of the enemy was at St. Quentin and that I was to move up the river and from the north bank cover the crossing of the 3rd Division who would use the bridges south of Ham.

To this day I have never been able to understand the reason for this order. Probably that part of the order directing me to be on this north bank was framed by some junior officer, although it appeared over the signature of the Deputy C.G.S., but why I should have been sent towards Ham at all I don't know. All our cavalry were north of the river and they were quite sufficient to cover the retirement of the 3rd Division without dragging my Division, after a long night march, about six miles out of its way.

The other order was still more remarkable and was sufficiently alarmist to turn the retreat into a rout. It was to the effect that 'all ammunition on wagons not absolutely required and other impediments such as officers' kits, etc., are to be left off-loaded and officers and men carried to the full capacity of all transport both horse and mechanical'. This order inflicted the greatest hardship on officers and men for months and naturally lowered their morale. The effect on the enemy when he saw what had been done must have been to raise his morale a hundred per cent. I do not know who was the author of this blunder. General Smith-Dorrien says that had he seen it before it was passed on he would have torn it up. I know the effect on my own morale when I saw half-burnt valises, bedding, greatcoats, etc. lying in heaps and I cannot bear even now to think of the delight such a sight must have been to the Germans.

About this time General Hunter-Weston and the remainder of his Brigade rejoined us and we also got touch of our missing Field Companies, Signal Company, Cyclists and Field Ambulances. We badly

wanted the first three and ordered them up, but again G.H.Q., or some
officious underling in their name, prevented them from joining us.

The 3rd Division crossed the river unmolested while my main body
waited about Esmery Hallon, and the cavalry gradually withdrew to
the south bank of the river. We knew nothing of the whereabouts of
the cavalry except what we could see and just as we were going to
blow up a bridge over the canal a large body of our cavalry arrived
from the north. How all the cavalry got across in the end I cannot
imagine. At one time in the morning a whole brigade appeared from
the direction of Voyennes and for a long time we were in doubt as to
whether they were our own people or Germans.

About this time we got an order to cross the Oise at Pont l'Eveque
that night. This was a stiff proposition. The bridge in question was
twelve miles distant as the crow flies and only twisting second class
roads to go by. The men were dead tired, only having had a few
hours' rest at Vendhuile on the night of the 26th/27th and marching
all night on the 27th/28th. However, after a longish halt at Esmery
Hallon we set forth.

We marched on as long as we could keep the men on their feet but
had to stop long after dark in and around Muirancourt. We established
touch with the 3rd Division.

Everyone was so tired that they dropped down where they were
and got several hours refreshing sleep.

Sempigny, just south of Noyon, was given us as our billeting area
for the night of 28th August and we moved off about 8 a.m. [on the
29th] and halted at Beaurains, a strong position.

It was about this time that the rumour, started at G.H.Q., got about
that we were to halt behind the River Oise to rest and refit. Why the
Oise was supposed to afford us protection I don't know, and as it
turned out we hardly halted there at all, but similar rumours kept on
being circulated, and the Aisne, and afterwards the Marne, and later
the Seine, were all held out as havens of rest which we were marching
for. It was not good for the troops. The mention of rest and refitting
began to be a subject for joke and the men were quite certain that it
was intended to retire to Marseilles with every river between held up

as haven of refuge, a refuge which they knew would never materialise. At first I was taken in myself and did forced marches to reach these havens, but when I found that these havens of rest disappeared when one reached them I soon attached no importance to rivers.

Hearing that Noyon was congested with troops I remained all day at Beaurains and set off in the evening for Carlepont, with the whole Division except the 10th Infantry Brigade and some guns which I left north of the river to collect all stragglers before blowing up the Noyon bridges. I had to send Major Montgomery my G.S.2 back to General Haldane with a message and I told him to rejoin me in the morning with the latest news of General Haldane's movements. My other G.S. Officers had been sent off on various duties leaving only Colonel Edmonds with me. On arrival at Carlepont Captain Burnett Hitchcock went off to prepare the next day's route, but before doing so pointed me out the route on the map and the road we should take to get us clear of the village as it is impossible to find your way out of a village by a small scale map if there are many exits. Colonel Edmonds and I then began to write the orders. I sent my A.D.C. to bed as I wanted him early.

No sooner had we begun than Colonel Edmonds said he could write or think no more. He was utterly done up which was little to wonder at considering what he had been through and how he had worked since the 25th instant with practically no sleep or rest. His loss was irreparable.

To find oneself practically alone with not sufficient detail at hand to make the task of writing orders easier, dog-tired, and with a flickering candle to work by, and yet knowing that the safety of the whole Division depended on the rapidity with which orders were got out and the accuracy of those orders, is not an enviable position and how I got through the task I don't know: but General Milne was most attentive and plied me with food during those anxious hours. However, somehow the orders were completed and issued.

About half an hour before the troops were due to arrive at the starting point, while it was yet dark, Colonel Taylor, my 'Q' Officer, an officer in whom I placed the greatest reliance, came in and told me that the villagers said that the road we were going by was not the best road to Tracy-le-Mont and that they pointed to another road as the correct one. Both roads I could see went more or less westward but to identify the roads on the map was impossible. At length I decided to follow the advice of the villagers and I diverted the head of the column accordingly.

We had not gone a mile when I saw the road we were on was bending to the westward whereas I knew that the right road should have turned to the southward, and I not only realised that we were on the wrong road but that the road went through a dense wood and would bring us down to the Oise again at Bailly. I admit being very anxious until I heard that our cavalry were holding Bailly Bridge. We turned southward at Bailly and reached Tracy-le-Mont about 11 a.m. [30 August] having come some three or four miles out of our way.

On arrival at Tracy-le-Mont General Smith-Dorrien visited us and told me that the situation was much easier and that the necessity for hurry had more or less disappeared but he hoped we would cross the Aisne that night. He was also very flattering in his remarks on what the Division had done.

We had a long halt at Tracy-le-Mont and when we set out again we formed up on the plateau in more or less battle formation and resumed the order of march from that. I think this had a good effect on the men.

We reached the Aisne that evening south of the river about Berneuil and Attichy. Headquarters were in a most sumptuous Chateau near Couloist, everything just as the owners had left it. We slept in lovely empire beds in the finest of linen sheets and stewed ourselves in marble baths. One unfortunate thing happened. A belated order was received ordering us to blow up Bailly Bridge. I did not see the order but Major Barstow, R.E. and a small party set off to try and carry it out although it was eight hours too late. They got to the bridge but were challenged and received with a volley, and only one transport officer and a few men who were with the lorry got back.

That evening we came under the command of General Pulteney, who had been appointed to command the III Corps consisting of the 4th and 6th Divisions, the latter being still in England.

The 19th Brigade was attached to this Corps in the place of the 6th Division. The 19th Brigade was composed of four battalions originally intended for lines of communication troops, but which were hurriedly called up and formed into a brigade immediately after the battle of Mons.[5] The Brigadier and the Brigade Major were both on the sick list and the brigade was merely four battalions without any staff of cohesion. How they were even fed I cannot imagine. They had had a great deal of fighting at Mons and Le Cateau, were quite worn out, and their morale, for the moment, was low.

The orders we received for the 31st were that we were to march westward through the Forest of Compiègne to Verberie about 15 miles distant. Verberie is on the Oise, or practically so, and is 10 miles south-west of the junction of the Oise and the Aisne. This order meant for us a flank march within striking distance of the enemy and moreover a flank march through a thick forest with plentiful rides, mostly grass, but some of a more solid foundation, both from north to south and from east to west. I am not in a position to say whether such a march could have been avoided, probably it could not, but it was a movement of such alarming danger that it must have cost G.H.Q. and Corps Headquarters as much anxiety as it caused me. They were in a better position to judge than I was, as they knew we had a cavalry brigade in the direction of Compiègne, a fact I did not know, and they did not consider it necessary to inform me about, but it would have eased my anxiety if they had. However, there was the order and it had to be carried out. There was one good metalled road from Attichy to Verberie via Pierfonds and I determined to send all my wheeled transport and guns by that road, escorted by the 11th Infantry Brigade while I marched the 10th and 12th Brigades by a woodland grass track which ran about two miles to the north of the main road and parallel to it. Why I ever came to such a decision, or why my staff allowed me to do so, I cannot imagine; it was a badly conceived idea as it was much harder marching by the track than by the main road and was

---

5   In fact the 19th Brigade was formed before Mons: see Notes to Part One below, p. 64.

two or three miles further. It afforded no greater security to the main body than if I had covered my flank with a battalion.

The start was bad. Either a good many Uhlans really got close enough to fire at us as we were breaking bivouac or our outposts imagined they saw Uhlans, but any way there was a great deal of firing going on though I could not find out what it was about even though I sent back to see.

It was one of the hottest marches I have ever known. The main body got to St. Sauveur about noon and remained there till we could clear up the situation, as we heard that at least two divisions of Germans were through Compiègne. The spot where the 10th and 12th Brigades were to emerge on to the Compiègne–Verberie road was at St. Croix, about midway between the two places and it was not till six in the evening that the head of the column reached that place. I had heard some hours before that one of our cavalry brigades was at St. Croix and I had many rumours of cavalry fights at that place, all of which were more or less imaginary. At about 6 p.m. I sent my guns and all transport up on to the plateau south of the small river which runs through St. Sauveur and into the Oise at Verberie, and I sent one battalion from each brigade as the brigades arrived as an escort. I was much disconcerted in seeing the enemy's aeroplanes notifying the position of our guns, by dropping various coloured light balls on them, but nothing came of it. Gradually my infantry arrived and we were in a fairly strong position behind the Oise and the tributary stream. There was, however, no less than 6 miles between my right and the 3rd Division. Our cavalry retired behind us for the night and our infantry held the bridges.

Soon after dark about six motor cars arrived from the westward carrying a French brigade staff. These cars were fitted out with head lights so dazzling that the sky was illuminated. This was very annoying as I did not want the Germans to know where we were. Many more cars, equally illuminated, soon arrived carrying a portion of the brigade. The officers and men got out of these cars and made such a noise and created such a panic among the inhabitants that I was quite delighted when they got back into their cars and drove off. They were a fair sample of French Territorials, almost off their heads with excitement, and quite useless.

We had not at that time realised that the only French troops we came across were Territorials of the worst class, and we imagined that all French troops were the same; and we were only anxious to get them out of the way. It was not till the advance began and the battle of the Ourcq was in full swing that we saw the French Regulars. We then quickly recognised what grand fighting soldiers the French are.

Somehow both General Milne and I got a great horror of that position, and I had named it the 'Valley of the shadow of death'. I felt that the sooner we were out of it and on the plateau, the better. I put the marching hour on about 2 hours, making it just before daylight [1 September] and I myself started for the plateau half an hour earlier. As I was ascending the hill through a dense wood, which covered the slopes, a terrific gun and rifle fire opened on the plateau, apparently directly on our line of march. I was hardly on the plateau before I was the centre of a galloping mass of unsaddled, maddened horses, some loose, some ridden by half-dressed men, many of them wounded. They drew up when they got near me and after some moments General Milne told me that, as far as he could ascertain, there had been an action at Néry between the 1st Cavalry brigade, with which was 'L' Battery, and a German cavalry brigade which had got through the gap between my right and the 3rd Division during the night, with our guns as their objective. Report said that the Germans were in possession of Néry. I sent General Haldane, whom I met at that moment, with 2 battalions to retake Néry at all costs, but when he arrived at that village he found that we had got the village and the enemy's guns, and that the hostile brigade had disappeared. It afterwards appeared that this hostile brigade came quite unexpectedly on the 1st Cavalry Brigade and after the fight could only get away to the southwards, where they broke up into small parties and hid in the woods, making raids for food. It was very many days, almost it may be said weeks, before all these scattered parties were accounted for, and it was their doings which caused the report that the Uhlans were always pushing through our lines and annoying our rear, which was quite true but by no means intentional on the enemy's part.

It took a long time withdrawing the 11th Brigade, which got rather heavily engaged at St. Sauveur, but I got them on to the plateau at last and went on with the retirement.

Headquarters of the III Corps was some miles in rear of us and, on being sniped by the fugitives from Néry, sent a message to me to send the 12th Brigade to them at once. Now if, at any staff tour at which the staff of the III Corps were acting as directors, any one of the players had sent a message asking for a brigade or any other unit by name without leaving the selection to the officer in command, the directors would have been horrified and a great deal would have been said or written on the enormity of the request; yet here you have a thoroughly trained and experienced staff, on the first day of their taking part in real war, perpetrating the very mistake they had so often corrected in others. It was bad, very bad. As a matter of fact at this moment I could not send the 12th; so I sent another brigade which, as was to be expected, was sufficient to overawe the snipers, and we heard no more of them.

We got safely into billets about Barron and Rosières, but our cyclists were much annoyed by the sniping fugitives and suffered some loss.

It was on this day [1 September] that I became aware of a very extraordinary thing which had happened, not extraordinary as regards the happening but extraordinary as regards the way the authorities dealt with it. It was in this way:

It appears that, after Le Cateau, Colonel 'A' with about 200 men of the 'A'shires and Colonel 'B' with about 30 men of the 'B'shires, both in my Division, after having lost their way, finally found themselves at St. Quentin, hungry and thoroughly done up, just as the last of the English troops had left that place. The men could go no further and threw themselves down and slept. The Mayor of St. Quentin came and interviewed Colonel 'A', telling him that the town was full of women and children, and that if Colonel 'A' and his troops remained, no doubt the Germans would fire on the town. Colonel 'A' could do nothing to rouse the tired-out men, and finally, persuaded by the

Mayor, made out a treaty between Colonels 'A' and 'B' on the one part and the German Emperor, etc., etc., giving themselves up as prisoners of war on certain conditions which were laid down. Now it is very difficult to know what else Colonel 'A' could have done. Probably the right course would have been to refuse to do anything until the Germans arrived: but Colonel 'A' imagined they were now before the town. He could not get his men on their legs to move out of the town; it is not unnatural that he gave way to the Mayor's entreaties and signed the papers. This paper he gave to the Mayor to give to the Germans on arrival. Colonel 'A' was a man of rather theatrical nature, and one can imagine him saying 'at any rate they will always quote my action as the proper thing to do in such circumstances'. Now if the matter had stopped there nothing more would have been heard of it; but the Germans did not arrive that night.

In the morning the men having been well-fed and rested were very different men from what they had been the night before. At this moment a cavalry subaltern, commanding one of the last of our patrols, rode through the town and asked the men what they were doing. By this time the men were ready to do anything and wanted to go with the cavalry subaltern, but unfortunately there was the treaty in the Mayor's hands. Here again was a predicament. It must be remembered that all this happened before we found out that war was not conducted on that gentlemanly and chivalrous system which we had always been led to expect, and no doubt Colonel 'A' was in doubt as to what would be the right thing to do. At any rate in the end he allowed the cavalry subaltern to go to the Mayor, explain matters, and ask for the return of the paper. The Mayor consented. Here again all would have been well had the cavalry subaltern torn up the document; but a senior officer arrived to whom he handed the paper, and this officer said that he would only give it into the hands of Sir John French himself.

And so it happened that I got orders to put both Colonel 'A' and Colonel 'B' under arrest.

After they had been carted about in an ambulance for some ten days, first during the retreat and then during the advance, they were tried, convicted and sentenced to be cashiered. Colonel 'A' retired to England and seclusion; Colonel 'B' at once enlisted in the Foreign Legion of the French Army, in which after having done many deeds of valour and having been more than once wounded, he got such a splendid reputation that at the end of the war he was reinstated as a Colonel in the Army and given back all his distinctions and decorations. These are the facts as they are known: but what I always want to know is what should Colonel 'A' have done, firstly when approached by the Mayor, when his men were dead to the world, secondly when he found next morning that escape was possible and that his men had recovered. As far as I can see he behaved perfectly correctly on both these occasions. All through the war the correct thing to do seemed to depend on the point of view of one's immediate senior. Later in the war, when men found themselves in an isolated position and retired, it depended on the point of view of the senior officer whether they got D.C.M.'s for gallant conduct in a difficult position, or whether they were shot for cowardice.

The next morning, the 2nd September, we marched before daylight. It was on this day I began to notice how discipline had deteriorated. As I said earlier, many men had parted with their badges and buttons at Boulogne. This started them on the downward path. After the order to burn kit at Noyon, many others things followed the buttons, and I regret to say that greatcoats, valises, and a great deal of equipment were thrown away during the night marches. What the roads must have been like I don't know, but I can imagine, and it is easy to see why the Germans put the B.E.F. down as a routed and negligible rabble which, stripped of all poetic licence, is exactly what it was. The officers did their best, but they were done to a turn; so done were they that they could only talk in a hoarse whisper. I have often been told by staff and cavalry officers that the 4th Division was in a far better state than any other Division, possibly because it had not been at it so long; but if this is correct, what the other divisions must have been like I cannot imagine. Certainly the state of the 19th Brigade was ten times worse than anything I had in my Division; but so extraordinary is the British character that I knew perfectly well that if it came to a fight, the men would fight as well as ever, and I have always blamed the authorities for the bolt we made of it. Had we retired more slowly fighting rear-guard actions, we should have taken immense toll out of the enemy and kept our men in better hand. We may have been prevented from doing this owing to the hasty retirement of the French, but I doubt it. This day we saw a great deal of the cavalry. I retired to Dammartin, a town on a very high hill, from which there was a magnificent view. From there we saw a good deal of shelling, but did not know what it was all about.

That evening, 2nd September, we marched off about 9.30 p.m. or a little later. Dammartin was a difficult place to get out of owing to the scarcity of the roads. I imagined we were fighting a rear-guard action on the outskirts of the town: but 2 or 3 years afterwards I was assured by the inhabitants, when I visited the place, that no Germans had ever been within 3 miles of Dammartin, but passed the hill without ascending it. Early next morning, 3rd September, our march was much hindered by fugitives, and roads were more or less blocked. It was only as we got near Paris that I noticed this wholesale flight. There were a few people at Dammartin; but at Lagny and all places south of the Marne the entire population had fled.

On the 4th September we remained at Lagny in comparative security, as we had the Marne on our Front, most of the bridges over which were destroyed. I have never been quite able to make out the arrangements as regards the blowing up of the bridges over the Marne. I have always been taught that a retiring force, if there is any likelihood of its being in a position to turn the retirement into an advance, should be very careful what bridges, if any, should be destroyed. This was not the case with us. Little attention was paid to the bridges. Sometimes they were destroyed, sometimes they were not. There may have been a plan but it was not apparent.

The day's rest at Lagny was very welcome. We understood that the situation was changing, but we knew little details, and it would have caused no more surprise to hear we were to advance on the 5th than if we had heard we were to retire. As a matter of fact we retired.

The reason for this further retreat is obscure, and a careful study of the official history of the war does not help to elucidate the matter.

Sir John French's Order No. 16 of 4th Sept. (6.35 p.m.) reads:

Columns of the enemy, probable strength 3½ Corps and 4 Cavalry
Divisions, have been marching all day across our front in a south-
easterly direction, their left on Chateau Thierry, their right on La
Ferté sous Jouarre. By noon the leading troops had begun to attack
XVIII Corps of the 5th French Army at St. Barthélemy. The enemy's
right flank guard, directed on Barcy, may be expected to cross the
Marne to-night or to-morrow morning near Germigny.

Now, if the above was given as a situation in a war game and the
question was asked 'What should the B.E.F. do?' the only possible
answer would be to carry out the scheme Galliéni put forward
during his visit to British Headquarters on the 4th, which was to
advance what he called his 'Army of Paris', namely the 6th Army and
the Paris Garrison, in an eastward direction and, on the following
day, the 5th, to attack in conjunction with the B.E.F. the right flank
of the German Army.

However, the second paragraph of Sir John's Order No. 16 shows
that he did not agree with this suggestion as it reads 'The Army will
move S.W. to-morrow – September 5 – pivoting on its left'. The
only redeeming point in the above, the four words 'pivoting on its
left', is negatived by the details laid down for the march causing the
retirement to be due south with hardly a touch of west in it, and no
pivoting on the left whatever.

The Official History tries to show that Joffre agreed with this move
as it quotes a letter from Joffre to Sir John saying:

In case the German Armies should continue the movement south-
south-east, thus moving away from the Seine and Paris, perhaps you
will consider, as I do, that your action will be most effective on the
right bank of that river between Marne and Seine.

    Your left resting on the Marne, supported by the entrenched camp
of Paris, will be covered by the mobile garrison of the capital, which
will attack eastwards on the left bank of the Marne.

There is also a suggestion that Joffre wanted more room for
Galliéni's Army about Lagny.

I can find nothing in Joffre's letter, or in the situation, to justify this retirement. Had Sir John pivoted back slightly on his left so as to ease the pressure on the right, if such pressure ever existed, and to open the jaws of the trap wider, well and good; but to withdraw the left 14 miles was a serious mistake, and put the III Corps one day behind in all subsequent operations till the Aisne was reached, a day's march they were always trying to make up but never could.

And so on the morning of the 5th we marched to Brie–Comte Robert. We threw out a line of outposts just south of the main line from Paris to the eastward along which line the French were moving trains at six minute intervals bringing troops from Alsace to reinforce Galliéni. No doubt the authorities knew that the line in question was in perfect safety; but it did seem strange to leave such an important line outside the protected zone, and I, being ignorant of the situation, moved the outposts forward to include the line.

So ended the retreat. It speaks volumes for the British character that the way it was conducted did not change it from a retreat to a rout. I am convinced that the only way to conduct such a retreat without loss of morale is to turn and rend the pursuer whenever he gives you a chance, and that every effort should be made to hide the appearance of hurry.

As can be seen from the above story we did none of these things. We were never allowed to fight, and were always being urged to move faster.

The strange part is that during the whole retreat I am convinced that every officer and man was certain that all would turn up right in the end, and I think that our feelings were similar to those of one of our men who, running before the enemy at the rate of 20 miles a day, almost done to the world, after one of our worst marches, was overhead to say 'Well if I don't give those blankety blank Germans what for for this when I get to Berlin, may I be for ever blankety blanked!!!'

Notes to Part One

The 4th Division from Mobilisation to the End of the Retreat from Mons

All dates are 1914 unless otherwise stated. All references to volume one of *Military Operations, France and Belgium, 1914*, are to the 1933 edition and not the 1922 edition, and are abbreviated: *MO, 1914, v. 1*. German units are italicised: *IV Reserve Corps*, etc. Figures in square brackets at the start of each note refer to page numbers in the text.

[8] '. . . *it was not until about the 29th of July that soldiers realised that the time had come when they would have to give an account of themselves.*'
    At midday on 29 July the cabinet authorised the 'precautionary period' in case of war: officers and men on leave were recalled to their regiments, and coastal defences manned. It was still uncertain, however, that war would be declared, and, if it were, what use would be made of the army: as late as 2 August a majority of the cabinet still believed 'that Britain was embarking on a naval war' (Strachan, p. 198).

[9] '*On August 9th we received orders for Headquarters of the Division to move to Bury St. Edmunds and the Division to move to various places on the east coast . . .*'
    Before the outbreak of war 4th Division headquarters were at Woolwich, and the headquarters of the 10th, 11th and 12th Brigades at Shorncliffe (near Folkestone), Colchester and Dover, respectively. After the declaration of war the division was assigned to defensive duties on the east coast – the 11th Brigade remaining

at Colchester while the 10th was dispatched to York and the 12th to Cromer, each with a battery of field artillery.

[11] '... *Mrs.Winston Churchill was playing golf at Sheringham, a few miles from Cromer, where she was joined by her husband. The First Lord of the Admiralty, seeing no troops about ... telegraphed for a Brigade.'*

General Snow's unlikely explanation of the reason why the 12th Brigade was sent to Cromer has a basis in fact. That summer the Churchills rented a seaside cottage in Overstrand, near Cromer, where Clementine remained after the declaration of war. Churchill wrote to her on 9 August: 'It makes me a little anxious that you should be on the coast. It is 100 to 1 against a raid – but still there is the chance: & Cromer has a good landing place near.' She wrote that day that the local authorities 'in a frantic effort to stem the ebbing tide of tourists' had projected onto the screen at the local cinema the message: 'Visitors! Why are you leaving Cromer? Mrs Winston Churchill and her Children are in residence in the neighbourhood. If it's safe enough for her, surely it's safe enough for you!' (Mary Soames (ed.), *Speaking for Themselves: The Personal Letters of Winston and Clementine Churchill* (London, 1998), pp. 92, 100–1.)

[11–12] *'On the 16th [August] we had completed mobilisation and I reported to the War Office ... I gathered that ... the 6th Division, which was the next Division due to start, had not yet finished mobilising. The 4th Division was therefore to assemble at Harrow and the 6th was to relieve us on the East Coast.'*

It had been agreed by the cabinet on 6 August that the 4th Division, not the 6th, would be next to France; and the division was relieved on the east coast not by the 6th Division, which remained mostly in Ireland, but by Yeomanry and Territorials.

[12] *'Nothing could have been better done than the arrangements for entraining and embarkation and the whole thing was a great triumph for the Quartermaster General.'*

Sir John Cowans: see Biographical Notes.

[12] *'We got out of Southampton Dock about 3 p.m. [22 August] . . . we were not formed into convoys, neither had we any escort . . .'*

The German Navy had no intelligence of the BEF's crossings, but neither was it encouraged to disrupt them. The German Chief of the General Staff personally informed his naval counterparts that 'it would even be of advantage if the armies in the West could settle with the 160,000 English at the same time as the French and Belgians', a perspective 'shared by many during the favourable commencement of the offensive in the West' (*MO, 1914*, v. 1, p. 10, n. 3).

[14] *[night of 24–5 August:] 'Had we arrived 24 hours later we certainly could have taken no part in covering the retirement of the 3rd and 5th Divisions on to the Le Cateau position, though I don't think that would have mattered much.'*

Although the 4th Division was not heavily engaged at Solesmes on 25 August, the troops retreating towards that town from Mons were engaged in 'a running fight' with the enemy, which by nightfall was close by, and Smith-Dorrien was always grateful to it for 'remaining out and allowing our tired rearguard to come through, and acting as a pivot for our cavalry to fall back on' (Ballard, p. 167). For the heavy losses of the 3rd and 5th Divisions 23–24 August see Appendix 5 below, p. 160.

[15] *'I was also told [afternoon of 24 August] that the idea was to fall back on the Le Cateau–Cambrai position and there accept battle, and that the position was being prepared by impressed labour . . .'*

'. . . a long, low spur running south of the Cambrai–Le Cateau road had already been sited as part of a general line, and some feeble trenches dug by civilians, but it was in no sense a prepared system, and the British suffered severely from the overwhelming artillery fire to which no adequate answer was possible' (Cruttwell, p. 23).

[15] *'On my return to Headquarters [late afternoon 24 August] we modified the orders slightly . . .'*

The effect of this was to move all three brigades of the 4th Division further north around Solesmes: by dawn on 25 August they were in place.

[16] *'We had information [25 August] that a strong force was advancing on us from Saulzoir.'*

Most probably General von der Marwitz's *Cavalry Corps*, which had as its objectives Haspres, Solesmes and Le Cateau, bringing it against the British left flank from the direction of Saulzoir. Its 'overtaking pursuit' failed to materialise (*MO, 1914*, v. 1, p. 126, n. 1).

[16–17] *[25 August] 'We certainly should have prevented any turning movement from the north-west, but whether any German troops were near enough to try such a movement I doubt.'*

While the enemy were not yet close enough to turn the British flank they were massing in great strength, a situation imperfectly conveyed by GHQ to its commanders in the field. A 'very accurate' summary compiled that night, 25 August, from air reports, and pointing to a build-up of enemy troops near Valenciennes, 'does not seem to have been communicated to the corps or divisions, or to the cavalry' (*MO, 1914*, v. 1, p. 129).

[18] *'Sir John asked [Archibald] Murray whether anything more had been heard of a large force . . . reported as entering the northern edge of the Forêt de Mormal in the early dawn [25 August]. Murray told him the Intelligence Dept. thought it was a false report, but in view of what happened at Landrecies that night I have often wondered . . .'*

During 25 August advanced guards of *III. Corps* had entered the forest, while those of *IV. Corps* had marched along its western flank. Elements of the latter had moved in the direction of Landrecies, ignorant of the British presence there, and a chance encounter led to a short but intense fight that went on until past midnight.

[18] *'This view was confirmed by a private letter from General [Henry]Wilson. This letter, later confirmed by Operation Order No. 8 of 25th . . .'*

For Wilson's 'private letter' and the content of 'Operation Order No. 8' see Appendix 2 below, pp. 149–50, 153–4.

[19] *[25 August] 'The night was very dark and the whole sky to the northward was lit up by what we thought were burning villages. As a matter of fact they were probably only big fires lighted to dry the men's clothes after the soaking rain.'*
    The official history suggests otherwise: 'As the three brigades marched off south-west rain was falling heavily and the darkness was only relieved on the northern horizon by the red glow of villages fired by the enemy' (*MO, 1914*, v. 1, pp. 138–9).

[21] *[c. 5.30 a.m. 26 August] 'I told Colonel Edmonds to say "Yes" [to Smith-Dorrien] and we agreed there was no necessity to issue further orders as the orders of the night before would now hold good.'*
    The 'orders of the night before' refers to General Snow's Operation Order No. 1 of 5 p.m. on 25 August: see Appendix 2 below, pp. 147–8, 152–3.

[21] *'About this time [a.m. 26 August] we got an order placing the Division under command of General Smith-Dorrien, commanding II Corps.'*
    Around 6.55 a.m. on 26 August 4th Division was warned by GHQ 'that it was to cover Sir H. Smith-Dorrien's left flank', a message repeated in GHQ's *written* reply to Smith-Dorrien sent 11.05 a.m.: '4th Division must co-operate' (*MO, 1914*, v. 1, p. 142).

[22] *[6 a.m. 26 August] 'The Germans brought up a large number of machine guns, and the King's Own and, immediately afterwards, the Lancashire Fusiliers came under a heavy fire . . . Both these battalions, together with two companies of Inniskilling Fusiliers, who came to their help, lost heavily before getting into fighting formation.'*
    Because of the absence of divisional cavalry and cyclists (see below, p. 59, and Appendix 1, p. 145), the 1st King's Own before Longsart were unable to verify French cavalry reports that their front was clear: they were taken completely by surprise when the enemy opened fire from the direction of Cattenières shortly after 6 a.m.

The enemy then turned on the 2nd Lancashire Fusiliers, west of the King's Own. Although the Lancashires initially brought their two machine guns to bear with good effect, one soon jammed, while the enemy had twenty-one with which to answer: the Lancashires were enfiladed 'with deadly effect' (*MO, 1914*, v. 1, pp. 165–6). Two companies of the 2nd Inniskillings gave support to the Lancashires, but General Snow appears to have confused them here with two companies of the 1st Warwickshires: it was the latter that 'swarmed up the hill' to save the King's Own, but were 'swept back upon reaching the crest with very heavy loss'. According to one member of the battalion: 'They had attained nothing, and had not even seen the men they set out to help. We lost half the battalion in that wild attack.' (*MO, 1914*, v. 1, pp. 165–6; Purdom, p. 12). Another of those involved was the future Field Marshal Bernard Montgomery, First Viscount Montgomery of Alamein, then a subaltern; he recalled that seven officers and forty men were lost for nothing: there had been 'no reconnaissance, no plan, no covering fire . . . Nobody knew what to do, so we returned to the original position from which we had begun the attack. If this was real war it struck me as most curious and did not seem to make any sense' (B. L. Montgomery, *The Memoirs of Field Marshal Montgomery* (Barnsley, 2010), p. 32). In spite of its heavy losses the 12th Brigade, with support from the 10th in reserve, withstood for ninety minutes an enemy cavalry division (the *2nd*) and two *Jäger* battalions, and withdrew in good order to the line Ligny–Esnes.

[22] *'I had not been told anything [on 26 August] about overwhelming forces being in the neighbourhood, or that there was any chance of an encircling movement from the north-west, all of which was known at G.H.Q. and probably at H.Q. II Corps . . .'*

During the battle of Mons, and more so Le Cateau, GHQ was out of touch with events. When it was in possession of accurate information regarding the enemy, it did not always pass it on: the official history notes this (*MO, 1914*, v. 1, p. 129), but does not speculate on the reasons for this.

[22] '. . . *although Colonel Bowes had told me of the existence of General Sordet's cavalry [on 26 August] I knew little about it and no one thought fit to enlighten me.*'

In the course of Tuesday 25 August General Sordet's Cavalry Corps marched westwards, across the line of the BEF's retreat, bivouacking that night just south of Esnes, where the 12th Brigade had its outposts. It had been constantly on the move since the outbreak of war, carrying out reconnaissance deep in Belgium, and on the night of the 25th men and horses were 'dog-tired and soaked with rain'. The next morning it moved to south of Cambrai, from where it overlooked the developing battle.

[23] '. . . *[c.9 a.m. 26 August] the 12th Brigade fell back on Haucourt with its left about Esnes. I never quite understood the necessity of this retirement . . . The German account implied that no pressure was brought to bear in this area till about 2 p.m.*'

The retirement was forced by the outflanking movement that grew out of the initial assault on the 1st King's Own and 2nd Lancashire Fusiliers (see above). By about 8.45 a.m. 'the German progress towards Wambaix . . . had gone so far that a retirement seemed to Br.-General H. F. M. Wilson imperative' (*MO, 1914*, v. 1, pp. 164–7). Wilson lacked any means of communication with divisional headquarters, and this withdrawal to the line Esnes–Ligny was made without reference to his superior, General Snow. It is not clear to which 'German account' General Snow here refers, but it is evident that the enemy made a very determined attack that morning; and that, after a lull, this was renewed around 1.40 p.m., with increased artillery fire and strong infantry reinforcement (*MO, 1914*, v. 1, pp. 164–7, 210–11).

[24] *[after noon, 26 August]* '. . . *the 12th Brigade advanced on Longsart towards our original position in order to withdraw as many wounded as possible, and was successful in moving a considerable number.*'

The official history suggests otherwise: though rescue parties did gain the north side of the Warnelle ravine they 'were driven back

by a steady fire from the enemy before they could collect many'
(*MO, 1914*, v. 1, p. 181).

[24] *[26 August] 'About 3 p.m. the advanced posts of the 11th Brigade had to
retire as their right was exposed owing to the retirement of the 3rd Division.'*
Companies of the 7th Brigade, 3rd Division, had in fact successfully
counterattacked at Caudry between 2.30 p.m. and 3 p.m., but
were unable to dislodge the enemy completely; Brigadier General
Hunter-Weston therefore withdrew the 11th Brigade across the
Warnelle ravine towards Ligny. The 7th Brigade was not finally
withdrawn from Caudry until around 4.30 p.m. (*MO, 1914*, v. 1,
pp. 181–2).

[25] *[afternoon of 26 August] 'There were some gallant, and what appeared
to be impossible, deeds done in getting out the guns . . . To quote two instances
out of many.'*
General Snow quite literally quotes here: the next two paragraphs,
and some of the sentences dealing with the beginning of the retreat,
are taken almost verbatim from *MO, 1914*, v. 1 (pp. 190–1).

[28] *'[Sir John French] dismisses the 4th Division with the remark that "the
4th Division was comparatively fresh". . .'*
Two very different descriptions of the state of the 4th Division in the
early morning of 26 August are given by French (as quoted above,
MO, 1914, v. 1, p. 77) and Smith-Dorrien: 'They were very weary,
having journeyed straight from England, detrained at Le Cateau on
the 24th, and marched thence at 1 a.m. on the 25th eight or nine
miles to Solesmes, been in action there all day, and marched back
over ten miles in the dark to their position, which was reached
after dawn' (Smith-Dorrien, *Forty-Eight Years*, pp. 401–2).

[29] *'General Sir Archibald Murray some years after 1914 . . . said that
the G.H.Q. idea was that the 3rd and 5th Divisions should have continued
the retirement before dawn on the 26th under cover of a strong rear-guard
composed of the 4th Division and the guns of the three divisions. This*

suggestion seems to show that G.H.Q. was not aware of the position of the
4th Division at dawn on 26th . . .'

Sir Horace Smith-Dorrien later observed: 'The unfortunate part of this Division was that it lacked the very essentials for a modern battle. It had none of the following: Divisional Cavalry, Divisional Cyclists, Signal Company, Field Ambulances, Field Companies R.E., Train and Divisional Ammunition Column, or Heavy Artillery. Let the reader think what that means – no troops to give warning, neither rapidly moving orderlies nor cables for communication, no means of getting away wounded, no engineers, who are the handy men of an army, no reserve ammunition, and no long-range heavy shell fire – and yet the Division was handled and fought magnificently, but at the expense of losses far greater than if they had been fully mobilised' (Smith-Dorrien, *Forty-Eight Years*, p. 402).

[29] *'There has been a good deal said at various times as to why the left flank of the 4th Division was not turned at Le Cateau. Lord French, in his book "1914", gives the credit to General Sordet although in his original despatch he said General Sordet gave no help and he severely blamed him for withholding that help. Sir Horace Smith-Dorrien also seems to imply that General Sordet saved the left . . .'*

While Sir John French may have been implicitly critical of General Sordet in his despatch of 7 September, he did not overtly censure him, as General Snow here implies. The Commander-in-Chief wrote: 'The French Cavalry Corps, under General Sordet, was coming upon our left rear early in the morning [of 26 August], and I sent an urgent message to him to do his utmost to come up and support the retirement of my left flank; but, owing to the fatigue of his horses he found himself unable to intervene in any way' (John French, *The Despatches of Sir John French: I. Mons, II. The Marne, III. The Aisne, IV. Flanders* (London, 1914), p. 13). Later on, however, he noted that Sordet, among others, 'saved the 2nd Corps' at Le Cateau, and accounted for his failure to acknowledge this on 7 September by stating: 'At the time the dispatch was written, indeed, I was entirely ignorant of the material support which was rendered throughout the day by Generals Sordet and d'Amade' (John French, *1914* (London, 1919), pp. 78–80). The implication was that Smith-Dorrien had misled him.

The latter became aware of Sordet's presence around 4.30 p.m. on 26 August when he heard heavy gunfire to the north-west, and feared that the enemy had turned General Snow's flank. In fact it was Sordet's guns just west of Esnes, covering Snow's retreating flank, and Smith-Dorrien was 'much relieved, on galloping to a hill about a mile in that direction, to recognise the short sharp crack of the famous "seventy-fives"', and in an order of the day, published on 29 August, he acknowledged 'our indebtedness to General Sordet's Corps' (Smith-Dorrien, *Forty-Eight Years*, pp. 408–9).

From General Snow's perspective, however, Sordet had done too little, too late, having left the British flank in the early morning, as the battle began, and only returning late in the day. Snow's evident resentment towards the Frenchman is not entirely unjustified: by mid-morning Sordet was 'fully conversant with the situation' but nevertheless moved his forces away from the British flank, only returning after a message from General Joffre, timed 1 p.m.: 'General Joffre requests that you will not only cover the left of the British Army, but do more and intervene in the battle with all the forces at your disposal.' The page of Smith-Dorrien's memoir dealing with this controversy is revealingly entitled 'Sordet's Tardy Help' (*Forty-Eight Years*, p. 409).

[31] *'In the end the [French Territorial] garrison of Cambrai and the 4th Division began their retirement about the same time, that is 3 p.m. and this retiring together was a matter of luck not of arrangement.'*
General Snow is mistaken here: according to Smith-Dorrien, d'Amade's Territorials 'finally left Cambrai . . . about 2 p.m.', while *MO, 1914*, v. 1, gives as 5.00 p.m. the hour at which the brigades of the 4th Division received their orders to retreat (Smith-Dorrien, *Forty-Eight Years*, p. 408; *MO, 1914*, v. 1, p. 189).

[31] 'We are told that about 2 p.m. on the 26th the 1st Division [of Sordet's Corps] moved forward . . . to within a short distance of Cambrai, where its guns engaged hostile infantry (II. Corps) coming out of the town about 6.30 p.m., by which time the 4th Division was beyond all need of support . . .'

General Snow is again mistaken: at around 6.30 p.m. General Sordet broke off, rather than began, his action against the *IV Reserve Corps*, and his help undoubtedly assisted the 4th Division, albeit very late in the day.

[32] 'Why Lord French suddenly altered his opinion and was so profuse in his thanks to General Sordet I do not know . . .'.

By magnifying the role of General Sordet's cavalry in protecting the British left flank at Le Cateau, Sir John French emphasised the degree to which Smith-Dorrien's success depended upon factors that lay beyond his control. In his memoir French pointedly credits practically everyone but Smith-Dorrien with having 'saved the 2nd Corps' (French, *1914*, p. 78).

[34] *[At Le Cateau]* 'A very large portion of my Division, including two Brigadiers, was separated from the Division and rejoined me by driblets during the next two or three days.'

Some did not rejoin until much later: seventy-eight officers and men, from a party that originally numbered about two hundred, comprising 'soldiers from nearly every battalion of the 3rd, 4th and 5th Divisions – and even two men of the 1st Division', eventually reached Boulogne, having escaped north and passed through the German lines (*MO, 1914*, v. 1, pp. 196–7; Haldane, pp. 25–6).

[34] *[26 August]* 'I can only say that whoever was responsible for not rushing up my signal company and field ambulances, when it became evident that a battle was imminent, made a very great and serious error . . .'

The responsibility lay with GHQ: the divisional troops missing from the 4th Division (see below, Appendix 1, p. 145), less the 60-pounder battery, arrived at St Quentin early on the 26th, but at 8.10 a.m. the OC signal company sent a message to divisional headquarters to the effect: 'detained here by order of GHQ'. These troops were afterwards formed into a column and ordered to retire, eventually joining the division when it came south of the Somme at Voyennes on the 28th (*MO, 1914*, v. 1, p. 147, n. 1).

[35] *[27 August]* '*Horses having been watered we retired to the Hancourt plateau, a very strong position, where several of our wandering parties joined us, noticeably General Haldane and his party.*'

Leading a party principally made up of 2nd Seaforth Highlanders and 1st Royal Irish Fusiliers, Haldane had fallen as much as seven hours' march behind the division. In the time that it took to catch up he did not see 'a single German infantryman', and the defensive positions being made on the plateau struck him 'as being somewhat unnecessary' (Haldane, pp. 35–6).

[36] '*Orders were received to retire to Voyennes and then cover the crossing of the Somme. We marched off at 7 p.m. [27 August], 10th Brigade leading . . .*'

Brigadier General Haldane recalled: 'I shall never forget this night march. It was the fifth night I had passed without sleep, except for some three hours, and as I found that to keep awake on horseback was impossible and would only lead to tumbling off, I was forced to tramp along on foot' (Haldane, p. 37).

[37] *[Voyennes, c.10 a.m. 28 August]* '*There Colonel Edmonds showed me two orders which had been received in my absence . . .*'

The two orders referred to were in fact parts 1 and 6 of GHQ Operation Order No. 9. For their contents and General Snow's thoughts on them see Appendix 3 below, pp. 155–7.

[38] '*At one time in the morning [28 August] a whole brigade appeared from the direction of Voyennes and for a long time we were in doubt as to whether they were our own people or Germans.*'

'Ignorance of the German Army proved a serious handicap in the early part of the campaign. British soldiers imagined that every German wore a spiked helmet, so that *Jäger*, who wore a kind of shako, and cavalrymen in hussar busbies and lancer caps were mistaken for Frenchmen or Belgians; machine-gun crews, carrying their weapons into action with trestle legs turned back, were thought to be medical bearers with stretchers, and were not fired on' (*MO, 1914*, v. 1, p. 11, n. 4).

[38] *'Sempigny, just south of Noyon, was given us as our billeting area for the night of 28th August and we moved off about 8 a.m. [29 August] and halted at Beaurains, a strong position.'*

On the night of 28/29 August 4th Division halted five miles short of the designated billeting area at Sempigny, and next morning prepared to make up the distance. Around 8 a.m., however, there came reports that German infantry were crossing the Somme in force, and General Snow prepared strong outposts in the neighbourhood of Beaurains, while sending a battalion to Muirancourt in support of the 2nd Cavalry Brigade, which was retiring south after engaging the enemy. By early afternoon it had become plain that the Beaurains outposts would not be tested.

[39] *'I remained all day at Beaurains [29 August] and set off in the evening for Carlepont, with the whole Division except the 10th Infantry Brigade and some guns which I left north of the river to collect all stragglers before blowing up the Noyon bridges.'*

Among the 'stragglers' was a company of the 1st Royal Irish Fusiliers who had not received the order to withdraw with the rest of the brigade across the Oise. General Haldane was loath to leave them behind, and sent cyclists to retrieve them while preparing the bridges for demolition. At 10.15 a.m. on 30 August the missing fusiliers appeared, after a skirmish with Uhlans, and soon afterwards the bridges were blown up, more than four hours later than planned (Haldane, pp. 45–7).

[40] *[30 August] 'One unfortunate thing happened. A belated order was received ordering us to blow up Bailly Bridge ...'*

The bridge at Bailly was prepared for demolition on the night of 29 August but not destroyed on a written order from II. Corps. At 7 p.m. the next day the necessary order was finally given, and at

9 p.m. a demolition party of the 9th Field Company Royal Engineers set out by lorry 'to find their way in the dark by unknown roads, to a village they had never seen, to blow up a bridge that had not been reconnoitred by any of the party' (R. U. H. Buckland, 'Demolitions Carried Out at Mons and During the Retreat, 1914', *Royal Engineers Journal*, vol. XLVI (March) 1932, pp. 18–39, 220–50, p. 228). Their infantry escort did not materialise, and as they approached the bridge, which was already in possession of the enemy, they were fired upon. The CO, Major Barstow, was killed and four of his party wounded, one seriously, (*MO, 1914*, v. 1, p. 242, n. 3, and corrigenda).

[41] *'19th Brigade was composed of four battalions . . . formed into a brigade immediately after the battle of Mons.'*
In fact it had been arranged on 19 August, before Mons, that the four battalions employed on lines of communication should make up the 19th Brigade: the brigade gathered at Valenciennes on 22 August and the next day occupied the extreme left of the British line at Mons (*MO, 1914*, v. 1, pp. 50, 71).

[43] *[1 September] 'I was hardly on the plateau before I was the centre of a galloping mass of unsaddled, maddened horses, some loose, some ridden by half-dressed men, many of them wounded.'*
These horses were likely to have been from the 1st East Lancashires and 1st Hampshires of the 11th Brigade, which had encountered the *2nd Cavalry Division* on the heights east-north-east of Verberie, at St Sauveur at dawn – an engagement separate from that fought at Néry (see below) (*MO, 1914*, v. 1, p. 258).

[43] *[1 September] '. . . after some moments General Milne told me that, as far as he could ascertain, there had been an action at Néry . . .'*
Just after dawn on 1 September, in thick fog, horsemen from the German *4th Cavalry Division* ran into a patrol of the 11th Hussars and pursued them back to their base at Néry, about two miles south of St Sauveur. As a result of this chance encounter a fierce fight ensued, during which L Battery distinguished itself against much

superior odds. In response to an appeal from Brigadier General C. J. Briggs, CO 1st Cavalry Brigade, strong reinforcements began to arrive at Néry, and by 8.45 a.m. the action was over. It was then that Haldane's composite battalion of 1st Warwickshires and 2nd Dublin Fusiliers (formed after Le Cateau), dispatched to Néry by General Snow, appeared from St Sauveur (*MO, 1914*, v. 1, pp. 256–7). After being repulsed at Néry and finding their routes east and west blocked by the sound of guns, the brigades of the *4th Cavalry Division* sought safety by moving independently southwards, and hiding in the great forest around Rozières as the British marched past.

[44] *'It was on this day [1 September] that I became aware of a very extraordinary thing which had happened . . .'*
A detailed account of the incident at St Quentin that General Snow narrates here is to be found in Peter T. Scott's *'Dishonoured': The 'Colonels' Surrender' at St Quentin* (London, 1994).

[44] *'. . . after Le Cateau, Colonel "A" with about 200 men of the "A"shires and Colonel "B" without about 30 men of the "B"shires, both in my Division, after having lost their way, finally found themselves at St. Quentin [on the afternoon of 27 August], hungry and thoroughly done up, just as the last of the English troops had left that place . . .'*
Colonel 'A' was Lieutenant Colonel Arthur Edward Mainwaring (1864–1930), commander of the 2nd Royal Dublin Fusiliers, and Colonel 'B' Lieutenant Colonel John Ford Elkington (1866–1944), of the 1st Warwickshires. When they entered St Quentin they had perhaps two hundred men between them. The town was by no means empty of British troops when they arrived, and Mainwaring later stated on oath that he had had a discussion with Smith-Dorrien there. Arthur Osburn, a medic with the 4th Royal Dragoon Guards, remembered seeing the two colonels at St Quentin: 'Middle-aged men, both of them looked utterly exhausted. From their appearance they were suffering severely from the sun' (Arthur Osburn, *Unwilling Passenger* (London, 1932), p. 83).

[45] *'In the morning the men having been well-fed and rested were very different men from what they had been the night before. At this moment a cavalry subaltern, commanding one of the last of our patrols, rode through the town and asked the men what they were doing.'*

The cavalry subaltern was probably Major 'Tom' Bridges' interpreter, Lieutenant A. C. G. Harrison, who arrived in St Quentin on the afternoon of 27 August. General Snow is mistaken in suggesting that the men were rested the next morning: the events here described took place in the afternoon and evening of a single day. Bridges had been instructed to give cover around St Quentin to troops still retiring from the battlefield, and led two squadrons of his own regiment, the 4th (Royal Irish) Dragoon Guards (Scott, pp. 55–6).

[45] *'Here again all would have been well had the cavalry subaltern torn up the document; but a senior officer arrived to whom he handed the paper, and this officer said that he would only give it into the hands of Sir John French himself.'*

Mainwaring was present when the 'surrender document' was retrieved from the mayor of St Quentin by a cavalry subaltern. He later recalled: 'I was too proud to argue with him [the subaltern] for possession of it, as I was still upheld with the conviction that I had done my duty. They took it and sent it to their General' (Scott, pp. 55–7).

[45–6] *'After they had been carted about in an ambulance for some ten days, first during the retreat and then during the advance, they were tried, convicted and sentenced to be cashiered.'*

The two colonels were found guilty at a court martial held at Chouy on 12 September, of 'behaving in a scandalous manner unbecoming the character of an officer and a gentleman' (Scott, p. 69).

[46] *'Colonel "A" retired to England and seclusion; Colonel "B" at once enlisted in the Foreign Legion of the French Army . . .'*

Elkington (Colonel 'B') subsequently served in the Foreign Legion and was discharged after being severely wounded in September

1915; he was awarded the Croix de Guerre avec Palme. In October 1916 his rehabilitation was complete when he was received by the king and made a companion of the DSO. Mainwaring's military career ended with his court martial, and he never had the opportunity to recover his reputation in the field, although he wrote, and privately circulated, a statement justifying his conduct at St Quentin (Scott, pp. 69–73).

[46] *'All through the war the correct thing to do seemed to depend on the point of view of one's immediate senior . . .'*

General Snow's obvious sympathy for the plight of colonels Elkington and Mainwaring was shared by Arthur Osburn, who blamed their predicament on the inadequacy of GHQ staff work: 'To put it mildly, it looks as if the two colonels, as so often happens, were made the scapegoats for the want of imagination of General Staff' (Osburn, pp. 83, 87).

[47] *'I have never been quite able to make out the arrangements as regards the blowing up of the bridges over the Marne . . . There may have been a plan but it was not apparent.'*

The demolition of bridges during the retreat was a haphazard affair, in part because events had taken GHQ by surprise, but also because pre-war manuals paid little attention to the subject. One engineer remembered: 'We were always being sent back *towards* the enemy to reconnoitre and prepare demolitions; it seemed as if the Staff never thought of them as tactical operations. They seemed to say to themselves when they crossed something: 'By G——! Here's a bridge, let's blow it up! Where's a sapper?' All their arrangements were very confusing – order, counter-orders, disorder' (Buckland, p. 21). The example of Bailly Bridge, which cost the life of Major Barstow, has already been noted above (p. 40). The Marne bridges were blown up on the authority of General Joffre, and GHQ's Operation Order No. 14 (issued at 7.30 p.m. on 2 September) made each of the corps commanders responsible for the British (as opposed to French) demolitions in a given sector (*MO, 1914*, v. 1, pp. 273, 533–4).

[48] *'The reason for this further retreat [on 5 September] is obscure, and a careful study of the Official History of the war does not help to elucidate the matter . . .'*

The 1933 edition of *MO, 1914,* v. 1, covers the subject of the continued retirement of the BEF on 5 September in considerably more detail than the 1922 edition, to which General Snow here refers, and most of the additional material concerns the visit of General Galliéni, military governor of Paris, to GHQ on the afternoon of 4 September (*MO, 1914*, v. 1, pp. 276–81; text of Operation Order No. 16, pp. 540–1). Galliéni visited with the purpose of suggesting that 'the British Army should cease to retreat, and take the offensive next day in co-operation with his forces'. Sir John French was, however, absent when he arrived, and after three hours of waiting Galliéni left without the agreement he had sought. Later that day, at 6.35 p.m., Sir John French issued orders for the army to 'move S.W. to-morrow – September 5th – pivoting on its left'. He had been alarmed by what he saw as the contradictory plans emanating from the French and he was troubled too by the gap between his right flank and the French Fifth Army. He also believed that he was conforming to General Joffre's wish that the BEF should retire to allow room on its left for the 'Army of Paris' south of the Marne, although his interpretation of Joffre's wishes is disputed.

In General Snow's opinion Operation Order No. 16 took the BEF decisively away from the German flank, and thus delayed its engagement with the enemy during the counter-offensive that was clearly imminent. This episode elicited his strongest criticism of the Commander-in-Chief during the retreat, and he would have doubtless concurred with the judgement that, under his charge, the BEF did not take 'adequate advantage of the opportunity for penetration' during the counter-offensive starting on the Marne: 'This was partly due to a rearward march of some twelve miles on the 5th, which Joffre's instructions had not reached French in time to prevent. But the advance towards the Marne was not pushed with the utmost energy, and the use of the cavalry was weak' (Cruttwell, 33).

Part Two

The 27th Division at St Eloi, and During Second Ypres

Those who remember the Salient only in the last years of the campaign, when it had become a sodden and corrugated brickyard, can scarcely conceive what the place was like during the throes of the Second Battle. The city of Ypres was dying, but not yet dead, and its solemn towers still stood, mute protestants against the outrage of war. To the east of it the meadows were still lush and green, and every hedgerow and garden bright with lilac, laburnum, and guelder-rose. It was a place of terror, but also a place of blossom. The sickly smell of gas struggled with the scent of hawthorn; great riven limbs of flowering chestnuts lay athwart the roads; the cuckoo called continually from the thickets. The horror of war seemed increased a thousandfold when shells burst among flowers, and men died in torture amid the sounds and odours of spring.

John Buchan,
Francis and Riversdale Grenfell: A Memoir (London, 1920), p. 228

Ypres is within the region where, when soldiers enter it, they abandon hope, because they have become sane at last, and their minds have a temperature a little below normal. In Ypres, whatever may have been their heroic and exalted dreams, they awake, see the world is mad, and surrender to the doom from which they know a world bereft will give them no reprieve.

H. M. Tomlinson,
Waiting for Daylight (London, 1929), p. 21

A NARRATIVE OF THE DOINGS OF THE 27TH DIVISION FROM THE DATE OF FORMATION TO THE END OF ITS TOUR ON THE WESTERN FRONT

On the 9th September 1914, during the Battle of the Marne, my horse fell with me, and I fractured my pelvis. This accident necessitated giving up command of the 4th Division and, after some weeks in the American Ambulance in Paris, I reached Woolwich on the 19th October.

On the 15th November, when I was still being treated as an invalid, I received a telegram directing me to go up to Town and see Lord Kitchener at once. On my arrival at the War Office, I was shown into Lord Kitchener's room, where he told me that he had selected me to command the 27th Division, which Division was to be formed at Winchester of regular battalions and batteries from India. These units were at that moment nearing England.

I told Lord Kitchener that I had not nearly recovered from my accident, and that I doubted whether I was yet in good enough health to carry out such an arduous task. He said that that had nothing to do with the matter; I was to see what I could do and, if later I found that I could not carry on, I should be relieved. There was nothing to be done but to accept the situation.

I. The Formation of the 27th Division

My Staff, which was a good one individually, consisted, so far as the principal officers were concerned, of Colonel H. L. Reed, V.C., G.S.O.I, Colonel H. J. Everett, who used to be my assistant adjutant in the Somerset L.I., A.A. and Q.M.G., with Colonel Stokes C.R.A. The subordinates were all able and experienced officers but for the most part strangers to each other, and of course had never worked together, which is essential for the smooth working of a Division. I telegraphed to France for my A.D.C., Colonel H.I.R. Allfrey, Somerset L.I., who joined me at once.

The Infantry Battalions were to be formed into three Brigades:

> The 80th Brigade: 2nd K.S.L.I., 3rd K.R.R.C., 4th K.R.R.C., 4th R.B. To which the P.P.C.L.I. was attached.
>
> The 81st Brigade: 1st Royal Scots, 2nd Gloucestershire Regt., 1st Argyll and Sutherland Highlanders, 2nd Cameron Highlanders. To which the 9th Royal Scots and 9th A. and S. Highlanders were attached in France.
>
> The 82nd Brigade: 1st Royal Irish, 2nd D.C.L.I., 2nd Royal Irish Fusiliers, 1st Leinster Regt. To which the 1st Cambridgeshire Territorials were attached in France.

The Princess Patricia's Canadian Light Infantry was a splendid Battalion composed of old soldiers who had settled in Canada.

Lord Kitchener told me that I could select anyone I liked to command the brigades, provided they were not on active service at the time. This proviso was a great mistake, as the Division would have been better served had officers with experience of fighting in Flanders been sent to command the brigades. However, I had little to grumble at, and three very good officers were nominated as my Brigadiers, namely, Col. Hon. C. G. Fortescue, Col. D. A. Macfarlane, and Col. L. A. M. Stopford.

The artillery had to be formed from cadres, each battery expanding to a brigade. Two territorial engineer companies were sent to me as my field companies, and Field Ambulances, Ammunition Column, etc. were provided by the War Office. The Field Ambulances consisted of Territorial Units, and the material with which they were provided was somewhat quaint. The Ambulance wagons consisted of old horse 'buses, while the harness was only held together with string. However before we started these deficiencies were put right.

On the 19th November, the Staff assembled at Winchester and the Units to compose the Division began to arrive the next day. I received orders that officers and men were to be granted a short furlough, but only one third at a time, as we were the only Regulars in the country and we were to act as a reserve to the troops on the east coast in case of invasion.

The camps which had been prepared for us were on the Downs south of the town, and no one would have supposed that even the heaviest rain could have much effect on them. However we were mistaken. The weather we experienced at Winchester, was the wettest within the memory of any of the inhabitants, and in a few days the camps were a sea of liquid mud, far worse than anything we experienced in Flanders afterwards. Warm clothing in the place of Indian Khaki was soon forthcoming, but this was not the case as regards boots. The men had arrived from India with boots almost worn out, and there were no new ones in stock to replace them, a fact which resulted in great discomfort and injury to the health of the troops.

I inspected the new arrivals and saw that they were a fine body of men of the right age, but their notions of training were far behind what one had been accustomed to in England. We managed to get through a good deal of training at Winchester, but were much handicapped by the weather, the mud, bad boots, and a general absence of all that we required. We had a few horses and no harness. Horses however, soon began to arrive, many good ones, but some which should never have been mobilised. How the harness and equipment was collected I don't know. It reflects great credit on the Q.M.G., for by the time we started for France, I had little to complain of as regards equipment, except for the scarcity of boots.

As soon as the troops had arrived at Winchester, Lord Kitchener began asking me daily by letter or wire, whether I was ready to start, though I can hardly believe he meant it seriously. He ordered me to report personally to him at the War Office twice a week. At each of my visits he expressed astonishment when I said I was not ready to start. One visit I well remember. I told him that one of the things that I was still in need of was a Divisional Ammunition Column. Now a Divisional Ammunition Column consists of 568 men, 709 horses and 110 vehicles. He seemed surprised, and sent for the Q.M.G. On

General Cowans presenting himself, Lord Kitchener said: 'What does Snow mean by saying he has no Ammunition Column?' General Cowans answered: 'That is perfectly correct as you sent the one earmarked for the 27th division to India last week'. Lord Kitchener replied: 'So I did. Well, send him down another to-morrow.' How the Q.M.G. was to provide 568 men, 709 horses and 110 vehicles by the next day, I do not know, and I cannot help thinking that Lord Kitchener thought that a Divisional Ammunition Column was something in the nature of a box of tools. He certainly was very ignorant, or pretended to be, on certain subjects. Two days before we started, when we had just received our harness in bulk, I told him that I could start in two days' time, by which time I should have fitted the harness. He said: 'Why not fit it when crossing the Channel?' I wonder whether he realised what a horse deck on a short sea voyage was like.

However, by the day we started, the 19th of December, we were very fairly equipped, and to look at were a fine Division; but I knew how impossible it was for a collection of Units, however good the material, to be of much value as a Division, except after months of training. The proof of this showed itself at once. We marched from Winchester to Southampton, a distance of about 12 miles by an excellent road. How many men fell out I do not know, but the road after the Division had passed, resembled very much the road on the line of the retreat from Mons; men lying about at the sides of the road, and the whole route strewn with equipment which had fallen off or had been thrown away. It was a discouraging sight after my 4th Division experiences when it was a rare occurrence for a man to fall out, and seldom even was one seen out of dressing.

I had received one shock previously, just before we left Winchester. His Majesty accompanied by Lord Kitchener inspected the Division. His Majesty expressed himself as highly pleased with what he had seen. I wonder if he really was. The day was delightful, one of those calm sunny days you sometimes get in December. Till the early morning it had rained heavily for 24 hours. The result was that the horses were badly groomed, the harness dirty, and the vehicles caked with mud. Very little effort was made to smarten up, which showed that morale was low. It was the first time, and the last, that I have ever seen troops allow themselves to be defeated by the weather. For any inspection, not to speak of a royal one, troops, especially Gunners, turn out spick and span whatever the weather or other difficulties they have to contend with.

II. In the Line at St Eloi

The arrangements for the voyage were excellent, and we assembled in due course at St Omer. We were at once set to dig a line of defence not far east of that place. The weather was very wet and the ground for the most part boggy. We had no R.E. stores, and the trenches must have fallen in within two or three days of making them, as there was no material for revetting them. The whole thing was a shocking waste of time, and the wet ground laid the seeds of that terrible scourge, Trench Feet, which was almost to destroy the Division later. Had we been given a little time to get the mens' feet into order, it would have been a very different story in the line at St. Eloi.

After a fortnight's stay at St. Omer, we received orders to reconnoitre the trenches near St. Eloi with a view to taking them over, and officers and N.C.O.'s went into the line with the French for tours of 24 hours each. The French Division which we were to relieve arranged these tours, and they put the N.C.O.'s and men into the most habitable trenches; and thus we got no idea of how bad the trenches round St. Eloi itself really were. We had heard a good deal of trench life and the various methods of fighting the water and mud, but when we did go into the line, we were not connected with an Engineer park or even given trench stores, while our boots were very bad, and the men had only two, or at the most, three pairs of socks. We bought as many old boxes as we could, hoping to use them for the men to stand in, or on, and so keep them out of the water, but we had none of the luxuries which were a necessity to trench life in later years.

The actual taking over was terribly bungled by the Staff of the 2nd Army, who arranged that the first Brigade to go into the trenches was to march 17 miles before reaching them. The men on the march got hot and tired, and then had to undergo the cold and misery of the trenches. The paved roads made a march of 17 miles a serious undertaking even if troops could look forward to a comfortable billet and a change of socks at the end of it; but to march troops right into the trenches after a 17 miles march was bound to end in disaster. Not only did men suffer from cold after getting heated on the march, but it took a good deal out of them, and thus vitality was not at its highest at the end of it. The paved roads knocked about the men's feet and got them into a condition which made them an easy victim to an attack of Trench Feet. I know I ought to have objected to the arrangement, but I hesitated to do so as I was a new-comer to trench warfare and quite inexperienced, whereas I was dealing with a staff who knew, or should have known, everything there was to know about it. Some four hundred men, though I am not sure of the exact number, reported sick the next morning, and there were many others who ought to have done so, but whose pluck kept them going.

The best method of occupying the line was difficult to arrive at. The French held it very lightly, relying entirely on their guns. We, having an inexperienced Artillery and very little ammunition, had to hold the line in far greater strength. It took about a brigade actually in the front line and support trenches to make the position anything like secure. The trenches themselves were either barricades of earth too thin, as a rule, to keep out bullets, or shallow broad trenches more like water courses, which as a matter of fact they soon became. Half a mile behind the trenches were the ruins of the village of Vormezeele which afforded some shelter; otherwise there was no cover for anything until the village of Dickebusch was reached, one and a half miles from the line. Dickebusch and its surroundings provided shelter for a brigade which we took advantage of, even though we knew the village could be blown to pieces if the Germans had so willed. The nearest shelter behind Dickebusch was Westoutre about 8¼ miles in rear. As men could not remain in the front line more than 48 hours at a time, and indeed that was far too long, the marching and counter-marching between the line, Dickebusch, and Westoutre became very tiring, especially as there were only paved roads by which to march.

The paved roads of Belgium during the winter are a veritable nightmare. The paved portion only extends over about one third of the width of the road and does not often exceed eight feet in breadth. The road on each side of this paving is not metalled and a vehicle, if it gets off the paving, often sinks in up to the axle. The difficulty of keeping every vehicle of a long convoy on the paving can be imagined, and if another vehicle is met coming in the opposite direction there is nothing to do but to build a passing place with timber, branches or stones. The delays which ensued were very annoying. I once saw a convoy of sixty motor buses held up for some three hours because the leading bus slipped off the paving.

The only place the Army could find for my headquarters was Boeschepe, some 9 miles behind the line. Why this place was chosen I don't know. It was certainly not for the accommodation, as the village was small and dirty with no decent buildings. It took me over two hours to get anywhere near the line, as the roads were congested with traffic and all paved. I soon established temporary headquarters at Reninghelst, only 8 miles behind the line; but I could only get one small house there as the French were in occupation. Later when the French left I brought up the whole of my headquarters to Reninghelst, and that place proved most convenient, though why we were not shelled out of it I don't know. Not a shot was fired into it while I was there, though later the village was destroyed. We had a lot of trouble with the inhabitants. They were as disagreeable as they could be, and there is little doubt that they were to a man pro-German. They got every penny they could out of us, and when they worked for us they did as little as they dared for the money. I think that the thing they disliked about us most was that we insisted on villages which we occupied being kept in a sanitary condition. Being a very dirty people they naturally resented this.

The handing over by the French was badly managed. As soon as our men reached the trenches, the French made a bee-line to the rear without explaining anything. I am very doubtful if we ever took over the front line in the vicinity of St. Eloi. My impression is that the French had either lost their front line trenches in that part of the field shortly before we took over, or that they only held their front line with a few look-out men. At any rate the trenches that we were shown into were more like support than fire trenches, for the most part covered in, and the first thing we had to do was to make them into fire trenches. The mud in those trenches beggars description. We lost several men on the first night, drowned or smothered. The boxes which we had purchased we found to be no good as they simply disappeared through the bottom of the trench. The men had either to stand in water, knee deep, with every prospect of sinking in deeper still, or hang on the side of the trench. These trenches compared very unfavourably with the worst of the trenches we met later. We found out later that we had been unlucky enough to relieve a Division which was proverbially one of the worst in the French army. The greater part of the line which we held was unimportant but in and around the village of St. Eloi there was always hard fighting. On the enemy's side of the village, just within our lines, was a large mound, in reality a brick-yard; it was about 30 feet above the surrounding terrain, and covered about an acre. As the country was flat it made a good observation post and so became a bone of contention. It was described in the English papers as: 'the heights of St. Eloi'!

A rather interesting episode happened the second day we were in the line. A Belgian priest came to me and asked if he might go down to St. Eloi that night and, with our help, retrieve a sacred relic which was in the vaults under the ruins of St. Eloi church. It appeared that the relic had been removed from somewhere on the front, on the advance of the Germans, and placed for safety in St. Eloi church. Later when St. Eloi became the cockpit of a battle, the relic could not be removed, and the Belgians, as long as St. Eloi was in the hands of the French, said nothing about the relic, fearing the French might take it, as it was so highly treasured among Roman Catholics. I gave the necessary leave, and the next day the priest showed me the relic. It was about a foot in height shaped rather like an hour glass, the material which held the glass in the centre being of gold or filigree. It was evidently very antique. In the centre of the globe there was some red or yellow substance which was said to be a drop of the blood of Christ. The priest took the relic back to Poperinghe. I thought for a long time that this relic was identical with the sacred relic kept in Bruges at the Church of the Sacred Blood, which relic is of world-wide fame. The relic I saw at Dickebusch was exactly similar to the Bruges one, and when Colonel Allfrey saw the Bruges relic being carried procession some years after the war, he was convinced it was the same which we had seen at Dickebusch. After very careful enquiry I have come to the conclusion that the relic we were dealing with was not the Bruges one, as it appears that there is a replica of the Bruges relic in Vormezeele where it had been before the war, and where it now is.

We were holding a line about 3,500 yards in length. We had no communication trenches and so all reliefs had to be carried out over the top. Behind the centre portion of the line movement by small parties could be carried on, even by day, with care up to within 200 yards of the line owing to woods and the uneven nature of the country. On the left and right the country was open and flat, and no movement could be carried out by day, except here and there by individuals within half a mile of the trenches. The enemy's trenches were in places not more than 20 yards distant, and this made reliefs on a moonlight night very difficult. Curiously enough we did not suffer many casualties during reliefs. The left half of the line could only be approached by a single paved road so narrow that vehicles could only pass each other with the greatest difficulty. All reliefs and supplies had to pass along this road, and to step off the road meant being hopelessly bogged. Luckily in those days the Germans did not barrage the approaches as both sides did later in the war. Had they done so St. Eloi could not have been held.

The Germans opposite us had communication trenches; but they were on drier ground.

The mistake about the whole trench system was that everyone had dug in where they were held up in October '14. At that time we had been attacking, and when the deadlock occurred we were for the most part on inferior ground to the Germans. What we ought to have done was to prepare a good line in a defensive position somewhere in rear, and to have abandoned the water logged and overlooked ground. Such a manoeuvre would have placed the Germans, if they attacked, on inferior and so wetter ground to what we held. At that time there was a notion at Headquarters that to give up a yard of ground was bad for morale, and we were ordered to stick to our original trenches at all costs. What casualties were caused by this idea I do not know, but they were considerable. In many places our trenches were close to and immediately below the German trenches, and the Germans were able to drain their trenches into ours, and flood us out.

We did manage to dig some support trenches when we could find dry ground, and we constructed quite a good reserve line about a mile in rear of the front line; but we never managed to dig communication trenches. We did make some attempts to do so, but they were of no avail as they filled with water and we had no pumps. Later in the war we should have overcome the difficulty but at this time the men were overworked in keeping the front trenches in order, and we were all inexperienced. On one occasion one of my staff said to a Corporal of the Engineers: 'Now you are an engineer; cannot you devise some method of draining this trench?' to which he replied: 'I am afraid Sir that I cannot; you see before the war I was a Christmas card maker by trade'.

Our position was a very dangerous one. We had our front trenches (it would be fairer to call them mud holes) crowded with men. We had practically no supports handy, though a few men were hidden in the cellars at St. Eloi, and more men in the cellars of Vormezeele half a mile back. The only way to reinforce was over the top, and the supports from Vormezeele could not move off the causeway.

Later in the war such dispositions would have been impossible as the Germans would have put down a barrage behind the trenches and destroyed the trenches with heavy shell fire. At the time I am speaking of, the Germans as well as ourselves had a good deal to learn, and they were content to shell the trenches with high velocity guns which did comparatively little harm.

It was a weird but fascinating experience to get on some high ground, such as the Scherpenberg, which overlooked the trenches, from which you could see the two opposing lines and the country in rear of each line. Except for a shrapnel bursting here and there in the air, or a fountain of mud thrown up by a heavier shell, all seemed deserted and derelict. Not a man was to be seen, and it was hard to imagine that hundreds of men were living and working in the country you were gazing at.

As soon as darkness fell the scene, if it could have been observed, would have looked very different. The country would have been seen to be almost alive with men, some coming out of the trenches carrying back the wounded, some going into the trenches and taking up trench stores, food, and all that was required. Every road would have been seen to be blocked with traffic; still not a light would have been visible. This busy scene would have gone on all night, till daybreak again showed nothing but the two lines of trenches apparently deserted and desolate.

The wet trenches soon began to tell on the men's feet, and after we had been in the trenches a couple of days the men reporting sick increased to an alarming extent. Very soon an average of three hundred men a day were being evacuated, and there was little chance of any of these men returning for months. We did all we could, but the Division rapidly became a skeleton of what it had been. Nothing was done to help us. We were not provided with wood wherewith to make trench-boards, and no extra socks or waterproof boots were forthcoming. We were only censured for having so many sick.

About this time the list of honours for the retreat was placed before Lord Kitchener. I happen to know that my name was on the list of those recommended for a K.C.B. Lord Kitchener himself put a blue pencil through my name, the only name so struck out, saying I should not have a K.C.B. owing to the sickness in my Division at that moment. True I got a K.C.B. six months later; but all those who were recommended for a K.C.B. for the retreat, and got one, were promoted in the Gazette when I was gazetted a K.C.B., and the majority, who were junior to me, went over my head.

G.H.Q. made a great effort in February to provide huts, and a good many were erected in the wood near Dickebusch and in woods between Dickebusch and Westoutre. This relieved the situation, but it was difficult to find places for these huts as the woods were for the most part bogs, and if huts were erected in the open they were shelled. We did not at this time realise the length of range of the German guns. A veritable town of huts was erected by 5th Army [i.e. Corps] south east of Vlamertinghe for general use, which soon afterwards became quite untenable owing to shell fire.

Thus we carried on till the middle of February 1915. Two or three raids were made by us, the chief ones being made by the Princess Patricia's Canadian Light Infantry and the K.R.R. They were called successful at the time, as the troops did actually penetrate into the enemy's trenches. Owing, however, to the absence of ammunition wherewith to establish a barrage, and the lack of bombs, our raiding parties were very quickly bombed out of the enemy's trenches and suffered losses quite out of proportion to anything gained by the raid. Indeed these raids did harm to our morale, as the men began to think the Germans were their superiors in hand-to-hand fighting, which at that time I am inclined to think was probably the case.

In the middle of February in a blinding hailstorm at about 4 p.m., the Germans rushed three of our trenches and drove out the garrison. Owing to the absence of support trenches we were unable to restore the situation by an immediate counter-attack; but after dark we brought up the reserve brigade, and before daylight captured the lost trenches. The only mistake we made was that we employed too many troops thereby incurring unnecessary loss and certainly much waste of energy.

Things quieted down after this and for a month were normal.

There now began to be rumours of the enemy mining but this seemed impossible to believe owing to the wet nature of the soil. We knew very little about mining in those days. Something had however to be done in the way of counter-mining, and about twenty miners were brought out from home. They worked well, but complained that the soil was not what they were accustomed to as it appeared to consist of barbed wire and dead bodies. This was not surprising as in October '14 there had been fierce fighting round St. Eloi. Our miners concentrated on the 'Mound', a prominent feature in the village, and drove a good shaft down the centre hoping to be able to reach firmer soil and so make galleries from thence under the German mines. We were however too late, as on 14th March, after a particularly quiet Sunday afternoon, the Germans at about 4 p.m., commenced a very heavy bombardment, much heavier than anything we had yet experienced. At the same time they exploded several mines destroying the shaft which was luckily not being worked on by our miners on that day. Some three trenches together with the Mound fell into the enemy's hands. The Germans also bombarded our back areas very heavily. In spite of that, the Irish Brigade, who were occupying the trenches at the moment, brought up some support from the Irish Fusiliers from Vormezeele and a daylight battle ensued in which our men, though they could not retake the trenches, held the enemy to the newly captured trenches.

We were inundated by telegrams from higher authority to retake the trenches at all costs, which we did within 36 hours, with some loss, and we again brought up the reserve brigade and thus used many more men than was necessary. The corps sent a brigade from Ypres to assist us which was not required. We made an effort to retake the captured Mound both on that and the succeeding night, but failed to do so, and it remained in the enemy's hands. The Germans, who were far more experienced than we were at that time, very quickly made the Mound impregnable. The loss of the Mound was a great blow to us as it enabled the Germans to overlook the immediate neighbourhood and most of our trenches. The papers declared that the loss of the Mound was a great threat to Ypres, as the Mound overlooked the Ypres–Poperinghe road by which everything going into Ypres had to pass. This was not the case. The Mound was three and a half miles from the road in question, was only some 20 feet high, and there was a good deal of enclosed land between the Mound and the road. Certainly you could not see the Mound from the road, as I often tried to do so, and therefore I am pretty sure the road could not be seen from the Mound.

The ignorance which superior authorities showed as to local conditions was astonishing. Why this was the case I do not know. Staff Officers from the Corps and the Army, and even now and then from

G.H.Q., were constantly in the trenches, and exposed themselves much more recklessly than any of the garrison of the trenches.

Very soon after this the Division was relieved and sent back to rest and refit. Very few men of the Division, as it came out three months before, were still with it. We had suffered heavily both from shell fire and trench feet, and though we knew we had more than held our own under appalling difficulties, higher authorities did not seem to be aware of the difficulties which we had encountered, and we were somewhat in disgrace for losing the Mound.

The 28th Division which was formed immediately after the 27th, and was, like the 27th, composed of units from India, took over the trenches immediately north of us about the middle of January.[1] Their experience was far worse than ours. They suffered far more heavily from trench feet, and they were very unlucky in the fighting they experienced. When they took over the trenches in Sanctuary Wood, they lost direction by some mistake, and two parties came in contact, each mistaking the other for Germans; heavy casualties were the result. By the end of February it was found necessary to reorganise this Division, and two brigades were exchanged for experienced ones of other divisions.

About this time there was a great epidemic of 'stellenbosching'. It almost looked as if the higher commands were determined to whitewash themselves for the unsatisfactory state of affairs by making scapegoats of subordinates, and many brigadiers were relieved of their commands. Two out of three infantry brigadiers who had started with me from England were sent home, the third had been invalided almost as soon as we arrived at St. Omer. I fought hard for these officers, both keen and hard working Brigadiers, and on account of my defence of them I nearly suffered the same fate. The whole proceeding was most unjust and to be regretted. I admit that the Brigadiers whom they sent me in their place were more experienced, as they were commanding officers who had been through the retreat and the fighting on the Aisne; but that does not remove the injustice to those who suffered.

---

1   In fact the 28th Division moved into the line at the beginning of February: see Notes to Part Two below, p. 119.

III. The Ypres Salient

We had only been resting a few days when we received orders to relieve a French division in the salient of Ypres. This was welcome news as that part of the line, which had been fairly quiet since the first battle of Ypres, was held by a very good French division, and the trenches were reported to be good.

At that time the salient consisted of a semi-circle east of Ypres with a radius of about three miles, the centre of the circle being the Menin Gate. Ypres itself had not been much damaged, as although the Cloth Hall and the Cathedral and some buildings round the square had been somewhat knocked about in October, the place had not been shelled since. Even the Cloth Hall was solid enough to provide shelter for a couple of battalions. The place was full of people, the market square being a busy scene daily. The villages of St. Jean and Potijze, both a mile east of the Menin Gate, were full of inhabitants.

The portion of the line we were to take over was from near Hill 60 south of Zillebeke on the right, to a point on the high ground south-east of Zonnebeke on the left. On our right was the 28th Division, on our left the French, relieved shortly afterwards by the 28th, who were relieved on our right by the 5th Division. Potijze, about a mile east of the Menin Gate, was divisional headquarters. The chateau at Potijze was a comfortable house of the villa type with another chateau or villa, built, I believe, for the eldest son in the same grounds. There was excellent stabling. The chateaux stood in very pretty and carefully tended grounds, well timbered, with an artificial lake, islands, bridges etc., the lake containing a collection of wild fowl and ducks of all description. About four hundred yards east of the house, at the end of the shrubbery, stood a summer-house which overlooked the greater part of the salient. This summer-house was some twenty-four feet in height with a tea-room on the top floor which was reached by a circular iron staircase. From the tea-room there was a wonderful view, and all our spare moments were spent in it watching the shelling and the aeroplanes. We used to say that 'all the crowned heads of Europe' called on us to see the sights, and certainly everyone who came out joy-riding from England paid us a visit.

These two chateaux were the only two buildings of importance left intact so far east of Ypres. They were clearly visible from the air and must have shown signs of occupation. We used to think that they belonged to a German, or someone in German pay, but that was not the case. Probably the enemy was quite aware that they were used as a Divisional Headquarters, but allowed us to live in fancied security till the time came. The chateaux were exactly as the inhabitants had left them, books, ornaments and even letters lying about as they had been left when the storm broke in 1914. The gardens were delightful and the gardener supplied us with all we wanted in the way of vegetables. Forced strawberries were just ripening when the second battle of Ypres destroyed the place.

Nothing could have been better arranged than the handing over. Everything was explained to us, and most elaborate plans and sketches, not only of what had been constructed but also what it had been intended to construct, were given to us. The French Staff officers seemed determined not to leave us to ourselves till we were firmly established and the French Artillery remained with us for some days, being relieved gradually by our batteries.

While the French batteries were supporting us we were given a good example of their excellence. On the S.O.S. being signalled, the batteries fired a perfect tornado of shells over our trenches putting down a most effective barrage. It was unlike anything to which we were accustomed.

The trenches were very different from anything we had experienced. They were in good order and dry, all, or almost all, being floored with trench boards. Plentiful communication trenches existed and it was quite safe to go to and from the front line in daylight. Tents and shelters had been put up in the woods to house sufficient supports, and the remainder of the division lived either in the barracks or in private houses in Ypres.

Shell-proof dug-outs unfortunately were lacking, but at that period such things were hardly known to the French or ourselves, though the

Germans had them in their lines. There was a more or less prepared support or reserve line running due south from immediately west of St. Julien to Zillebeke. This line had been made by the French. It was in no way continuous but consisted of a line of redoubts at intervals of four to six hundred yards. Each redoubt was intended for a garrison of about fifty men. The best feature of this line was a continuous line of wire which was some ten yards or more deep and put up in the best French style. The French were remarkably good at wiring. This line was a valuable addition to our defences as they stood when we took over, but later when the Germans took St. Julien the northern section of this wire was a great embarrassment to us as it impeded reinforcing and, in the vicinity of St. Julien, was a great help to the Germans against our counter-attacks. More will be said about this later. This line was always known as the G.H.Q. line.

All the cafes and shops in Ypres were open and the men thoroughly enjoyed themselves. Hooge the headquarters of one of my brigades was a delightful place. It is true that the Chateau itself had been practically demolished in October 1914 but the stables were standing and the grounds delightful. There was a beautiful lake and really fine trees in the park and shrubberies. I often used to ride down there in the early morning, and on a sunny day when the birds were singing, the water-fowl splashing, and now and again a cock pheasant strutting across a ride, it was impossible to realise that a war was going on. Very few shells came over during the twenty-four hours and never one in the early morning. The Germans had certain hours during which the artillery was in action and we soon got to know them.

In these pleasant circumstances the health of the men rapidly improved and a case of trench feet was a rare occurrence. Movement anywhere within the lines was possible by day which relieved the congestion at night. On the right the wooded nature of the country provided a screen even against aeroplane observation. On the left, except near the trenches, the country was open though undulating, and a good deal of our back areas could be overlooked from the north-east. The 28th Division held the crest of the hills to within a mile of Passchendaele, but there the line quitted the high ground.

No doubt the Germans had observation posts on the high ground immediately west of Passchendaele, and Passchendaele's church tower could be seen from our back areas between Potijze and Hooge. That the Germans had a look-out post on this tower is quite certain but they never seemed to derive any advantage from it as, even when troops were moving in fairly dense formations in view of it, nothing happened. However there the tower was, and it was rather a thorn in our flesh and gave one a rather naked feeling when riding about in view of it. These were happy days. I got up about 5 o'clock and rode to within a few hundred yards of the line and, leaving the horses, visited anything I wanted to see, in perfect safety. I usually got back to the Chateau about 8 or 9 a.m., and after a bath and breakfast, either did office work or visited the troops in the back areas. The afternoons were almost always taken up in receiving distinguished visitors, military and otherwise, and showing them the sights from the summer-house. We busied ourselves constructing what we in the innocence of our hearts called dug-outs. As a matter of fact they were only splinter-proofs, if that. They mostly consisted of a hole in the ground covered with timber over which was piled three or four feet of earth. Neither the French nor ourselves ever built dug-outs, as we knew them later, in those days, and we did not do so till we drove the Germans back in 1916 and learned, from what we then found, how real dug-outs should be constructed.

The French had made two so-called dug-outs near the Chateau at Potijze, one close to the road about 20 yards west of the chateau, the other a burrowing in a mound near the house. The one near the road was about 12 feet deep, twenty feet long, and six broad, covered with stout timber with five or six feet of earth heaped on top. It would not have been much protection from a direct hit from a 5.9 and was sited east and west so that a shrapnel bursting near the door would have raked the whole interior. We did not attach much importance to this dug-out at the time but looked upon it as one of the show sights of Potijze. Little did we think that it was to be our means of salvation within the next few weeks, or how hastily we should erect a traverse at the door to protect us from the too frequent shrapnel.

Our artillery units were very busy making dug-outs. They wanted them I admit, as our guns were pushed well forward. I visited most of these dug-outs, they were not even splinter-proofs but were merely a protection from view and to a certain extent from the weather. One battery I particularly remember, dug, or I should rather say, erected a wonderful labyrinth in Railway Wood. In the battle a few weeks later this shelter became a death-trap and, being crowded with men who thought that they had found safety, was turned into a veritable shambles.

The ramparts of Ypres covered the city on its east and south sides. These ramparts were of solid earth about thirty feet high and thirty yards broad. They offered grand opportunities for securing dug-outs proof against any shells, with a minimum of labour. We neglected to take advantage of this opportunity until after the battle began.

Shortly after we took over the salient a memorandum was sent round from G.H.Q. saying that intelligence agents reported the preparation of poisonous gases in the forest a few miles north-east of our position and that this information was to be passed round for what it was worth. I cannot say that I attached much importance to this information but also passed it on at its face value.

The town of Ypres during this period had a quiet time. I cannot say it was quite a safe abode, as now and again a stray shell fell in the streets, but there was no systematic bombardment.

About the 17th of April when I was in the garden at Potijze I heard a noise which was quite new to me. It sounded like that which a runaway tram car would make running on badly laid rails. The noise seemed to be very high up in the air and the shell, for there was no doubt it was a shell, seemed to be travelling very slowly. I heard the explosion in the direction of Ypres and so I took up my position where a fair view of the town could be procured. In about half an hour the noise occurred again and I got a good view of the burst. Smoke, stones, planks and debris of all sorts were thrown high in the air, seemingly as high as the spires of the churches. We found on investigation that the shell was a 17-inch. It made a crater, if it hit the ground, some 20 yards in diameter and 12 feet deep. If it hit a building it brought down everything in the vicinity. It was fired from a very long distance. During the next few days and during the ensuing battle some half dozen of these shells were fired into the town every afternoon.

At this period the 27th and 28th Divisions formed 5th Corps commanded by Lieut.-General Sir Herbert Plumer. The Corps was part of Lieut.-General Sir Horace Smith-Dorrien's second army. On the right of the 27th Division lay the 5th Division engaged, day and night, at Hill 60 which was in full view from the roof our chateau. The three brigades of the 27th Division were all holding part of the line in order from right to left, 82nd – Br.-General J. R. Longley, 81st – Br.-General H. Crocker, 80th – Br.-General W. E. B. Smith. The headquarters of these brigades were situated, the 82nd and 81st at Hooge and the 80th at Verlorenhoek. Each brigade had 2 battalions in the line and immediate support, one battalion in Ypres as brigade reserve, while one battalion of each brigade, billeted either in the outskirts of Ypres or in Vlamertinghe, found the division's reserve. The Senior Officer took command of this reserve but a permanent adjutant was appointed. On the left of the 28th Division was the Canadian Division and on the Canadians' left, the French. My Q. Staff were quartered in Ypres just inside the Menin Gate.

We were or course occasionally visited by the Corps and Army Commanders. Sir Horace Smith-Dorrien was very unlucky in his visits. On one afternoon when he was with me in the summer-house the Germans began dropping shells on a hill about three hundred yards away. What they thought they were doing I cannot imagine; they never had dropped shells on that position before, and nothing was there worth shelling. Perhaps they were registering, but the fire was too rapid for that. Anyway, it made the summer-house an unhealthy spot that afternoon. Another day directly Sir Horace had arrived they bombarded a farm three hundred yards from the chateau. There could not have been any connection between Sir Horace's visits and the bombardments, but Sir Horace began to think our headquarters were not altogether a health resort.

About this time the weather was glorious, one of the finest Springs that I can remember.

On the 19th April I went into Ypres, arriving about 9 a.m., to visit the battalions billeted there. No sooner had I begun my inspection than the Germans started a fairly heavy bombardment with 8-inch and lighter guns. In the convent, where we had a battalion billeted, a large shell exploded just before I arrived, killing and wounding some thirty men. I was much impressed with the behaviour of the sisters who went about their work and helped with the wounded as if nothing unusual was happening. I sent them back to safety shortly afterwards. It was quite impossible to go on with the inspection so I took refuge in the house occupied by our administrative staff just inside the Menin Gate. Two eight-inch howitzers were firing on the Menin gate and the place was rather lively; stones, bricks, and splinters of all sorts being thrown about, some even through the windows as each shell burst. We were quite aware that if one of these shells hit the house it would shatter it. However no shell did hit it and about noon the bombardment ceased. This bombardment came as a surprise to the inhabitants and they at once began to clear out of the town.

Mr A. J. Balfour and Mr. F. E. Smith were coming to lunch that day and I wired to Vlamertinghe to try and stop them entering Ypres, but somehow the message miscarried and they arrived about 1 o'clock having come through Ypres after the bombardment had ceased. I took them to the summer-house in the afternoon, and during the whole of their visit, not one shell burst in the salient and not one hostile aeroplane appeared. It was perfectly peaceful and a most glorious afternoon. I was impressed by the knowledge Mr. Balfour showed regarding explosives and indeed in military matters generally.

On the 21st Mr. Winston Churchill came to see me. His experience was very different from that of Mr. Balfour. Of course I took him to the summer-house and from there we witnessed the liveliest afternoon's work both in shelling and in the air that I had as yet experienced. Mr Churchill thoroughly enjoyed himself and evidently spent a happy afternoon. I was impressed by his saying that the war would go on till we had over-run Germany and smashed up all her factories. This idea was prevalent at the time except with people who were in or near the trenches who did not quite see how such a happy result could be achieved.

About this time it became clear that the German artillery was getting more active and that they were paying special attention to Ypres and our back areas, but there was nothing to show we were on the eve of a great battle; and the Germans themselves, so it now appears, did not anticipate a battle of the nature of the one which followed and had no reinforcements at hand.

As a result of the shelling on the 21st April the town of Ypres became so unhealthy that during the night of the 21st to 22nd I moved most of the troops into the fields west of the town, leaving in Ypres only those troops who had good cellar accommodation. Of course the troops I moved into the fields had to bivouac but the weather was very fine and it was better than being under constant shell-fire. I also arranged that the Q. staff should move to Busseboom some 3 miles south-west of Ypres.

IV. Second Ypres

The morning of the 22nd of April was fine and warm. I motored through Ypres taking the northern road as things round the Menin Gate were somewhat lively. I visited the battalions bivouacked in the fields and found them fairly comfortable. I returned to Potijze for lunch, where everything was normal except that some shells were falling on the Potijze–Ypres road.

In the afternoon I went with some of my staff to the summer-house and enjoyed a lovely afternoon which was perhaps quieter than usual.

At about 5 p.m., the German guns to the north-east and the French guns north of us began a somewhat rapid fire but I could see no shell bursting in our area. While watching I noticed a whitish blue mist to the north-east of us over the French lines. It was the sort of mist one expects to see over water meadows on a frosty night. We were rather puzzled by it. We soon noticed a peculiar smell which made our noses and throats tingle, but it was some time before we realised that this was the much talked of gas. Later, black colonial troops began to filter through Potijze and, although we could not understand what they said, we gathered from the way they coughed and pointed to their throats that they were suffering from the effects of gas and were thoroughly scared, and as these fugitives became thicker and thicker, we soon realised that something very serious had happened. I felt fairly comfortable as the French seventy-fives were firing very regularly to the north of us. However at about 7 p.m., the French guns suddenly ceased and I then became very anxious. I could not find out why these guns had ceased fire, and I have never actually heard what did happen, but I believe that they were captured. I heard at about 7.30 p.m., from 5th Corps that the French right had been slightly driven back and that they were organising a counter-attack.

From what I heard from other sources I realised that the situation was more serious than would appear from 5th Corps' message and I felt sure that there was a bad break in the French line. I knew that if the French had, as I supposed, been broken, the Germans would get round the left of the Canadians and so be in a position to roll up the whole salient. Indeed if the break was as serious as I thought, I realised that there would be no necessity for the Germans to roll up the troops in the line as there was literally nothing between them and Ypres except my Headquarters, and if they could reach Ypres, the 27th and 28th Divisions and the Canadians would be cut off. As a matter of fact this was the actual situation at about 8 p.m.; but for some reason or other the Germans did not exploit their success. Whether it was that they ran into their own gas, or whether it was that they had not anticipated that their gas would be successful and so had no reserves handy, I don't know. Anyway, they took no advantage of the situation, and Ypres, which was at their mercy till after midnight at least, remained in our hands.

The reports which I received from my own front during the evening of the 22nd showed that conditions on that front were normal; but I could get no definite information from the 28th Division, and from the Canadian Division I heard nothing.

I was perfectly aware that if a bad break in the line had occurred there was no time to lose, and that all my reserves and even supports must be thrust into the breach whether that was on my front or anybody else's; so at 7.45 p.m., I ordered the 4th Rifle Brigade from the fields west of Ypres to a position between Potijze and St Jean, and the 9th Royal Scots from Vlamertinghe to fields west of Ypres. I sent two and a half companies of the 2nd King's Shropshire Light Infantry, which regiment was bivouacking west of Ypres, to the grounds of Potijze, and one and a half companies of the same battalion to the Headquarters of the 80th Brigade as their Headquarters were as exposed as my own.

These moves were completed by about 9 p.m., and shortly afterwards I had reliable information that the 28th Division was holding their original trenches, but that the left of the Canadians had fallen back to Kitchener Wood a mile west of St Julien, some Canadians being in the G.H.Q. line near that place. There was no news of the French.

During the night my Division was attacked, but not seriously, probably with a view to preventing the Division reinforcing the troops where the breach had occurred. The night on the whole was fairly quiet and we at Headquarters managed to get some sleep.

The Canadians made some attempts at counter-attacking during the night, and some eleven battalions were engaged under General Turner and Colonel Geddes, the latter commanding a force composed of units of the 27th and 28th Division which had been hurried into the gap. These counter-attacks had little, if any result.

It was not till the early hours of the 23rd that I ascertained that the Canadian Division Head Quarters were in Brielen, two miles north-west of Ypres. The Headquarters of the 28th Division were still in Ypres about three hundred yards north of the Grand Place.[2]

The situation was very obscure all through the 23rd April, little information reaching us either from the front or the rear.

A lamentable counter-attack was ordered by Headquarters of the 2nd Army at the instigation of G.H.Q. The French were supposed to be conforming. Of my Division, the 4th Rifle Brigade,

---

2   The headquarters of the 28th had in fact moved west of Ypres on 20 April: see Notes to Part Two below, p. 127.

2nd King's Shropshire L.I., 2nd Duke of Cornwall's Light Infantry and the 9th Royal Scots were involved. I knew little or nothing of this counter-attack, except that I was told to support it with my artillery. The losses were very heavy, and it never had any chance of success. No one knew the situation and there was practically no artillery support worthy of the name. We wasted some of our all too scarce ammunition in shelling the supposed objective, but as far as my Division was concerned we were not told definitely what the objective was and had no real information as to the hour of attack. The situation was quite out of hand. The Headquarters of the 2nd Army were miles in rear, those of the 28th and the Canadian Divisions were also back and the only connection between those Commanders and their Divisions was by telephone, the wires of which were for the most part out of action on account of the shelling. I was in a position, my Headquarters being well up in the Salient, to know more of the situation than anyone else, but I knew very little as the reports I received were so conflicting.

During the day of the 23rd I took every man out of the trenches who could be spared and by evening, I was holding the line very thinly with hardly a man behind my front trenches. All my other troops I had hurled into the breach or had massed them near Potijze, ready to move in any direction they were required. In the evening I sent the 2nd Wessex R.E. Co. to put Wieltje in a state of defence, though that village was not in my area.

There was considerable confusion in the matter of command; owing to the distance away of the Commanders of the 28th and Canadian Divisions another command had cropped up, which came by the name of Geddes' Detachment. It was composed of battalions which had drifted into the breach near St. Julien. It was commanded by Lt. Col. Geddes of the Buffs, a first rate man who was killed shortly afterwards. Who Col. Geddes was under I don't know, and I don't think he knew either.

Reports kept on coming in, at one time that the Canadians were back in the G.H.Q. line west of St Julien, at another that they were holding on to their original positions. Both reports were true as some troops had fallen back while others had kept on.

That night the Commander of a Canadian brigade came to my dug-out and informed me that his men were fed up with fighting all day and that he had ordered them to fall back to the G.H.Q. line. I explained to the Brigadier in rather a forcible manner that if he had done so, the sooner he counter-ordered the order the better. He told me that he had covering orders from his Divisional General and on investigation I found that the order read: 'If forced to retire, retire into the G.H.Q. line'. I explained to him that if he considered these words constituted an order he was to consider it cancelled by me and that he was to get his men back into their original trenches or as nearly as was possible and to stick to that position at all costs. I also impressed on him that there was no question of retiring. He carried out my orders. This is a good instance of the danger of even mentioning a line of retirement in orders, as such mention is liable, as in this case, to be accepted as an order, or any way as a provision to retire.

By the night of the 23rd/24th we made certain that, though units were mixed up, the British line was almost intact, but that left of the Canadians the line was somewhat in rear of the old line, and further again to the left isolated British units were holding ground originally occupied by the French. What the French were doing beyond talking of grand counter-attacks we knew little.

During the early hours of the 24th the enemy's artillery was increased considerably and all back areas especially in the vicinity of Potijze and St. Jean were heavily bombarded. Up to this time the Chateau had escaped injury though the stables and the small chateau adjoining had been frequently struck with shrapnel.

About 8 a.m. on the 24th the shelling became so heavy that I ordered all wires to be connected up with the dugout close to the road and just west of the Chateau, and we retired into this dugout shortly afterwards. The dugout was far too small for what was required of it. It was only about 20 feet long by 6 broad, of which space the signals took up quite half. However we managed to get in most of the essential members of the Gen. Staff, the remainder still occupying the safest parts of the Chateau. The Administrative Staff which had always been accommodated in Ypres, just inside the Menin Gate, were sent back to Busseboom.

1 Lieutenant General Sir Thomas D'Oyly Snow (*right*) pictured on exercise after the war. Although age was one reason given for his departure from the Western Front he lived until 1940, outlasting nearly all his contemporaries.

Payne   Ethelston   Otway   Justice   Poynton   Snow   Lovett   Sturt
Kintsch   Waldly   Knox Leet VC   Thurlow   England   Wellington   Maddison
Hilla   Pearce   Watch   R Gray

2 Snow and his brother officers on their return from South Africa. He is the giant figure sixth from the left. His height proved a powerful genetic legacy: the shortest of his five grandsons was 6'4". (Somerset Military Museum)

3 Snow with his luxuriant moustache again stands squarely in the middle of the photograph with the regimental officers. Snow had performed well against the Zulus – he was made adjutant and a promising career lay ahead. The nature of Britain's imperial entanglements meant that subalterns like Snow saw plenty of active operations. (Somerset Military Museum)

IN COMMAND OF THE 4TH DIVISION OF THE BRITISH EXPEDITIONARY FORCE AT THE FRONT: MAJOR-GENERAL T. SNOW.

4 (*Above*): The terse missive sent by Snow to his wife just after the Battle of Le Cateau. The paucity of the language must have jarred with the scale and complexity of the events that the men of the BEF had witnessed.

5 (*Above right*) and 6 (*right*): The picture and short biography published in the press about Major General Snow, commander of the BEF's 4th Division. For a professional lifelong officer, it was a dream command.

Major General Snow, commanding the 4th Division since 1911, served in the Zulu Campaign; the Soudan Expedition (1884-85), being severely wounded in the action at El Gubat; and the Soudan Campaign of 1898, when he was present at Atbara and Khartoum, and was twice mentioned in despatches. His first regiment was the Somerset Light Infantry; he was promoted major into the Enniskilling Fusiliers; and he has commanded the 2nd Battalion Northampton Regiment.

7 (*Bottom right*): A copy of the Special Order issued by the staff of 4th Division on the departure of General Snow. He was invalided back to the UK having suffered a broken pelvis after a fall from his horse. His recuperation was by no means complete when he bowed to Kitchener's order to command another hastily assembled division.

(All taken from the collected letters of Gen Snow. IWM 76/79/1)

SPECIAL ORDER.

On temporarily relinquishing the command of the 4th Div. to Major General Sir Harry Rawlinson, Maj.Gen. Snow wishes to express his great appreciation of the gallantry and endurance of all ranks of the Division since their arrival in France, during which time he has had the honour to command them.

He also wishes to express his thanks to all officers and men for their loyalty and support both in peace and war, since he took over command of the 4th Div.

LA CARRIERE L'EVEQUE FE.   Lt.Col.
23/9/14.   Gen.Staff, 4th Divn.

8 Soldiers of the British Expeditionary Force arrive in Le Havre on 16 August 1914. The mobilisation and transportation of the BEF was a triumph of meticulous staff work while the surface ships of the German navy, the second largest in the world after Britain's, was unable to interdict the deployment. (By permission of the Imperial War Museum, ref Q051472)

9 French civilians besieging men of the 1st Battalion, Cameronians at Le Havre. Snow complained about the soldiers swapping away their shoulder boards, cap badges and buttons. (Imperial War Museum, ref Q051473)

10 The day after the Battle of Mons, exhausted British troops enjoy a brief break from what will become one of the most notable retreats in British military history. (Imperial War Museum, ref Q051478)

11 British forces retreat down a quintessentially French poplar-lined road. Despite extreme temperatures, enemy action and exhaustion, the BEF never lost its cohesion and was able to play its part in the vital autumn battles. (Imperial War Museum, ref Q051486)

12 A rare action shot from the earliest weeks of the war. Men of the 1st Battalion, Middlesex Regiment, 19th Brigade, come under shrapnel fire from German artillery during the Battle of the Marne on 8 September 1914. The peaked caps of peacetime offered no protection. (Imperial War Museum, ref Q051489)

13 One of the few surviving shots of the Battle of Le Cateau. A staff conference of the battalion officers of the 1st Cameronians. The commanding officer, Lieutenant Colonel P R Robertson, is mounted. In August and September 1914 it was still customary for senior officers to traverse the battlefield by horse. The practice was unthinkable just a few weeks later. (Imperial War Museum, ref Q051480)

Lt. E.J.Bruford.   Lt. R.G.F.Besley.   Lt. I.N.Jackson.   Lt. I.F.Marshall,   2/Lt. F. Moore.   Capt. J.A.Gould.   Lt. R.G.A.Mitchell.   Capt. I.Stevens.   Lt. J.A.Banwell.   Lt. R.J.W.Marr.   2/Lt. J.Sealey.
                                                                 M.C.

Capt. S.A.Elder.   Capt. J.A.Blake.   Capt. J.B.Taylor.   Major C.H.Goodland.   Lt. Gen. Sir T.D.O'Snow   Capt. G.P.Clarke.   Capt. J.R.Ware.   Capt. J.A.Dale.   Lt & Q.M.C.R.Davis.
                                                                          K.C.B., K.C.M.G.   M.C.

        2/Lt. C.W.Hirst.   2/Lt. I.S.Daniel.   2/Lt. A.M.Ashford.   Lt. B.D.Byers.   2/Lt. G.J.Pollard.

14 Snow as a corps commander midway through the war. He was promoted partly in response to his handling of the dogged response
to the German attack at the Second Battle of Ypres. However, his attack on Gommecourt as part of the Somme Offensive in 1916 was
the lowpoint of his career. His assault on 1 July 1916 was a bloody and futile failure even by the standards of that terrible day.

I only hope they don't go your way,
but I don't see why they Should.–

<u>20th June '15</u>

"Tomorrow I shall be able to say tomorrow's
I hope.– I don't think the Boches will
interfere as they are very tame here
& much too busy down South.–
It's quite an easy journey from here
motoring to Boulogne.– I don't leave here
till 12.– I shall take 2 motors for fear of
one breaking down.– It's odd arriving
22nd, just exactly 6 months.–

T.D'O.S. arrived home
on June 22nd; & on the
24th received the K.C.B.
in the Birthday Honours
list.–

Photo taken at Blackheath
where we had a small
house for 6 months.–

R.J.S.   J.J.S.   T.D.O.S.   G.D.O.S.   June 1915.

15 A page from the transcribed collection of Snow's letters home. The letters refer to June
1915. Glued in is a picture of Snow with his children. His son John, second from right,
followed his father into the Somerset Light Infantry and ended his career as a brigadier.
(Taken from the collected letters of Gen Snow. IWM 76/79/1)

About 9 a.m. I had a long talk with General Plumer on the 'phone. I did not hear much more of the situation from him than I knew myself, but he told me that the 13th Brigade were being brought up to the immediate north of Ypres, that the 13th Reserve Cavalry Brigade had been sent for, and that the York and Durham Brigade had arrived at Ypres. Gen. Plumer directed me to send two more of my battalions to the Canadians which I did, leaving me practically without any reserves for my own Division. General Plumer gave me to understand that, as I was the only senior officer on the spot, I was to have more or less a free hand to use any troops I could lay my hands on to re-establish the situation, and that I was to be in actual command of all troops arriving in the Salient but not allocated to certain units. Indeed all such troops were to constitute Corps Reserve and to be under my orders. This made matters much easier for me.

During the morning the bombardment became so heavy that practically all communication with the rear was severed, and not only was I out of touch with Corps Headquarters, but the 28th Division and the Canadians were cut off from their Divisional Headquarters for hours at a time. My dugout being practically in the centre of the Salient became a sort of rendez-vous for everyone seeking instructions, and so I found myself forced to take upon myself responsibilities which were not really mine.

I had a wonderful signalling officer, Lt. E. N. Eveleigh, R.E., and he kept my line open not only with my own Brigade but with the Brigades of the 28th Division and Canadians (except for short intervals), and so these Units came to look to me for instructions. The worst of it was that communications between these Units and their own Commanders became operative at intervals, and so orders were transmitted to the Units which I did not become aware of, orders which were often at variance with what I had issued.

I arranged with 5th Corps that a Staff Officer of the 28th Division should be attached to my Headquarters through whom I could deal with the 28th Division and this helped matters, at least it made it appear that any orders I issued to the troops of the 28th Division had the sanction of the Divisional General.

I established a most useful method of communication by means of some cyclists under Lt H. F. Otway, Leinster Regt., which was invaluable. Before I acted on any report I sent a cyclist patrol to verify the information, which saved much unnecessary movement. As an instance of this, one day I received an urgent message from G.O.C. 28th Division during one of the intervals when the wires were working, saying his front had been broken-in near Broodseinde and asking for me to detail battalions of the Corps reserve to re-establish the situation. Before acting I sent up my usual patrol to verify the report, and the patrol shortly arrived back with the report that there was no break in the line and that the troops in the vicinity of the reported breach were having a comparatively quiet time.

We had one thing to be thankful for and that was the weather. Ever since the morning of the 22nd it had been beautiful, the most perfect Spring weather I have ever known; the birds, quite undismayed by the noise of the guns or the explosion of shells, sang merrily.

I was very anxious to know what was happening on the French front, but I could get no information. I had no news either direct or through our own Army Headquarters, and all I did find out was through patrols which I sent out in the direction of the French line or where these lines ought to have been.

Whenever I did hear from the French, the reports were very optimistic, showing that a great counter-attack was shortly to be delivered which ought to do more than re-establish the original situation. This grand counter-attack never materialised then or at any other time, although the rounds we expended on its behalf were something enormous and of course all wasted. Several times I was told that the French were going to attack such and such a place at such and such a time and this information [was] coupled with a request that I should assist with my artillery. I turned on all my guns at the given hour or half an hour before, often giving the necessary lifts to allow for the French advance. An hour or so later I would get a message to say that the counter-attack had been postponed to such and such an hour and again asking me to afford artillery support at that hour. There was nothing for me to do but comply and so waste more ammunition. Even as regards our own troops, many local counter-attacks were made quite unsupported by artillery, and at other times vast quantities of ammunition were expended in supporting counter-attacks which never took place. Had we had more telephone wire and more experienced forward observing officers, such a thing could not have happened.

Although by the 23rd/24th we had come to the conclusion that for some reason or other the Germans had not been able to follow up their success, there was nothing to show us that they would not bring up reinforcements from other parts of the line to attack us in great superiority of numbers while the line was in a fluid state, and therefore we could only work hard to establish ourselves in some sort of tenable position before the arrival of those reinforcements.

However if the enemy lacked infantry they certainly did not lack guns or ammunition. They bombarded us day and night, not only our Headquarters and the trenches but all the approaches. Such was the shape of the Salient that we could be bombarded from any point of the compass from north, east and south. We had little or nothing to reply with. As regards the field guns, we were supposed to be cut down to 3 rounds per gun per diem, and as for heavy guns, all we had was some 5-inch howitzers and some 4.7", which latter were as dangerous to friends as foes, as their range could not be depended on to within hundreds of yards. Our ammunition was so scanty that at one time I told the C.R.A. that all rounds of 18 pounders fired were to pass just over the trenches so that the men could hear some shells going in the right direction. We also gave out that the reason of our lack of guns and ammunition was that we had sent all our guns south to assist in the break through there, which break through ended in a fiasco owing to lack of ammunition. There was a pair of hostile 6" or 8" howitzers which used to sweep the Zonnebeke–Ypres road regularly. They began at Zonnebeke and lengthened about 100 yards or so at a time right past Potijze. It was a tense moment when the last pair of shells had dropped about 100 yards short of the Chateau to see where the next pair would go.

We were very crowded in the dugout. I had a small table for myself, and there were two small tables for G.S. Officer, and another one or two for clerks, but the greater part of the dugout was given over to the signals. At night we cleared out the tables and slept on the floor packed like sardines. The noise was terrific, what with telephone bells ringing and shells bursting near by. The effect on me was to make me very sleepy and I snatched many a half hour's sleep in the intervals between receiving reports and issuing orders. It was well that I could do so, as anything in the way of prolonged sleep even at night, was an impossibility.

The question of supplies became very difficult. Supplies could only be brought up at night and the regimental transport which only had two alternative routes through Ypres suffered heavily.

The 27th Supply Wagons suffered less than those of other Divisions owing to the care of my divisional Cavalry Commander whom I appointed a guide to the Transport. This officer would make a study of where shells were falling and of the system on which the enemy's batteries were working. He used to give the transport a rendez-vous just west of Ypres and then lead the massed transport through Ypres by whichever road appeared to him to be safest at the moment. It was not so difficult as it sounds, as the enemy's Artillery were very conservative in their methods and generally shelled localities in the same order. Major Calvert seldom, if ever, made a mistake in his choice of routes and the losses of the 27th Divisional Transport were negligible. Units being so constantly moved away from their brigade and being often themselves split up added to the difficulty, but I cannot remember any instance of troops being reported short of rations.

By midday on the 24th, except for the shelling from which we suffered heavily, things were more or less in hand. All my reserve battalions had been absorbed into the line, or as supports, in the St. Julien direction, but we had a more or less continuous line or at any rate a line of posts between the Canadians' left and the right of the French or where that right professed to be.

About 2.15 p.m. on the afternoon of 24th April, there was a bad break in the line near Gravenstafel, so serious that I felt I must act at once. I sent an order to General Turner Commanding 3rd Canadian Brigade saying that as senior officer on the spot I directed him to take two battalions of the 28th and one of the 27th Division's and, adding every man he could spare, to counter-attack and re-establish the situation. I had so few troops of my own and the situation was so critical that I had to use these two battalions of the 28th Division reserve which were in the Salient. I was of course fully justified in doing so, as I was more or less responsible for the safety of the salient. Furthermore I was the senior officer on the spot.

There was a good deal of discussion on my action at a later date, and General Bulfin Commanding the 28th Division was much annoyed by it and complained to Sir John French. The latter said I was fully justified in my action.

The village of St. Julien was a puzzle during the first few days of the battle. It was not an important position, but was the biggest village in this area and was named on the map. It thus came into prominence, though no one ever seemed sure whether it was in ours or the Germans' hands, and every time an effort was made to regain lost ground it was called a counter-attack on St. Julien.

The biggest effort made against St. Julien was in the early hours of the 25th April. It was known as Hull's attack. The first I heard of it was at 11 p.m. on the 24th. At that hour I received instructions that such an attack was to be made at 3 a.m. on the 25th. I was ordered to detail two, or it may be three, battalions to assist and that the C.O.'s of these battalions were to be detailed to meet General Hull at midnight at the level crossing west of Ypres. It was quite impossible to get the orders to these Commanding Officers in time to allow them to be at the level crossing by midnight, but I issued the orders telling them to find General Hull as soon as possible.

I was directed to assist this attack with all the artillery I could get hold of and so all guns of the 27th, 28th and Canadian Divisions were turned on St. Julien at 2.45 a.m. and a brisk fire was kept up till 3.15 or after, by which hour I hoped St. Julien would have been taken, and certainly by that hour we had used up far more ammunition than was prudent. As a matter of fact, the attack was not launched till 5.30 a.m., and how General Hull managed to get his troops together as early as that has always been a mystery to me. The attack, when it was made, had little or no artillery support and it was a fiasco, and ended by making no progress and suffered heavy losses.

For this attack the whole of the 10th Brigade was used together with 3 Battalions of the Northumbrian Division and three of my battalions.

About 5 a.m., on the 26th I got back the D.C.L.I. and the 9th Royal Scots, and they went into the grounds of the Chateau which was getting too full of troops to be safe. The Lahore Division arrived near Wieltje. A cavalry brigade arrived on the night of the 26th, under Maj. Gen. Cis Bingham. They had a rough passage through Ypres as far as shelling was concerned, and Cis Bingham when he arrived at my dugout was very much done. A whisky and soda and an hour's rest put him all right again. I placed this Brigade in Corps Reserve.

The difficulty was where to find cover for all these troops. There was plenty of cover in the Sanctuary Wood and the adjoining coppices, but that was not where the reserves were wanted. Except for the grounds of Potijze Chateau, which was already crowded with troops, the whole country was open. It was impossible to use the ruined villages of St. Jean and Wieltje as they were constantly and heavily bombarded. The redoubts of the G.H.Q. line were also full to overflowing. The only thing to do was to make the reserves dig themselves in in any desirable spot; but the enemy's aeroplanes were so alert that heavy losses from artillery fire resulted. We later found that the best method was to dig in at night and cover the newly turned earth with boughs etc., and so camouflage the trenches.

Everybody of any importance who arrived in the Salient came to my dugout to report or consult, and many were the conferences held in it.

The gratuitous advice I received from people responsible and irresponsible was amusing. One section of officers kept urging me to take a firm hand, and being the only responsible person on the spot, to order all troops in the salient to retire on to the line of the canal which meant on to the outskirts of Ypres.

To a certain extent this advice was sound. By making such a retirement we should have got rid of the Salient and established ourselves in a really strong line and we should have freed ourselves of the embarrassment of the bottle-neck approach through Ypres, but though I was the man on the spot, such a movement would have laid open the flank of troops on my left over which I had no control, and so could only have been undertaken by Sir Herbert Plumer, and even then only if the French agreed. But to take it upon myself, with my limited information, to order such a retrograde movement was unthinkable and I never entertained it for a moment.

I have often wondered what the result would have been had Sir Herbert Plumer taken the proposed course. We should not, I feel sure, have lost Ypres, and thus there would have been no more loss of morale than we experienced in shortening the Salient as we did on the 3rd May; we should have saved those terrible losses which we suffered not only during the remainder of the 2nd Battle of Ypres, but during the battles in the Salient in subsequent years.

My G.S.I. Colonel Reed was hit in the face by splinters on the night of the 26th/27th and my servant, my groom, and one of my horses were wounded; so on the morning of the 27th I sent everyone not absolutely necessary back to Busseboom, merely keeping one A.D.C., three Staff Officers and sufficient clerks and servants to carry on.

Colonel Reed's wound was not serious but it was thought advisable to send him to the rear for inoculation. His place was taken by Major R. H. Hare, R.A. an imperturbable Staff Officer who was always cheery and alert. Major Hare remained with me till we moved back west of Ypres when Colonel Reed re-joined.

I felt relieved after I had got rid of everyone on my staff who was not absolutely necessary. Among the others whom I sent back was Lt. Colonel Frank Mildmay, now Lord Mildmay, who was my interpreter and acted as extra A.D.C. He had been fully employed since the battle began, carrying messages to exposed parts of the battlefields. He was one of those people who always insisted on being employed if a really dangerous job presented itself, and even when I elected to send someone else I generally found Frank Mildmay had accompanied him, even if it was only to show him the way! He had done more than his share of work, and I was glad to get him out of the turmoil. That afternoon Potijze was treated to a very heavy bombardment, and I was congratulating myself on having sent so many of my staff back when in walked Frank Mildmay. On my asking him what he was doing, he calmly said: 'Oh I just walked over to see how you were all getting on'. I did not know whether to reprimand him for unnecessarily exposing himself, or to thank him for his loyalty; but I know that I was at heart very pleased. I recommended this officer several times for a decoration, but he was never awarded one. No one more thoroughly deserved recognition.

The bombardment increased as the day wore on. Many of my guns were in a very forward position and, had my line been broken, would have been quickly overrun. All the horse lines were west of Ypres, and there would not have been time to bring the horses up to save the guns. I therefore had to keep some horses, though very few, somewhere near the guns. They suffered very heavily as the Germans guns searched every bit of cover in the area.

On the 28th April 5th Corps, or more properly 'Plumer's Force', consisted of the 4th, 27th, 28th and Canadian Divisions and the Lahore and Northumbrian Divisions.[3] There were also one, if not two, cavalry brigades (dismounted) east of Ypres. The battalions of my division, which I had thrust into the line to the north-eastward, began to return to me.

As a matter of fact the Salient was too congested with troops at this time. We had only artillery to fear, and the more troops there were in the Salient the better target they offered. It was a very difficult proposition for Sir Herbert Plumer, as if he kept the bulk of his troops west of the canal and the Germans brought up sufficient troops to enable them to advance, they could put down such a barrage on the few routes across the canal that the troops in the Salient would be isolated.

The action, or rather the lack of action, on the part of the French on the 27th, 28th, and 29th April must have been a source of great worry

---

3   For the composition of 'Plumer's Force', see Notes to Part Two below, p. 133.

to Sir Herbert Plumer and G.H.Q.; there were always rumours of a grand counter-attack, but it never came off.

As it became clear that the French were not going to re-establish themselves on the lost ground, G.H.Q. determined that the Salient must be made less pronounced. It was absolutely necessary to do something of this sort though it entailed giving up all the high ground east of Zonnebeke, thereby giving the enemy good observation over the whole of the area east of the canal. After much consideration it was arranged that a new line should be dug from the right of the 27th Division to pass through the eastern portion of Sanctuary Wood, east of the Hooge chateau wood, east of Bellewarde Lake, through Frezenberg, to the existing line near St. Julien.

I had no great objection to the line through my area as it was more or less covered, but I thought the Frezenberg position, which was to be occupied by the 28th Division, very exposed.

We immediately set to work to construct this line, and we were helped by working parties from the Northumberland Brigade. On some parts of the line we could work by day, and each night some 2,500 were employed. It takes a long time to construct a good line and furnish it with trench boards and other necessaries; but by the night of the 1st May the line was reported as habitable, though very lightly wired. It was very difficult digging in the woods, but owing to the lovely weather we were not impeded by water. A discussion was held on the telephone as to the best method of withdrawing. The 28th and Canadian Commanders voted for a sudden withdrawal leaving no rear-guard behind. I voted that we should leave rear guards to dispute every inch of ground between the old and the new line. The opposition vote gained Sir Herbert Plumer's approval. Rearguards might have been a difficulty in the 28th and Canadian areas as the ground was so open, but in my area we should have made the Germans pay heavily for every yard of ground gained.

During the night of the 3rd/4th the withdrawal to the new line was successfully carried out. The Germans did not detect the retirement till daylight and then followed up very cautiously. The retirement was accomplished practically without loss.

The withdrawal made it necessary to select new position for our guns, which was difficult as to withdraw them west of the canal made the ranges long, and there were not many hidden positions east of the canal. However we got fairly good positions, and during the remainder of the battle the guns did not suffer very heavily.

As the new line would bring the front trenches to within a few hundred yards of my Headquarters at Potijze, the Army Commander directed that I should transfer them to somewhere west of the canal, and we arranged to carry out the withdrawal at 3 a.m. on the 3rd May. We selected that hour as it was usually the quietest hour of the twenty-four.

During the afternoon of the 2nd May my Headquarters at Potijze were heavily bombarded for over 2 hours. The concussion caused by the bursting of big shells made the dugout rock like a ship in a storm, and when a particularly heavy explosion occurred all the lamps were put out. All wires were cut and we posted sentries over the dugout to warn us if the Germans were coming. However nothing happened and the bombardment in due time ceased. When we went outside and looked about us, we saw that many trees of 2 foot in diameter had been cut off or else blown out of the ground, and on top of our dugout was lying a 'dud' 6-inch shell. Had it burst when it struck the top of the dugout, it is unlikely that any of us would have escaped.

When we left on the morning of the 3rd May at 3 a.m. we nearly got into trouble at the Menin Gate, as when we were crossing the bridge a shrapnel exploded just in front of the bonnet of my car and another at the same moment burst between my car and the one following it, about 20 yards behind.

I had not been to Ypres for more than a week and the changes I noticed as I drove through were wonderful. Many houses were flat and the Cloth Hall only a ruined wall. It was like the city of the dead, no movement except a stray dog here and there, or a horse or two wandering aimlessly about with its harness dragging behind it. Shells were bursting among the ruins, but we all got safely through and reached our new Headquarters which we had established in a farm about a mile south of Vlamertinghe.

Nothing much happened that day except that there was an unusually heavy bombardment of back areas about 5 a.m., and we were glad we had selected such an early hour for our move.

The Corps Commander Sir Herbert Plumer and General Allenby visited me and were very complimentary on the work I had done. Sir Herbert told me that Sir Horace Smith-Dorrien had gone home, that he was to succeed him in command of the 2nd Army, and that General Allenby had taken over 5th Corps.

As the accommodation of the farm was very limited, we took over a farm south of Busseboom as retired Headquarters where we could get some rest when the situation allowed. As it turned out, the situation seldom did allow as long as we remained in the line.

Up to the date of the retirement, all the fighting had taken place in the vicinity of St. Julien or anyway north of the Ypres–Zonnebeke road, and my Division had only to endure the shelling. After the move, the enemy's activity was transferred south, and there was heavy shelling of the 27th and 28th Division front. From 12 noon onwards the new trenches were heavily bombarded.

Except for the shelling, which owing to the shallow nature of the trenches inflicted heavy casualties, nothing much happened till the morning of the 8th. In the meantime Hill 60 on our right fell into enemy's hands.

On the morning of the 8th the bombardment of the new front between the Menin Road and Mouse Trap Farm became intense. The 80th Brigade being on my left was the only one of my brigades to suffer. That Brigade held the front from the Menin Road to north of the Bellawaarde Ridge. The 28th Division holding the forward slopes near Frezenberg suffered most. This position of the 28th was an impossible one; it was on a forward slope overlooked from the Passchendaele Ridge. The 83rd Brigade which was holding this position broke after repelling several attacks, and fell back to a line near Verlorenhoek losing many men, missing and prisoners.

The 4th K.R.R.C. and the P.P.C.L.I. stood firm and drove off every attempt on their trenches, and the remainder of the [80th] Brigade had to be called up.

The 81st Brigade suffered very heavily from shell fire. From the 9th to the 12th May there were heavy bombardments and periodical infantry attacks, the enemy paying most attention to the front held by the 27th division. On the 12th, the 28th Division were relieved, and we had the Cavalry on our left.

The Cavalry and the 80th Brigade were heavily attacked on the 13th May, the cavalry being driven in and losing heavily in a counter-attack. The 80th Brigade again stood firm. So things went on till the 17th. The battalions of the 80th Brigade were reduced to skeletons, yet they were always ready, after a day in support, or perhaps two days, to relieve their comrades in the front line. In one of my messages I spoke of the 80th Brigade as the 'Stonewall Brigade', which epithet stuck to them ever afterwards and is referred to in the Official History. I do not think that to the end of the War I ever came across a better lot of fighting than that put up by the 80th Brigade during those days.

On the 17th the Cavalry began to relieve us, and by the 19th only our artillery was left in, and I handed over command.

I and my Staff retired to Apple Blossom Farm, the farm we had selected as our retired Headquarters when we first moved west of Ypres, but which we had hardly ever had time to visit, much less to sleep in.

On the 24th, there was a great gas attack all along the front of the Salient, and the 80th Brigade were called upon as Reserves and delivered a counter-attack on the night of the 24th/25th against Bellewaarde Chateau in conjunction with the 84th Brigade of the 28th Division. This counter-attack was supported by all the units of the 27th and 28th Division east of Ypres. It met with a certain amount of success, but finally had to retire on to the road east of Witte Poort Farm which they held. The brigade was finally relieved on the night of the 26th/27th May.

V. 'Review of the Operations'

On reviewing the 2nd Battle of Ypres certain points which are to be regretted force themselves into prominence. The chief of these are: —

1. The confusion of command.
2. The congestion of troops in the Salient.
3. The failure to provide buried cables and shell-roof dug-outs.
4. Want of cohesion between the artillery and infantry.
5. Mistaken tactics.

and a few lines must be devoted to each of the above.

1. First as regards confusion of command: when the battle began the chain of command seemed right enough. The Corps Commander was in a suitable position, and he had three Division Commanders under him, the 27th, 28th and Canadians. Unfortunately the 28th and Canadian Commanders, for lack of suitable accommodation, had taken up their positions too far back, and although this did not matter in quiet times when the wires were working and when the Brigade Headquarters could be reached in a few minutes by motor car, it did matter a great deal in the battle when all wires were down, and approaches, which practically only amounted to two, were swept by hostile fire. The G.O.C. 27th Division was on the other hand (suitable accommodation being available) well to the front, in the exact centre behind the three Divisions, and that fact alone forced him to take control of the 28th and Canadian Divisions, especially when he found that they were cut off from their own Divisional commanders. Had the G.O.C. 27th Division been more directly behind his own division he would not have been so much in the position of the man on the spot, and communications from the Corps to all parts of the fighting line would not so naturally have gone through him. In this case, although the advantage of a man on the spot would have been lost, there would have been less confusion of command, and the G.O.C.'s 28th and Canadian Divisions could have been the only people to whom their Brigadiers would have turned to for advice, difficult as it was to get at them.

It would have been better if, as soon as the battle began, the G.O.C.'s 28th and Canadian Divisions had established their advanced Headquarters somewhere in the Salient as far forward as those of the G.O.C. 27th Division. They could then have kept touch with their Brigadiers all through the Battle and much confusion would have been avoided. This confusion was intensified by the number of independent battalions which had been thrust into the fight irrespective of area. At one time the 27th Division had some six or seven of its battalions operating in the 28th, Canadian, and even in the French areas, and these battalions were more or less under two commanders, namely their own Divisional Commander and the Commander of the Division or Brigade in whose area they happened to be. It was owing to these circumstances that local Commanders and detachments were formed, for example Hull's detachment, and Geddes' detachment. Indeed the whole area over which Sir Hebert Plumer was exercising control as G.O.C. 5th Corps had so many troops sent into it that Sir Herbert's command was called 'Plumer's detachment', but whether Sir Herbert dealt with the whole detachment through his corps staff, or had a separate staff for this purpose, I for one do not know.

2. As regards congestion of troops in the Salient: it is difficult to see how this could have been avoided in the circumstances. Our artillery was not sufficiently experienced, and the supply of ammunition much too small, to leave the defence chiefly to that arm, and it was necessary therefore to have sufficient infantry available to repel any real infantry attack on the part of the enemy. Infantry sufficient for this purpose had to be kept much further forward than would have been the case in ordinary circumstances, because of the bottle-neck of Ypres through which ran the only two approaches to the Salient. Had these reserves been kept west of Ypres, the enemy's artillery was powerful enough to make the approaches through Ypres quite impossible. We were at that date very inferior in the air to the Germans, and so no long distance reconnaissance could be undertaken, and we were, during the whole battle, left in uncertainty as to the enemy's prospects of reinforcements. Unfortunately for us we were playing into the

Germans' hands, as their superiority in artillery, and their unlimited supply of ammunition, enabled them to inflict on us heavy casualties. A report was sent round from G.H.Q. during the battle that the German losses were enormous, and that train after train of wounded were seen going to the rear. I cannot believe this. Certainly very few German casualties could have been the result of gun-fire, and as for rifle-fire very few rounds were fired, at any rate the battalions of my Division, even by those who were in the thick of the fight.

3. As regards the failure to provide buried cables and shell-proof dug-outs: the only excuse is that neither had been much thought about so early in the war. At the same time, had we had buried cables, even if we went so far only as to bury the main cable from the Corps to the Divisions, and the Divisions to the Brigades, we should have been saved endless trouble and anxiety. We all learned later in the campaign that one of the fist things to assure success either in attack or defence was a cable so dug in that no artillery fire could possibly put it out of use.

4. As regards cohesion between the artillery and infantry: our artillery was very inexperienced. It had acquired some skill in firing over our trenches, but in that case the ranges were known and the wires from the forward observing officer to the guns more or less permanent. It was a very different thing in the open warfare of the battle under discussion. The targets were constantly changing, and it was difficult for inexperienced forward observing officers to find the right place to observe from. Moreover, we had not sufficient telephone wires to connect the forward observing officers with the batteries. Firing by maps was in its infancy, so most of the firing done was more or less chance work. Neither had infantry officers realised at that time the absolute necessity for artillery support in the attack, although they knew how necessary it was in the defence. Counter-battery work was almost unknown. But even had we had experienced artillery with plenty of wires we should have been little better off owing to the number of rounds available. The shortage of ammunition in itself was enough to lose the battle and Ypres.

5. As regards mistaken tactics: there can be little doubt that the tactics we employed were wrong. We made counter-attack after counter-attack. There are two distinct types of counter-attack. The first is the local counter-attack which is made by the reserves on the spot against the point of greatest pressure. The other is the grand counter-attack which to be successful should be aimed at the flank or in rear of the flank of the attack. As there was no open flank as a rule in the Great War, latter types of counter-attacks were aimed at the side of the bulge or salient which generally presented itself after a successful attack. Such a counter was made by Foch on the Marne, successfully, in 1918, and such a counter was intended at Cambrai in 1917 by the Cavalry from Epéhy on Villers Guislain. This latter counter never came off, as the Cavalry Corps were drawn off from the place of assembly to the point of greatest pressure at Gouzeaucourt. A counter-attack of this description was impossible in the 2nd Battle of Ypres, as the necessary troops would have had to be assembled in our salient where they would have been the target of German guns from north, south, and east. Thus the only type of counter-attack possible was the local one at the point of greatest pressure. The Germans knew where they were pressing us the most heavily and therefore knew exactly where the counter was to be expected and with their supremacy in guns, and apparently unlimited ammunition, they were able to pump lead on that locality to their heart's content, thereby causing us terrible losses.

What the Germans did all through the battle was to bring an overwhelming fire on a certain length of front trench literally blowing us out of it. This length of trench they occupied very lightly. They then concentred their guns in front of this trench, and when our counter began, they brought such barrage to bear that our troops generally failed to reach the trench, or if they did, only at enormous sacrifice. Had we contented ourselves, when we were shelled out of our trenches, with digging new ones and making no attempt at countering, it might have been bad for morale, but it would have saved us the enormous casualty roll which resulted from our counter-attacks. We had practically no artillery support, and we ought to have modified our tactics accordingly, instead of which we stuck religiously to the book which never had calculated on such disparity of artillery between two opposing forces.

Seldom has a more difficult operation devolved on any Commander than on Sir Herbert Plumer. It was the French front which was taken, and it was for them to restore it. They kept on for several days declaring that a huge counter-attack was being arranged, and they begged Sir Herbert to do all he could to hold the enemy who had broken through, until the grand counter should restore the situation. This grand counter never materialised, even if it was ever seriously contemplated. A few pitiful counter-attacks hardly worthy of the name were attempted by the French, but never anything serious, and when Sir Herbert saw there was no help to be expected from the French he had to shorten the line. Had he known that the French never intended business he might have shortened the line directly after the gas attack and so avoided all the losses incurred by our counter-attacks. Although, when the fight began, he was G.O.C., 5th Corps, in command of a properly composed force, before the battle had been going on for 48 hours he found himself nominated 'G.O.C. Plumer Detachment',[4] which not only included his old command but also a mass of detached units and stray battalions which had drifted in from other commands; some of these battalions were acting on their own, others were hastily formed with brigades or detachments under officers who had no staff or at any rate no machinery to help them to carry out their duties.

Added to this we had practically no heavy guns and our field guns were woefully short of ammunition.

It was a Herculean task which fell on Sir Herbert Plumer and right well he acquitted himself.

Throughout the war it was difficult to know how one's actions would be viewed by one's superiors. One was never sure whether for some particular action one would be promoted or stellenbosched. As

---

4   It was rather more than forty-eight hours before Plumer found himself thus nominated; see Notes to Part Two below, p. 138.

an example of this, shortly after the 2nd Battle of Ypres I met General Hull, and we fully discussed our action during the battle. At the end of the discussion I said: 'Anyway there are two people who ought to be 'stellenbosched', you are one, and I am the other'. He fully agreed. Within a few days, Sir John's despatch appeared from which I quote the following extract: '. . .and I wish to place on record the deep admiration which I feel for the resource and presence of mind evinced by the leaders actually on the spot. The parts taken by Major General Snow and Br. General Hull were reported to me as being particularly marked in this respect'.

After a short rest the 27th Division took over the Armentières front. Things were very peaceful in this area and the enemy not at all inclined to fight even when provoked. The trenches were excellent, and the billets first class. After about 4 weeks on this front I handed over the Division to General Milne in the middle of July 1915, as I was promoted to be a Corps Commander.

Shortly afterwards the Division moved to the Somme area and a few weeks later proceeded to Salonika, where it remained till the end of the war.

NOTES TO PART TWO

THE 27TH DIVISION AT ST ELOI,
AND DURING 'SECOND YPRES'

All dates are 1915 unless otherwise stated. All references to *Military Operations, France and Belgium, 1915.Volume I:Winter 1914–1915: Battle of Neuve Chapelle: Battles of Ypres*, are abbreviated to *MO, 1915,* v. 1. German units are italicised: *XXVI. Corps*, etc. Figures in square brackets at the start of each note refer to page numbers in the text.

[76] *[November 1914]* '. . . *three very good officers were nominated as my Brigadiers, namely, Col. Hon. C. G. Fortescue, Col. D. A. Macfarlane, and Col. L. A. M. Stopford.'*
    None of these was in post during Second Ypres; they had been replaced by Brigadier Generals W. E. B. Smith (80th Brigade), H. L. Croker (81st Brigade) and J. R. Longley (82nd Brigade): see Appendix 6 below, p. 163.

[79] *'After a fortnight's stay at St. Omer, we received orders to reconnoitre the trenches near St. Eloi with a view to taking them over . . .'*
    As the BEF expanded in the winter of 1914–15, so the front that it occupied lengthened. On the nights of 5/6 and 6/7 January 1915 the 27th Division took over, from the French 32nd Division, the trenches from the Kemmel–Wytschaete road north-east to St Eloi, roughly three and a half miles. On the nights of 1/2 and 2/3 February the 28th Division moved into the line immediately left, relieving the French 31st division, and thus extending the British front approximately two miles northwards, from St Eloi to the Ypres–Zandvoorde road.

[86] *[February] 'Indeed these raids did harm to our morale, as the men began to think the Germans were their superiors in hand-to-hand fighting . . .'*

On 5 February the Commander-in-Chief issued a memorandum drawing attention to 'the importance of constant activity and of offensive methods in general', and giving official sanction to small-scale localised attacks, or 'raids' (*MO, 1915*, v. 1, pp. 33–4). At a time when the BEF was forced onto the defensive the Commander-in-Chief saw raids as playing an important part in a psychological battle: 'they relieve monotony and improve the moral of our own troops, while they have a corresponding detrimental effect on the moral of the enemy's troops.' The Germans, though, were at this time far better equipped for trench warfare than the British, making it difficult for local commanders to satisfy the key caveats in the Commander-in-Chief's memorandum: 'These minor operations should . . . have a reasonable chance of success, and be commensurate with the losses likely to be entailed.'

[86] *[February–March] 'There now began to be rumours of the enemy mining . . . Something had however to be done in the way of counter-mining, and about twenty miners were brought out from home.'*

With the onset of siege warfare on the Western Front the BEF began to organise specialist mining units, and in February eight tunnelling companies were formed, comprising men recruited for the purpose at home, and augmented by the transfer from their existing units of miners already serving at the front.

[87] *[14 March] 'Some three trenches together with the Mound fell into the enemy's hands. The Germans also bombarded our back areas very heavily. In spite of that, the Irish Brigade, who were occupying the trenches at the moment, brought up some support . . .'*

The surprise German attack at St Eloi on 14 March, beginning at 5 p.m., was directed at trenches held by the 80th Brigade – and not the 'Irish Brigade', by which General Snow means the 82nd. Because of heavy shelling no reinforcements were to hand, and a counterattack, which was only partially successful, was not launched until after midnight. A further German attack in this sector on 17 March was 'repulsed with great loss' (*MO, 1915*, v. 1, p. 31).

[88] '*The 28th Division . . . took over the trenches immediately North of us about the middle of January.*'
In fact it was in early February (see above, p. 119).

[88] '*By the end of February it was found necessary to reorganise [the 28th] Division, and two brigades were exchanged for experienced ones of other divisions.*'
The 83rd Brigade of the 28th Division had been attacked on 4 February, directly after moving into the line, and the 2nd East Yorkshires 'suffered considerably' in fighting that went on for many days (*MO, 1915*, v. 1, p. 31). The division was also depleted by sickness, and on 18 February its three brigades were temporarily relieved by the 9th, 13th and 15th brigades.

[88] '*About this time [March–April] there was a great epidemic of "stellenbosching". . . Two out of three infantry brigadiers who had started with me from England were sent home . . .*'
It is unclear from General Snow's account which of the original 'very good officers' nominated as his brigadiers (see above) were removed. For 'Stellenbosching' see the Glossary, below.

[89] '*We had only been resting a few days when we received orders to relieve a French division in the salient of Ypres . . .*'
In the first half of April the BEF extended its front northwards, taking over roughly three-quarters of the Ypres Salient from the French, as far as the Ypres–Poelcappelle road. The 27th Division moved into the line on 2–8 April; the 28th Division on 8–11 April; and the Canadian Division (assigned to V. Corps from First Army as from 7 April) on 15–17 April. The 27th occupied the front from just left of Hill 60 to midway along Polygon Wood; the 28th from that point to just left of Berlin Wood; and the Canadians from that point to the Ypres–Poelcappelle road. From the Canadian left to the canal

at Steenstraat the line was held by two French divisions, the 45th (Algerian) and 87th (Territorial). Neither was considered a first-rate unit. The 45th came into the line on 16 April, while the 87th had been in the vicinity of Ypres ever since the fighting in October–November 1914. North of Steenstraat the Belgian sector began.

[90] *[early / mid-April] 'These two chateaux [at Potijze] were the only two buildings of importance left intact so far East of Ypres . . . Probably the enemy was quite aware that they were used as a Divisional Headquarters, but allowed us to live in fancied security till the time came.'*

The Germans planned to bombard headquarters in the Salient during the attack of 22 April, but the concrete base of the 15-inch long-range gun specially brought up for the purpose did not set in time (*MO, 1915*, v. 1, p. 187 n. 2).

[91] *'There was a more or less prepared support or reserve line running due south from immediately West of St. Julien to Zillebeke.'*

This was the so-called GHQ Line, see Glossary.

[91] *'[The GHQ] line was a valuable addition to our defences . . . but later when the Germans took St. Julien the northern section of this wire was a great embarrassment to us as it impeded reinforcing . . .'*

The heavy wiring of the GHQ Line proved an encumbrance in particular to 'Hull's Attack' on 25 April, contributing to its delayed start: it was intended as a night attack but was eventually launched in daylight.

[91] *'Hooge the headquarters of one of my brigades was a delightful place.'*

The headquarters of the 82nd Brigade were at Hooge, and those of the 81st close by; the 80th's headquarters were at Verlorenhoek, almost one and a half miles north-north-west.

[92] *'Neither the French nor ourselves ever built dug-outs, as we knew them later, in those days, and we did not do so till we drove the Germans back in 1916 and learned, from what we then found, how real dug-outs should be constructed.'*

General Snow alludes to the German dug-outs on the chalk lands of the Somme that were captured during the 1916 offensive. Some, for example at La Boisselle, were discovered to be forty feet deep. In the waterlogged clay soil of Flanders the construction of such defences was more difficult.

[93] *[early April]* '*Shortly after we took over the salient a memorandum was sent round from G.H.Q. saying that intelligence agents reported the preparation of poisonous gases in the forest a few miles north-east of our position and that this information was to be passed round for what it was worth . . .*'

On 15 April Second Army forwarded to GHQ a report from its liaison officer with the two French divisions in the Salient, pointing to the imminent use of asphyxiating gas by the enemy. The intelligence came from a German prisoner from *XXVI. Corps*, who was found to be carrying a rudimentary protection against gas. His story was disbelieved, however – he appeared too forthcoming to be credible – and reconnaissance by an RFC squadron on the 16th revealed nothing out of the ordinary. It was presumed that the enemy was trying to gain some tactical or psychological advantage by misinformation.

But as early as 30 March the French Tenth Army, to the right of the BEF, had learnt from prisoners that there were large supplies of an asphyxiating gas in cylinders along the front in the vicinity of Zillebeke, and on 16 April GHQ learnt from Belgian sources that the Germans were mass producing 'mouth protectors . . . against the effects of asphyxiating gas' in Ghent. The rumour of gas was apparently discussed at a meeting of senior medical officers in V. Corps on 15 April, but no special action taken. While the British were prepared to give credence to the reports of an impending attack, they did not think that this would involve gas, and General Plumer passed on to his divisional commanders the gas element in a general warning 'for what it was worth'. The official history notes that the devastating effects of 'cloud' gas (gas shells were already in use by this time) were not then understood and, moreover, that its use by the enemy could not be imagined: 'At that date no British officer believed that the enemy's leaders would deliberately depart from the usages of civilised warfare' (*MO, 1915*, v. 1, pp. 163–6, and notes).

[94] *[c.17 April] 'Sir Horace Smith-Dorrien was very unlucky in his visits . . . On one afternoon when he was with me . . . the Germans began dropping shells on a hill about three hundred yards away . . .'*

Losses among the general officers were not uncommon: on 31 October 1914 Major-General Monro was nearly a casualty when a German shell hit Hooge Chateau, in which the staffs of the 1st and 2nd Divisions were meeting. The explosion mortally wounded Major-General Lomax, commander of the 1st Division, and killed six staff officers. Monro was stunned for some hours, but later made a complete recovery. Of twenty-nine infantrymen and cavalrymen of the rank of brigadier and above, twelve were killed, wounded or invalided by the end of 1914.

[95] *'On the 19th April I went into Ypres . . . Mr A. J. Balfour and Mr. F. E. Smith were coming to lunch that day . . .'*

In the original General Snow dates this '21st April', but correspondence to his wife makes clear that it was in fact the 19th.

[95] *'On the 21st Mr. Winston Churchill came to see me . . . Of course I took him to the summer-house and from there we witnessed the liveliest afternoon's work both in shelling and in the air that I had as yet experienced. Mr Churchill thoroughly enjoyed himself and evidently spent a happy afternoon.'*

Weeks earlier Churchill had talked with Asquith's daughter, Violet, about his plans for the Gallipoli campaign: 'He discussed every aspect of the strategy, military & naval, with zest & suddenly breaking off said quite seriously 'I think a curse should rest on me – because I love this war. I know it's smashing & shattering the lives of thousands every moment – & yet – I can't help it – I enjoy every second of it" (Mark Pottle (ed.), *Champion Redoubtable: The Diaries and Letters of Violet Bonham Carter, 1914–1945* (London, 1998), p. 25).

[96] *[18–21 April] 'About this time it became clear that the German artillery was getting more active ... but there was nothing to show we were on the eve of a great battle; and the Germans themselves, so it now appears, did not anticipate a battle of the nature of the one which followed and had no reinforcements at hand.'*

According to German accounts (*MO, 1915*, v. 1, pp. 187–90), the 'battles of Ypres ... had their origin ... solely in the desire to try the new weapon, gas, thoroughly at the front'; no reserves were made available to the *Fourth Army* by the supreme command 'either before the attack or during the fighting that continued on into May'. The *Fourth Army* nevertheless made its own arrangements for reinforcements, diverting units from other sectors of the line; it also had strategic goals for the 'gas attack' – notably the capture of the high ground near Pilckem (in which it was successful).

[97] *[evening of 22 April] 'Indeed if the break was as serious as I thought, I realised that there would be no necessity for the Germans to roll up the troops in the line as there was literally nothing between them and Ypres except my Headquarters ...'*

This is something of an exaggeration: the headquarters of the 2nd and 3rd Canadian Brigades stood between the German advance and 27th Division HQ.

[97] *'... for some reason or other the Germans did not exploit their success. Whether it was that they ran into their own gas, or whether it was that they had not anticipated that their gas would be successful and so had no reserves handy, I don't know.'*

The reasons are perhaps threefold: first, the Germans apparently underestimated the destructive potential of their new weapon, and did not have the reserves necessary 'to convert the break-in into a break-through'; secondly, their infantry was wary of traversing ground so recently swept by gas; thirdly, the Canadians offered stiff resistance, led by Brigadier General Turner, VC, GOC 3rd Canadian Brigade (*MO, 1915*, v. 1, pp. 178–83 and notes, pp. 191–2 and notes).

[98] *'I sent two and a half companies of the 2nd King's Shropshire Light Infantry, which regiment was bivouacking West of Ypres, to the grounds of Potijze . . .'*

In fact the 2nd King's Shropshire Light Infantry was east of Ypres (near Bellewaarde) when it was sent to cover divisional HQ at Potijze and 80th Brigade HQ at Verlorenhoek.

[98] *'During the night my Division was attacked, but not seriously, probably with a view to preventing the Division reinforcing the troops where the breach had occurred.'*

This supposition appears to have been correct, and the German strategy to have succeeded: the attacks against the 27th and 28th Division shortly after midnight made General Plumer 'hesitate to utilise all the reserves of these divisions on his threatened flank' (*MO, 1915*, v. 1, p. 184 and n. 1).

[98] *'The Canadians made some attempts at counter-attacking during the night, and some eleven battalions were engaged under General Turner and Colonel Geddes, the latter commanding a force composed of units of the 27th and 28th Division which had been hurried into the gap. These counter-attacks had little, if any result.'*

At midnight on 22 April the 10th Canadians, with the 16th Battalion (Canadian Scottish) in support, launched a successful counterattack, retaking Kitchener's Wood. It had been initiated at the request of the French, who sought support for their own counterattack by the 45th Algerians against Pilckem. When the French counterattack failed to materialise, the Canadians were left isolated. They dug in on the north-east edge of the wood but were eventually forced to withdraw, after suffering heavy casualties from shell fire. Around this time a new force, the 'Geddes' Detachment' – named after its CO Colonel A. D. Geddes – came into being, tasked with bridging, if possible, the gap between French right and the Canadian left. By early the following morning, Geddes' Detachment, along with Brigadier General Turner's 3rd Canadian Brigade, had thrown a poorly entrenched, discontinuous line across the gap from the

Ypres–Poelcappelle road south towards St Julien and then south-west towards the bridge on the canal at Brielen.

[98] *[early hours of 23 April]* *'The Headquarters of the 28th Division were still in Ypres about three hundred yards North of the Grand Place ...'*
The 28th Division headquarters had in fact moved from Ypres to the chateau at Vlamertinghe, about three miles west of Ypres, on 20 April, as a result of the shelling of the town. Nearby, just west of Brielen, were the headquarters of the Canadian Division. Of the three British divisional HQs, only the 27th was east of the canal when the battle began, a state of affairs that continued until its conclusion.

[98–9] *[afternoon, 23 April]* *'A lamentable counter-attack was ordered by Headquarters of the 2nd Army at the instigation of G.H.Q....We wasted some of our all too scarce ammunition in shelling the supposed objective, but as far as my Division was concerned we were not told definitely what the objective was and had no real information as to the hour of attack ...'*
At 2.40 p.m. on 23 April, at the behest of GHQ, Second Army issued orders to V. Corps for a 'general attack between Kitchener's Wood and the canal'. GHQ was acting in support of the French, who had proclaimed their determination to regain their line between. In fact the French attack did not happen. The British action, which was to due begin at 3 p.m., involved the 13th Brigade under Brigadier General Wanless O'Gowan, and the Geddes' Detachment. The 13th Brigade, however, was delayed in reaching the start and zero hour was postponed to 4.15 p.m. The artillery, not being informed of this delay, opened a preliminary bombardment at 2.45 p.m., and, because of the shortage of ammunition, could not repeat this at the later hour. The British eventually advanced in daylight, in excellent visibility, across mostly open countryside, against an enemy entrenched on higher ground, and with superior fire power: 'The attack to which the Second Army was committed by G.H.Q. order at the request of the French never had any prospect of success' (*MO, 1915*, v. 1, p. 203). A check had been forced on

the enemy's advance, but this came at a very heavy price, and no ground was gained on the afternoon of the 23rd 'that could not have been secured, probably without any casualties, by a simple advance after dark, to which the openness of the country lent itself' (*MO, 1915*, v. 1, p. 207).

[99] *'The Headquarters of the 2nd Army were miles in rear, those of the 28th and the Canadian Divisions were also back and the only connection between those Commanders and their Divisions was by telephone, the wires of which were for the most part out of action on account of the shelling . . .'*

During Second Ypres V. Corps' lines to 27th Division headquarters at Potijze were serviced by the joint labours of the 27th, 28th and Canadian Signal Companies, and this proved the most effective means of communication with the forces in the Salient. From Potijze messages could generally be sent by car to Wieltje, roughly a mile distant, and a central point behind the newly formed front line. In consequence 27th Division headquarters 'very soon became a focus of communications and the point to which corps reinforcements and reserves were directed' (*MO, 1915*, v. 1, p. 186–7).

[99] *'There was considerable confusion in the matter of command . . . [Geddes' Detachment] was commanded by Lt. Col. Geddes of the Buffs, a first rate man who was killed shortly afterwards. Who Col. Geddes was under I don't know, and I don't think he knew either.'*

The short history of Geddes' Detachment illustrates the central theme of the 'confusion of command'. In response to the break in the French line the commanders of the 27th, 28th and Canadian Divisions mobilised their reserves, and sent forward such battalions as they were able. At 12.30 a.m. on the 23rd April four of these battalions, all from the 28th Division (2nd Buffs, 3rd Middlesex, 5th King's Own, 1st York and Lancasters), were placed 'at the disposal' of the 1st Canadian Division, 'which put them under the command of the senior officer, Colonel A. D. Geddes of the Buffs, to form the "Geddes' Detachment"' (*MO, 1915*, v. 1, p. 181). When this force pushed north from St Jean in the early hours of 23 April (see above),

Geddes effectively took his instructions from Lieutenant General E. A. H. Alderson, GOC Canadian 1st Division, and thereafter acted as a part of what the official history calls Alderson's 'force' or 'command' (*MO, 1915*, v. 1, p. 248, n. 1, p. 257). This command also included the 1st and 3rd Brigades of Alderson's Division, as well as the 10th Brigade, 13th Brigade, and 149th (Northumberland) Brigade. Later on the morning of 23 April Geddes's own command expanded, as he was allocated the 2nd Duke of Cornwall's Light Infantry and 9th Royal Scots of the 27th Division, and the 2nd East Yorkshires of the 28th. Geddes now had 'seven battalions to command without the staff even of a brigade' (*MO, 1915*, v. 1, p. 200). As late as 3 p.m. on the 23rd, as he prepared to participate in the attack towards Pilckem, he did not know the location of the two battalions sent to him from the 27th Division. He was also unaware that, during this attack, he was to act under the 13th Brigade, the order not reaching him until forty-five minutes after it had begun: fortunately, he 'acted independently'. On 27 April, when the Ypres command was reorganised, Geddes' Detachment was effectively disbanded, and its battalions returned to their own brigades. Colonel Geddes closed his headquarters that night. He was killed early the next morning (see Biographical Notes, below).

[100] *'During the early hours of the 24th the enemy's artillery was increased considerably and all back areas especially in the vicinity of Potijze and St. Jean were heavily bombarded.'*
General Snow here describes the opening stages of the Battle of St Julien, during which the enemy attacked the apex of the Canadian line north of that place. At 4 a.m. on the 24th, after an hour-long bombardment, they released a thick cloud of gas along a thousand-yard front. The Canadian line held, although later that morning the Germans broke through the defences of the 3rd Canadian Brigade, north-east of St Julien, forcing a retirement.

[101] *'About 9 a.m. [24 August] I had a long talk with General Plumer on the 'phone. I did not hear much more of the situation from him than I knew myself,*

but he told me that the 13th Brigade were being brought up to the immediate north of Ypres, that the 13th Reserve Cavalry Brigade had been sent for, and that the York and Durham Brigade had arrived at Ypres.'

General Snow appears mistaken on two of these points: the 13th Brigade was already north of Ypres, having come up the previous afternoon, 23 April, and there is no mention of the 13th Reserve Cavalry Brigade in the official history's account of the battle. The 150th (the 1st York and Durham) Brigade had been ordered to Brielen to support the 13th Brigade by General Bulfin the previous evening.

[101] *'Gen. Plumer directed me to send two more of my battalions to the Canadians which I did, leaving me practically without any reserves for my own Division.'*

According to the official history Snow sent the only battalion remaining in his divisional reserve – the 1st Royal Irish, which had been reduced to 356 in the ranks.

[101] *'General Plumer gave me to understand that, as I was the only senior officer on the spot, I was to have more or less a free hand to use any troops I could lay my hands on to re-establish the situation, and that I was to be in actual command of all troops arriving in the Salient but not allocated to certain units . . .'*

It was suggested at Second Army headquarters that Snow should be placed in charge of all troops from St Julien to the canal, but this was not acted upon. He was, however, given effective command of the corps' reserve near Potijze, and thus was in a position to give support to the Canadians to the north of him.

[103] *'However if the enemy lacked infantry they certainly did not lack guns or ammunition . . . We had little or nothing to reply with. As regards the field guns, we were supposed to be cut down to 3 rounds per gun per diem, and as for heavy guns, all we had was some 5-inch howitzers and some 4.7".. .'*

The 5-inch howitzer and 4.7-inch gun are described in the official history as 'the ancient and obsolete weapons of the South African

War' (*MO, 1915*, v. 1, p. 211). Not only were the British guns inadequate, but supply of ammunition insufficient too. Around 24 April the daily ration of shells in the Second Army was: for each 13-pdr, 2; 18-pdrs., 3; 4-inch howitzers, 3; 4.7-inch, 10; 6-inch howitzer, 3. The shell shortage at Second Ypres was exacerbated by the preparations for the Dardanelles campaign, which began with the landings of 25 April.

[103] *'We also gave out that the reason of our lack of guns and ammunition was that we had sent all our guns South to assist in the breakthrough there, which breakthrough ended in a fiasco owing to lack of ammunition.'*

This is a reference to the offensive at Neuve Chapelle to the south, which had ended on 13 March, Sir John French reporting to Kitchener: 'Cessation of forward movement is necessitated today by the fatigue of the troops, and, above all, by the want of ammunition' (*MO, 1915*, v. 1, p. 149).

[104–5] *'About 2.15 p.m. on the afternoon of 24th April, there was a bad break in the line near Gravenstafel, so serious that I felt I must act at once. I sent an order to General Turner Commanding 3rd Canadian Brigade saying that as senior officer on the spot I directed him to take two battalions of the 28th and one of the 27th Division's and, adding every man he could spare, to counter-attack and re-establish the situation.'*

Around midday on the 24th the German infantry renewed its assault on St Julien, advancing from the north and north-west against the 3rd Canadian Brigade led by Brigadier General Turner (in the original, Snow confuses him with Brigadier General A. W. Currie, CO of the 2nd Candian Brigade). At 1.40 p.m. Turner was obliged to retire, splitting his brigade, with its left in the GHQ Line covering Wieltje, and its right east of St Julien on the Gravenstafel–Wieltje road. Should the Germans be able to push south, through Fortuin, in any force, they threatened to cut off the British and Canadian troops in the east of the Salient. Snow instructed Turner to defend Fortuin 'at all costs', and gave him effective command in the field. He also deployed the only reserves available to him, those of the 28th Division on the Zonnebeke front: the 1st Suffolks and the 12th London (Rangers) advanced to Fortuin with instructions to counterattack on contact. With vital reinforcement from two battalions of the 150th Brigade, and support also from the Canadians, Fortuin was secured, and the immediate crisis averted.

[105] *'The biggest effort made against St. Julien was in the early hours of the 25th April. It was known as Hull's attack . . . the attack was not launched till 5.30 a.m., and how General Hull managed to get his troops together as early as that has always been a mystery to me. The attack, when it was made, had little or no artillery support and it was a fiasco, and ended by making no progress and suffered heavy losses.'*

'Hull's Attack' had its origins in the Commander-in-Chief's order to the Second Army, issued at 4.15 p.m. on 24th April, 'at once to restore and hold the line about St. Julien'. Brigadier General C. P. A. Hull, CO 10th Brigade, was selected to lead fifteen battalions in the operation, which was one that displayed in a marked degree the many difficulties associated with 'counterattacks' during Second Ypres: it was to take place at night; it involved troops drawn from many different units; it was across unreconnoitred ground; the enemy had the advantages of terrain and fire power. So confused were the arrangements that, even though zero hour was put back from 3.30 a.m. to 5.30 a.m., not all of the units involved were in position even at the later hour: Hull proceeded with only his own five battalions (10th Brigade) and not the fifteen he had been allocated. Although the leading elements of the 10th Brigade advanced to within a hundred yards of the outskirts of St Julien, it proved impossible to reach the town itself, still less to drive the enemy from it, and the ground that had been retaken was surrendered in the general withdrawal on 3/4 May. The 10th Brigade's losses in this 'magnificent but hopeless attempt' were heavy: 73 officers and 2,346 other ranks, 'mostly irreplaceable, well trained men' (*MO, 1915*, v. 1, pp. 242–3).

[106] *'For [Hull's] attack the whole of the 10th Brigade was used together with 3 Battalions of the Northumbrian Division and three of my battalions.'*

For the composition of 'Hull's Attack', see Appendix 7 below, p. 169.

[106] *'One section of officers kept urging me to take a firm hand, and being the only responsible person on the spot, to order all troops in the salient to retire on to the line of the canal which meant on to the outskirts of Ypres.'*

The official history notes that there were 'many among the commanders of lower rank in the actual fighting line, brigadiers and commanding officers of battalions, who advocated a retirement back to the ramparts of Ypres and the canal, to get in line with the French' (*MO, 1915*, v. 1, p. 297). The decision, though, lay with the Commander-in-Chief, and so long as General Foch declared the French intention of recovering their line, Sir John felt an obligation to keep his forces in the Salient, and on the offensive.

[108] *'On the 28th April 5th Corps, or more properly "Plumer's Force", consisted of the 4th, 27th, 28th and Canadian Divisions and the Lahore and Northumbrian Divisions. There were also one, if not two, cavalry brigades (dismounted) East of Ypres.'*

In fact 'Plumer's Force' consisted of: the Cavalry Corps; V. Corps (27th, 28th, and Canadian Divisions); Lahore Division; 10th and 11th Brigades (4th Division); 149th, 150th, and 151st Brigades (50th (Northumbrian) Division); 13th Brigade (5th Division); two field companies of Royal Engineers (7th Division). It was discontinued at 6 a.m. on 7 May, when V. Corps returned to Second Army, of which Plumer had become the commander.

[109] *'After much consideration it was arranged that a new line should be dug from the right of the 27th Division . . . through Frezenberg, to the existing line near St. Julien. I had no great objection to the line through my area as it was more or less covered, but I thought the Frezenberg position, which was to be occupied by the 28th Division, very exposed.'*

On the night of 26/27 April work had begun on a defensive 'switch line' behind the Frezenberg Ridge. The line later selected by General Plumer, however, to which General Snow here refers, ran along the forward facing slopes of the ridge, making the position specially vulnerable to enemy artillery. It was, however, the first position that could be defended once a withdrawal from the Gravenstafel Ridge had been executed.

[110] *'I had not been to Ypres for more than a week and the changes I noticed as I drove through were wonderful.'*

General Snow means 'wonderful' in the sense of inspiring awe and wonder, and not the modern usage of admirable or especially good.

[111] *[5 May:] 'In the meantime Hill 60 on our right fell into enemy's hands.'*
On 1 May the Germans launched an attack against the 15th Brigade at Hill 60 using gas; for the first time it failed to secure them any advantage. When used again with a favourable wind on the morning of the 5th, however, it proved decisive. The Germans took Hill 60, and held it against a determined counterattack launched that evening by the 13th Brigade, which had just returned from an arduous time in the Salient.

[111] *'On the morning of the 8th [May] the bombardment of the new front between the Menin Road and Mouse Trap Farm became intense . . . The 28th Division holding the forward slopes near Frezenberg suffered most . . . The 83rd Brigade which was holding this position broke after repelling several attacks . . .'*

At around 10 a.m. on 8 May German infantry succeeded, at the third attempt that morning, in penetrating the 83rd Brigade's front either side of the village of Frezenberg, three miles east-north-east of Ypres. A two-hour artillery bombardment starting at 7.10 a.m. destroyed much of the British front line before lifting on to the support trenches, and eventually all of the 83rd Brigade in the front trenches were either 'killed, wounded or buried' (*MO, 1915*, v. 1, pp. 314–15). It proved impossible to reinforce them on the forward slope of the ridge, and General Snow ordered the 80th Brigade to extend its line north-westwards, behind the right of the

83rd Brigade, as a defensive line. This measure and the 'devoted stand' of troops in the 83rd Brigade contained the break-in.

[112] *[8 May] 'The 4th K.R.R.C. and the P.P.C.L.I. stood firm and drove off every attempt on their trenches, and the remainder of the Brigade had to be called up.'*

The 4th King's Royal Rifle Corps and Princess Patricia's Canadian Light Infantry (80th Brigade) were to the immediate right of the 83rd Brigade, defending Hooge woods and the Bellewaarde ridge; they too had suffered a 'perfect inferno' of enemy shell fire. With every reinforcement available – including 'signallers, pioneers, orderlies and batmen' – they eventually cleared their front 'of all Germans except a few snipers lying out in the long grass and ruins of buildings' (*MO, 1915*, v. 1, p. 317).

[112] *'On the 12th [May], the 28th Division were relieved, and we had the Cavalry on our left.'*

On the night of 12/13 May Major-General de Lisle's 'Cavalry Force', consisting of the 1st and 3rd Cavalry Divisions, relieved the 28th Division (including also the 2nd Royal Dublin Fusiliers and 1st Royal Warwickshires, 10th Brigade, which had been sent to reinforce it), and the 2nd Shropshire Light Infantry of the 27th Division, on the 28th's right. The Cavalry Force now held a sector from Bellewaarde lake to six hundred yards south-east of Mouse Trap Farm, where the 4th Division took over.

[112] *'The Cavalry and the 80th Brigade were heavily attacked on the 13th May, the cavalry being driven in and losing heavily in a counter-attack.'*

From 3.30 a.m. to 1 p.m. on 13 May German artillery fire pulverised the front between Hooge and the Ypres–St Julien road, which was held by the Cavalry Force and 80th Brigade. Heavy rain made the use of rifles by the defenders difficult, but in spite of this the German infantry attacks were mostly driven off by rifle fire. A sector lost by 7th Cavalry Brigade around 8 a.m., however, could not be regained. This was in spite of an organised counterattack by the 8th and 9th Cavalry Brigades, supported by survivors from the Leicester Yeomanry (7th Cavalry Brigade), commencing at 2.30 p.m. Ultimately a new line was established around a thousand yards in rear of the old one, stretching from Railway Wood north to the line held by the 1st Cavalry Brigade. The cavalry lost 'very heavily' in this engagement, with three commanding officers (all lieutenant colonels) killed, and five wounded, including a brigadier general.

[112] *'In one of my messages I spoke of the 80th Brigade as the "Stonewall Brigade", which epithet stuck to them ever afterwards and is referred to in the Official History.'*

By the middle of May the three brigades and divisional troops of the 27th Division had been in the line for four weeks without respite, and on being relieved (17–19 May) they were specially congratulated by the Commander-in-Chief 'on their steadfastness and endurance, the 80th Brigade, reduced, in spite of drafts, to a bare 1,628, being singled out as deserving, if ever a brigade did, the epithet of "Stonewall"' (*MO, 1915*, v. 1, p. 339).

[112] *'I and my Staff retired to Apple Blossom Farm, the farm we had selected as our retired Headquarters when we first moved West of Ypres, but which we had hardly ever had time to visit, much less to sleep in.'*

During the withdrawal of 3 May the 27th Division headquarters moved from Potijze to a farm a mile south of Vlamertinghe, west of Ypres.

[112] *'On the 24th, there was a great gas attack all along the front of the Salient, and the 80th Brigade were called upon as Reserves and delivered a counter-attack on the night of the 24th/25th against Bellewaarde Chateau in conjunction with the 84th Brigade of the 28th Division.'*

At 2.45 a.m. on 24 May the enemy launched its most extensive gas attack to date, in combination with heavy gun and rifle fire. The gas covered almost the entire length of V. Corps' front, from Turco Farm (the junction with the French) to just south of Hooge, around four and a half miles, and in the light winds it moved slowly, forming a bank up to forty feet off the ground with the density of a fog. In spite of this there was no break in the front on the scale of 22 April, although sections of line were ceded to the enemy, notably around Bellewaarde lake. In response General Bulfin sent up the 80th and 84th Brigades, and the latter of these counterattacked at 5 p.m. on the 24th, after considerable delays caused by the difficulties of communication on the battlefield. The 80th Brigade arrived too late for this zero hour, and was not in a position to advance in support of the 84th until 11 p.m. Though it came within yards of the enemy line, it was forced by enemy fire to retire to the line already established by the 84th Brigade on the road east of Witte Poort Farm.

[113] '. . . when the battle began the chain of command seemed right enough. The Corps Commander was in a suitable position, and he had three Division Commanders under him, the 27th, 28th and Canadians.'

During the fighting of Second Ypres both Smith-Dorrien and Plumer moved their headquarters nearer the fighting: at noon on 26 April Second Army headquarters were relocated from Hazebrouck to Poperhinge, seven miles west of Ypres, while the same day V. Corps moved to Goldfish Chateau, one and a half miles west of Ypres.

[115] 'A report was sent round from G.H.Q. during the battle that the German losses were enormous, and that train after train of wounded were seen going to the rear. I cannot believe this . . .'

German losses at Second Ypres are given as 34,933 (860 officers and 34,073 other ranks), and British losses as 59,275 (2,150 officers and 57,125 other ranks). Although direct comparison is not possible, for reasons set out below (see Appendix 8 below, p. 172), it seems beyond doubt that '[British] casualties were certainly heavier than the German' (MO, 1915, v. 1, p. 356).

[117] 'Seldom has a more difficult operation devolved on any Commander than on Sir Herbert Plumer . . . Had he known that the French never intended business he might have shortened the line directly after the gas attack and so avoided all the losses incurred by our counter-attacks.'

The decision to shorten the line lay ultimately with the Commander-in-Chief, and not Plumer, and in failing to order this – as the official history makes clear – Sir John French succumbed to pressure from General Foch, as well to his own misplaced sense of optimism. To these factors must be added his hostility towards his GOC Second Army, Smith-Dorrien, who on 27 April presented a detailed case for withdrawing in stages on to the GHQ Line, beginning that night. French dismissed Smith-Dorrien's arguments out of hand, but within days had authorised the withdrawal to a reduced line, which was concluded on the night of 3/4 May.

[117] *'Although, when the fight began, [Plumer] was G.O.C., V. Corps, in command of a properly composed force, before the battle had been going on for 48 hours he found himself nominated "G.O.C. Plumer Detachment"...'*
It was in fact rather more than forty-eight hours from the start of the battle, in the late-afternoon and early evening of 22 April, to Plumer becoming GOC 'Plumer's Force', at 5.30 p.m. on 27 April.

[118] *Shortly afterwards the Division moved to the Somme area and a few weeks later proceeded to Salonika, where it remained till the end of the war.*
German satirists dubbed Salonika their 'greatest Allied internment camp' (Cruttwell, p. 234), and a substantial Franco-British force was pinned down there waiting for the opportunity to make a decisive intervention in the Balkans.

Appendix 1

Order of Battle of the British Expeditionary Force, August 1914

General Headquarters

Commander-in-Chief: Field Marshal Sir J. D. P. French
Chief of the General Staff: Lieutenant General Sir A. J. Murray
Major-General, General Staff: Major-General H. H. Wilson
GSO1 (Operations): Colonel G. M. Harper
GSO1 (Intelligence): Colonel G. M. W. Macdonogh
Adjutant General: Major-General Sir C. F. N. Macready
Quartermaster General: Major-General Sir W. R. Robertson

Cavalry Division

GOC Major-General E. H. H. Allenby

1st Cavalry Brigade: GOC Brigadier General C. J. Briggs
  2nd Dragoon Guards (Queen's Bays)
  5th (Princess Charlotte of Wales's) Dragoon Guards
  11th (Prince Albert's Own) Hussars
  1st Signal Troop

2nd Cavalry Brigade: GOC Brigadier-General H. de B. De Lisle
  4th (Royal Irish) Dragoon Guards
  9th (Queen's Royal) Lancers
  18th (Queen Mary's Own) Hussars
  2nd Signal Troop

3rd Cavalry Brigade: GOC Brigadier General H. de la P. Gough
  4th (Queen's Own) Hussars
  5th (Royal Irish) Lancers
  16th (The Queen's) Lancers
  3rd Signal Troop

4th Cavalry Brigade: GOC Brigadier General Hon. C. E. Bingham

Composite Regiment of Household Cavalry
6th Dragoon Guards (Carabiniers)
3rd (King's Own) Hussars
4th Signal Troop
5th Cavalry Brigade: GOC Brigadier General Sir P. W. Chetwode, Bt.
2nd Dragoons (Royal Scots Greys)
12th (Prince of Wales's Royal) Lancers
20th Hussars
(with) J Battery RHA and Ammunition Column
4th Field Troop
5th Signal Troop
5th Cavalry Field Ambulance
Artillery:
III. Brigade RHA, D and E Batteries
III. Brigade Ammunition Column
VII. Brigade RHA, I and L Batteries
VII. Brigade Ammunition Column
Engineers: 1st Field Squadron, RE
Signal Service: 1st Signal Squadron
Army Service Corps: HQ 1st Cavalry Divisional ASC
Medical Units: 1st, 2nd, 3rd, and 4th Cavalry Field Ambulances

I. Corps
GOC Lieutenant General Sir Douglas Haig

1st Division: GOC Major-General S. H. Lomax
  1st Infantry Brigade: GOC Brigadier General F. I. Maxse
    1st Coldstream Guards
    1st Scots Guards
    1st The Black Watch (Royal Highlanders)
    2nd Royal Munster Fusiliers
  2nd Infantry Brigade: GOC Brigadier General E. S. Bulfin
    2nd The Royal Sussex Regiment
    1st The Loyal North Lancashire Regiment
    1st The Northamptonshire Regiment
    2nd The King's Royal Rifle Corps
  3rd Infantry Brigade: GOC Brigadier General H. J. S. Landon
    1st The Queen's (Royal West Surrey Regiment)
    1st The South Wales Borderers

1st The Gloucester Regiment

2nd Welch Regiment

Divisional Troops:

Mounted Troops: 'C' squadron of 15th Hussars; 1st Cyclist Company

Artillery:

> XXV. Brigade RFA, 113th, 114th, and 115th Batteries; XXV. Brigade Ammunition Column
>
> XXVI. Brigade RFA, 116th, 117th, and 118th Batteries; XXVI. Brigade Ammunition Column
>
> XXXIX. Brigade RFA 46th, 51st, and 54th Batteries; XXXIX. Brigade Ammunition Column
>
> XLIII. (Howitzer) Brigade RFA, 30th, 40th, and 57th (Howitzer) Batteries; XLIII. (Howitzer) Brigade Ammunition Column
>
> 26th Heavy Battery RGA and Heavy Battery Ammunition Column
>
> 1st Divisional Ammunition Column

Engineers: 23rd and 26th Field Companies

Signal Service: 1st Signal Company

Army Service Corps: 1st Divisional Train

Royal Army Medical Corps: 1st, 2nd, and 3rd Field Ambulances

2nd Division: GOC Major-General C. C. Monro

4th (Guards) Brigade: GOC Brigadier General R. Scott-Kerr

> 2nd Grenadiers Guards
>
> 2nd Coldstream Guards
>
> 3rd Coldstream Guards
>
> 1st Irish Guards

5th Infantry Brigade: GOC Brigadier General R. C. B. Haking

> 2nd The Worcester Regiment
>
> 2nd The Oxfordshire and Buckinghamshire Light Infantry
>
> 2nd The Highland Light Infantry
>
> 2nd The Connaught Rangers

6th Infantry Brigade: GOC Brigadier General R. H. Davies

> 1st The King's (Liverpool) Regiment
>
> 2nd The South Staffordshire Regiment
>
> 1st Princess Charlotte of Wales's (Royal Berkshire Regiment)
>
> 1st The King's Royal Rifle Corps

Divisional Troops:

> *Mounted Troops*: 'B' squadron 15th (The King's) Hussars; 2nd Cyclist Company
>
> *Artillery*:
>
>> XXXIV. Brigade RFA, 22nd, 50th, and 70th Batteries; XXXIV. Brigade Ammunition Column
>>
>> XXXVI. Brigade RFA, 15th, 48th, and 71st Batteries; XXXVI. Brigade Ammunition Column
>>
>> XLI. Brigade RFA, 9th, 16th, and 17th Batteries; XLI. Brigade Ammunition Column
>>
>> XLIV. (Howitzer) Brigade RFA, 47th, 56th, 60th (Howitzer) Batteries; XLIV. (Howitzer) Brigade Ammunition Column
>>
>> 35th Heavy Battery RGA and Heavy Battery Ammunition Column
>>
>> 2nd Divisional Ammunition Column
>
> *Engineers*: 5th and 11th Field Companies, RE
>
> *Signal Service*: 2nd Signal Company
>
> *Army Service Corps*: 2nd Divisional Train
>
> *Royal Army Medical Corps*: 4th, 5th, and 6th Field Ambulances

II. Corps

GOC Lieutenant General Sir James Grierson (died in train between Rouen and Amiens, 17 August); succeeded by General Sir Horace L. Smith-Dorrien (who took over command at Bavai, 4.00 p.m., 21 August)

3rd Division: GOC Major-General Hubert I. W. Hamilton

> **7th Infantry Brigade**: GOC Brigadier General F. W. N. McCracken
>> 3rd The Worcester Regiment
>> 2nd The Prince of Wales's Volunteers (South Lancashire Regiment)
>> 1st The Duke of Edinburgh's (Wiltshire Regiment)
>> 2nd The Royal Irish Rifles
>
> **8th Infantry Brigade**: GOC Brigadier General B. J. C. Doran
>> 2nd The Royal Scots (Lothian Regiment)
>> 2nd The Royal Irish Regiment
>> 4th The Duke of Cambridge's Own (Middlesex Regiment)
>> 1st The Gordon Highlanders
>
> **9th Infantry Brigade**: GOC Brigadier General F. C. Shaw
>> 1st The Northumberland Fusiliers
>> 4th The Royal Fusiliers (City of London Regiment)
>> 1st The Lincolnshire Regiment

1st The Royal Scots Fusiliers

Divisional Troops:

Mounted Troops: 'A' squadron 15th (The King's) Hussars; 3rd Cyclist
    Company

Artillery:

XXIII. Brigade RFA, 107th, 108th, and 109th Batteries; XXIII.
    Brigade Ammunition Column

XL. Brigade RFA, 6th, 23rd, and 49th Batteries; XL. Brigade
    Ammunition Column

XLII. Brigade RFA, 29th, 41st, and 45th Batteries; XLII. Brigade
    Ammunition Column

XXX. (Howitzer) Brigade RFA, 128th, 129th, 130th (Howitzer)
    Batteries; XXX. (Howitzer) Brigade Ammunition Column

48th Heavy Battery RGA and Heavy Battery Ammunition Column

3rd Divisional Ammunition Column

Engineers: 56th and 57th Field Companies, RE

Signal Service: 3rd Signal Company

Army Service Corps: 3rd Divisional Train

Royal Army Medical Corps: 7th, 8th, and 9th Field Ambulances

5th Division: Major-General Sir Charles Fergusson

13th Infantry Brigade: GOC Brigadier General G. J. Cuthbert

2nd The King's Own Scottish Borderers

2nd The Duke of Wellington's (West Riding Regiment)

1st The Queen's Own (Royal West Kent Regiment)

2nd The King's Own (Yorkshire Light Infantry)

14th Infantry Brigade: GOC Brigadier General S. P. Rolt

2nd The Suffolk Regiment

1st The East Surrey Regiment

1st The Duke of Cornwall's Light Infantry

2nd The Manchester Regiment

15th Infantry Brigade: GOC Brigadier General A. E. W. Count
Gleichen

1st The Norfolk Regiment

1st The Bedfordshire Regiment

1st The Cheshire Regiment

1st The Dorsetshire Regiment

Divisional Troops:

  Mounted Troops: 'A' squadron 19th (Queen Alexandra's Own Royal) Hussars; 5th Cyclist Company

  Artillery:

  XV. Brigade RFA, 11th, 52nd, and 80th Batteries; XV. Brigade Ammunition Column

  XXVII. Brigade RFA, 119th, 120th, and 121st Batteries; XXVII. Brigade Ammunition Column

  XXVIII. Brigade RFA, 122nd, 123rd, and 124th Batteries; XXVIII. Brigade Ammunition Column

  VIII. (Howitzer) Brigade RFA, 37th, 61st, 65th (Howitzer) Batteries; VIII. (Howitzer) Brigade Ammunition Column

  108th Heavy Battery RGA and Heavy Battery Ammunition Column

  Engineers: 17th and 59th Field Companies, RE

  Signal Service: 5th Signal Company

  Army Service Corps: 5th Divisional Train

  Royal Army Medical Corps: 13th, 14th, and 15th Field Ambulances

III. Corps
GOC Major-General W. P. Pulteney

4th Division: GOC Major-General T. D.'O. Snow

  10th Infantry Brigade: GOC Brigadier General J. A. L. Haldane

  1st The Royal Warwickshire Regiment

  2nd Seaforth Highlanders (Ross-shire Buffs, The Duke of Albany's)

  1st Princess Victoria's (Royal Irish Fusiliers)

  2nd The Royal Dublin Fusiliers

  11th Infantry Brigade: GOC Brigadier General A. G. Hunter-Weston

  1st Prince Albert's (Somerset Light Infantry)

  1st East Lancashire Regiment

  1st Hampshire Regiment

  1st Rifle Brigade (Prince Consort's Own)

  12th Infantry Brigade: GOC Brigadier General H. F. M. Wilson

  1st King's Own (Royal Lancaster) Regiment

  2nd Lancashire Fusiliers

  2nd Royal Inniskilling Fusiliers

  2nd Essex Regiment

Divisional Troops:[1]

Mounted Troops: B Squadron 19th (Queen's Alexandra's Own) Hussars*;
   4th Cyclist Company*

Artillery:

   XIV Brigade RFA, 39th, 68th, and 88th Batteries; XIV Brigade
      Ammunition Column

   XXIX Brigade RFA, 125th, 126th, and 127th Batteries; XXIX
      Brigade Ammunition Column

   XXXII Brigade RFA, 27th, 134th, and 135th Batteries; XXXII
      Brigade Ammunition Column

   XXXVII (Howitzer) Brigade RFA, 31st, 35th, and 55th (Howitzer)
      Batteries; XXXVII (Howitzer) Brigade Ammunition Column

   31st Heavy Battery RGA* and Heavy Battery Ammunition
      Column*

   4th Divisional Ammunition Column*

Engineers: 7th and 9th Field Companies, RE*

Signal Service: 4th Signal Company*

Army Service Corps: 4th Divisional Train*

Royal Army Medical Corps: 10th, 11th, and 12th Field Ambulances*

19th Infantry Brigade: GOC Major-General L. G. Drummond
   2nd The Royal Welch Fusiliers
   1st The Cameronians (Scottish Rifles)
   1st The Duke of Cambridge's Own (Middlesex Regiment)
   2nd Princess Louise's (Argyll and Sutherland Highlanders)

Royal Flying Corps
GOC Brigadier General Sir David Henderson
The 2nd, 3rd, 4th, and 5th Aeroplane Squadrons[2]

Source: *MO, 1914*, v. 1, pp. 471–84; French, *1914*, pp. 17–30, 'The First
Expeditionary Force'.

---

1   At the battle of Le Cateau, 26 August, the 4th Division was without the
units marked *.

2   The 6th Squadron landed at St Nazaire on 5 October, but did not come
into action until 16 October.

Appendix 2

Le Cateau Operation Orders,
24–25 August 1914

*Operation Order No. 7, by Sir John French, commanding British
Expeditionary Force. Issued at Bavai at 8.25 p.m., Monday 24 August.*

1. The Army will move to-morrow, 25th inst., to a position
    in the neighbourhood of Le Cateau, exact positions will be
    pointed out on the ground to-morrow.
2. Corps will march so that their rear guards are clear of the
    Maubeuge–Bavai–Eth road by 5.30 a.m.
3. Roads available:

    1st Corps (with 5th Cavalry Brigade attached). All roads
    east of, but excluding, Bavai–Montay road.

    2nd Corps. Bavai–Montay road (inclusive), up to but
    excluding the road Wargnies–Villers Pol–Ruesnes–
    Capelle sur Ecaillon–Vertain–Romerie–Solesmes.

    Cavalry Division, with *19th Infantry Brigade* attached, the
    last-named road inclusive and all roads to the westward.
4. Two brigades of the Cavalry Division with the Divisional
    Cavalry of the 2nd Corps, under command of a brigadier
    to be named by G.O.C. Cavalry Division, will cover the
    movement of the 2nd Corps.

    The remainder of the Cavalry Division with the 19th Inf.
    Brigade, under command of the G.O.C. Cavalry Division,
    will cover the west flank.
5. Reports to H.Q. Bavai up to 5 a.m., then to H.Q. Le
    Cateau.

6. A Staff Officer from Corps and Cavalry Division will report to G.H.Q. Le Cateau at 5 a.m. to receiver orders as to positions.

A. J. Murray, Major-General C.G.S.
for F.M. C.-in-C.

Operation Order No. 1, by Major-General T. D'O. Snow. Issued at 5.00 p.m., Tuesday 25 August.

1. 1st and 2nd Corps are taking up a position approximately on the line Avesnes–Le Cateau–Caudry (incl.). Third Div. on the left.

2. The Fourth Division will take up a position Caudry (excl.)–Fontaine au Pire–Wambaix–knoll just West of Seranvillers, and will commence entrenching as soon as it is light to-morrow.

3. Disposition of units will be:

    (a) *11th Brigade* Caudry (excl.) to station on railway between Fontaine au Pire–Wambaix (incl.).[1] *Temp. H.Q.* Carrières, just south of Fontaine au Pire. *Route* from present position Briastre–Viesly–Bethencourt–Beauvois.

    (b) *12th Brigade* station on railway between Fontaine au Pire and Wambaix (excl.) to knoll West of Seranvillers.[2] *Tempy. H.Q.* Longsart. *Route* from present position Bethencourt–Cattenières–Wambaix. The ½ Bn. R. Innis. Fus. must remain in position until the Tenth Brig. has passed through Beauvois. It may withdraw its detachment from Bevillers to Beauvois.

---

1   At 6.40 p.m., following instructions from GHQ, an amendment was issued shortening the length of 11th Brigade's line: the new line ran 'From Fontaine au Pire (inclusive) to railway station, instead of Caudry (exclusive) to railway station'.

2   As above, 12th Brigade's line was shortened: 'From railway line at Station between Fontaine au Pire and Wambaix (exclusive) to Wambaix (inclusive)'.

    (c) *10th Brig.* Haucourt (in reserve). *Route* – any route west of Caudry.

      Order of March of Inf. Brigs.:

      12th Brig., 11th Brig., 10th Brig.

    (d) *Irish Horse* Haucourt.

    (e) *Div. H.Q.* Haucourt.

    (f) *Div. Arty.* (less 32 Bde.) Ligny en Cambrésis.

      Tempy. H.Q. The Mairie at Ligny en Cambrésis.

    (g) *Fd. Ambces.* (on arrival) one at Ligny en Cambrésis, one at Mn. d'Haucourt.

4.   Outposts will be found by 11th and 12th Brigades:

    11th Brig. Caudry (excl.) to the line Estournel–Longsart.

    12th Brig. from the line Estournel–Longsart to Masnières.

5.   Refilling point will be notified later.

6.   Sick will be taken back with units in impressed wagons and will be handed over to the Fd. Ambces. when they arrive.

7.   Meeting place for the 2nd Line Transport:

    10th Brig.   East exit of Haucourt.

    11th Brig.   Railway Bridge on road Fontaine au Pire-Ligny en Cambrésis road.

    12th Brig.   North exit of Esnes.

    Arty.   Stand fast at Ligny en Cambrésis

8.   All First Line vehicles not required can be sent back at once to the position given in para. 3.

9.   Troops will *not* move from their present position to those mentioned in para. 3 until they receive further orders, but reconnaissances will be made with a view to carrying it out in the dark.

Issued at 5 p.m.

J. E. Edmonds, Colonel, G.S. 4th Division

*Operation Order No. 8, by Sir John French, commanding British
Expeditionary Force. Issued from GHQ at 7.30 p.m., Tuesday 25 August.*

1. The enemy followed our movement this morning and is also
    passing troops of all arms to the West and South.
2. It is the intention of the Commander-in-Chief to continue the
    retirement tomorrow with a view to covering his advanced
    base and protect his L[ines]. of C[ommunication].
3. For this movement the 19th Brigade will be taken from
    the Cavalry Division and placed under the orders of the II.
    Army.
4. The retirement will be carried out from left to right.
5. The 4th Div. will fall back on the western flank in the general
    direction of Péronne, the western column moving along the
    line indicated roughly by the line Seranvillers–Le Catelet.
    The movement to commence at 7 a.m.

    The billeting area for tomorrow night being around Le
    Catelet–Beaurevoir.

    Boundary roads for this force being:

    On the East.

    Fontaine–Ligny–Caullery–Elincourt–Serain–Beaurevoir
    inclus.

    On the West.

    Such roads as the G.O.C. 4th Div. wishes to use.

6. The II Corps, with the 19th Bde., will move in echelon and
    fall back in the general direction of Beaurevoir–Prémont–La
    Sablière.

    Boundary roads for this force:

    On the West.

    Fontaine–Ligny–Caullery–Elincourt–Serain–Beaurevoir
    exclus.

    On the East.

    All roads between the above and the Le Cateau–Busigny road
    exclusive.

The billeting area for tomorrow night being from Beaurevoir (exclus.) to La Sablière.

7. The I Corps will start at 5.30 a.m. and march to the area of Busigny, and connect with the II Corps at La Sablière.

   The I Corps can use the Le Cateau–Busigny road and roads to the East.

   Billeting area in Busigny and to the N. and E.

8. The Cav. Div., with the 5th Cav. Bde. Attached, will cover the movement on the N. and W. and will arrange their billets outside those already allotted.

9. G.H.Q. to St. Quentin at 7 p.m. to-night.

A. J. Murray, Lieut.-General, C.G.S.

The Three Operation Orders and the Battle of Le Cateau[3]

The three operation orders presented here help to illuminate General Snow's account of the battle of Le Cateau. They also reveal some of the recurring themes of the retreat: the poor quality of leadership and lack of clarity emanating from GHQ; the C-in-C's readiness to devolve urgent arrangements on his corps' commanders; and his tendency to allow them a degree of independence that undermined the cohesion of his small force. Above all, they reveal the speed with which events were moving on the night of 25/26 August, and the consequent difficulty experienced by all levels of command in ascertaining what was going on, and in issuing the appropriate instructions.

GHQ Operation Order No. 7

Sir John French's Operation Order No. 7 was issued at 8.25 p.m. on Monday 24 August. The Commander-in-Chief had correctly guessed that day that von Kluck's *First Army* was attempting not only to outflank the BEF on the left, but also to drive it east, and force it to take refuge

---

3   The three operation orders are in *MO, 1914*, v. 1, pp. 515, 516–17, 518–19.

in the old fortress of Maubeuge, where its line of retreat could be cut off. Sir John had no intention of being thus isolated, and, faced with the continued retirement of the French armies on his right, and the inadequacy of their deployments on his left, he decided to continue the retreat south the next day, 25 August, to a line drawn roughly west–east through the town of Le Cateau.

Having reached this decision, however, Sir John did not issue detailed instructions to that effect. This alarmed the commander of II. Corps, Sir Horace Smith-Dorrien, who feared a repetition of the events earlier that day, the 24th, when orders to begin the retreat from Mons 'had been issued too late to avoid the enemy coming to close grips'.[4] II. Corps had suffered heavily as a result. Around 6.00 p.m., therefore, Smith-Dorrien sought out his chief at the advanced headquarters in the *mairie* at Bavai and pressed him on the point. French assented to Smith-Dorrien's proposal to begin II. Corps' retirement early, but added that I. Corps' commander, Douglas Haig, 'could still do as he intended'.[5]

Worried that the BEF would lose cohesion, Smith-Dorrien went across the room and urged Sir Archibald Murray, French's Chief of Staff, 'to induce the Chief to issue an order for the whole force to move early and simultaneously. Murray said he would see what he could do later on, and he was evidently successful.'[6] The result was Operation Order No. 7. No mention is made in this order of the Commander-in-Chief's intention to make a stand at Le Cateau, although earlier that day General Snow had been told by Henry Wilson 'that the idea was to fall back on the Le Cateau–Cambrai position and there accept battle'. To this effect, the official history notes: 'a defensive line . . . had been partially prepared by civil labour, from Inchy south-eastwards to St. Benin (1¾ miles south of Le Cateau)'.[7]

---

4   Smith-Dorrien, *Forty-Eight Years*, p. 392.
5   Ibid.
6   Ibid.
7   *MO, 1914*, v. 1 p. 123.

If the BEF was to give battle at Le Cateau it was of the utmost importance that it remain a united force. The path south to Le Cateau, however, was blocked by the Forêt de Mormal – nine miles long, roughly three to four miles wide, and without any north–south road running through it. Sir John French was thus forced to divide his force, allocating to II. Corps the Roman road from Bavai to Montay (north-west of Le Cateau), and to I. Corps all routes to the east of this. As a result all contact was lost between I. and II. Corps at a crucial time. Although it was intended that they would meet up on the Le Cateau position the next day this did not happen, and direct contact was not regained until 1 September.

4th Division Operation Order No. 1

In the early hours of the 25th, while the BEF was travelling south, the 4th Division, having detrained at Le Cateau, was en route northwards, to positions around Solesmes. At this important junction all roads from the north converged, and the 10th, 11th, and 12th Brigades were deployed so as to guard the southwards retirement through the town of II. Corps, the Cavalry Division, and the 19th Infantry Brigade. While General Snow's account makes clear the difficulty he faced in finding out 'what was going on', he must have been informed at some point that afternoon of the contents of Operation Order No. 7, because at 5.00 p.m. he issued his own Operation Order No. 1. This instructed the 4th Division to take up a position at Le Cateau (on the line Caudry–Fontaine-au-Pire–Wambaix knoll) and to 'commence entrenching as soon as it is light tomorrow'. According to the official history General Snow's order is 'the only divisional operation order available for Le Cateau', and it indicates both that he expected that a stand would be made there, and also that I. Corps would be in the line.

At some point that afternoon, 25 August, General Snow also received a 'private letter' from his old friend Henry Wilson, the Commander-in-Chief's Deputy Chief of the General Staff, indicating a change of plan: there would be no stand at Le Cateau, only a continuation of the retreat. Reports of the continued retirement of the French on the right, and 'the strength of the enemy on his own immediate front', had convinced the C-in-C that 'he could not stand on the Le Cateau position, but must continue the retreat on St Quentin and Noyon'.[8]

In his narrative of these events General Snow is clear that he received Wilson's 'private letter' before he issued Operation Order No. 1, but it seems more likely that they came the other way around. The operation order gave no indication that the retreat would be continued, and to the contrary ordered 'entrenching' at first light, an unnecessary diversion for any force with instructions to keep moving. And Wilson's letter, in spite of its informality (it began 'Dear Snowball' and ended 'Yours Henry') 'amounted to an order pure and simple': the Commander-in-Chief meant not to stand, but to keep falling back.[9]

GHQ Operation Order No. 8

About 6.00 p.m. on 25 August Smith-Dorrien also received a note from Henry Wilson, written at 3.45 p.m., conveying in more formal terms essentially the same message sent to General Snow: 'The C.-in-C. has decided to continue the retirement to-morrow, the left (probably the 4th Division) being directed towards Péronne. He told me to let you have this private note of his intention. Orders will follow as soon as the details can be worked out.'[10] The resulting GHQ Operation Order No. 8 was issued at 7.30 p.m. that night, the 25th. It identified the billeting area for the BEF the following night, 26 August, as Le Catelet–Beaurevoir–La Sablière–Busigny. Smith-Dorrien received the order at 9.00 p.m., and at 10.45 p.m. he issued to II. Corps instructions 'for continuing the retreat instead of standing at Le Cateau'.[11]

---

8   Ibid.

9   Callwell, *Wilson*, p. 168.

10   *MO, 1914*, v. 1, p. 517.

11   Smith-Dorrien, *Forty-Eight Years*, p. 398.

Operation Order No. 8 did not, however, reach the 4th Division until midnight, when Colonel W. H. Bowes arrived from GHQ bearing a copy. The appropriate divisional orders for continued retirement were then drafted, but, because all three brigades were on the road south from Solesmes, they were not issued. At 5.00 a.m. the next morning, the 26th, Snow dispatched staff officers to make contact with his brigades, intending then to issue the orders should the situation permit. At this point he snatched a moment's sleep. Within a matter of minutes, however, Captain B. Walcot arrived from II. Corps with news of Smith-Dorrien's 2.00 a.m. decision to make a stand.

Smith-Dorrien later recalled: 'General Snow received my message about 5 a.m., just as he was issuing orders to retire, and readily consented to remain and fight under my orders.'[12] At 5.30 a.m. Snow sent staff officers to his brigades with instructions 'to take up the positions already ordered' the previous day (i.e. at 5.00 p.m.) – along the line Caudry–Fontaine-au-Pire–Wambaix knoll – and it was on this position that they fought at Le Cateau.[13] Within half an hour of General Snow sending out these instructions the 12th Brigade came under attack before Esnes and Haucourt, and one of his staff officers, Captain H. J. Elles, returned to report that the infantry were already 'at it hammer and tongs'.[14] General Snow later wrote to Smith-Dorrien: 'When you sent to me the morning of the 26th to ask if I would stand and fight, I ought to have answered: "I have no other choice, as my troops are already engaged in a battle of encounter, and it must be some hours before I can extricate them."'[15]

---

12 Ibid., p. 402.

13 *MO, 1914*, v. 1, pp. 148–9, 516–19; Smith-Dorrien, *Forty-Eight Years*, p. 402.

14 *MO, 1914*, v. 1, p. 149.

15 Smith-Dorrien, *Forty-Eight Years*, p. 402.

APPENDIX 3

THE RETREAT:
OPERATION ORDER No. 9

Around 4.00 a.m. on the morning of 28 August the 4th Division received by motor cyclist Operation Order No. 9, which had been issued by GHQ at 8.30 p.m. on the previous evening. It ran as follows:

1. It is reported on good authority that German Forces are in or near St. Quentin.
2. The 3rd and 5th Divisions and 19th Bde. will clear Ham and the other canal bridges by daylight, and will then march on Noyon and cross to the left bank of the R. Oise.
3. The 4th Division, under orders of II. Corps, will move to ground north of the bridges at Ham, starting immediately on receipt of order.
4. The I. Corps has been ordered to Pierremande (8 miles S.W. of La Fère), passing the R. Oise at La Fère, starting as soon after receipt of this order as possible.
5. The Cav. Div. now under orders of the C.-in-C. will cover the retirement of the II. Corps and 4th Division.
6. All ammunition on wagons not absolutely required and other impedimenta will be unloaded and officers and men carried to the full capacity of all transport, both horse and mechanical.
7. G.H.Q. will move to Compiègne at Y [sic] a.m. to-morrow.

H. Wilson, Major-Genl.,
Sub-Chief of Staff.[1]

---

1   *MO, 1914*, v. 1, p. 521.

The order caused General Snow consternation on two counts. First, there was the instruction to move to the north bank of the Somme at Ham, a manoeuvre that forced an additional march of six miles at the end of a night march that General Haldane, GOC 10th Brigade, described as the most demanding of the whole retreat. Of greater concern to General Snow, however, was the sixth part of the order, candidly summarised in GHQ files as an instruction 'to throw away unnecessary impedimenta and ammunition not absolutely required and carry exhausted men on vehicles'. Snow considered it 'sufficiently alarmist to turn the retreat into a rout', and II. Corps' commander, Smith-Dorrien, on learning of it, at once ordered that it should be disregarded. He was first informed of the order by his old friend Brigadier General Hunter Weston, the commander of the 11th Brigade:

> [Hunter Weston] went on to say that the order had had a very damping effect on his troops, for it was clear it would not have been issued unless we were in a very tight place. I told him I had never heard of the order, that the situation was excellent, the enemy only in small parties, and those keeping at a respectful distance, and that I was entirely at a loss to understand why such an order had been issued.

Smith-Dorrien assumed that the order must have been a mistake on the part of GHQ, but when he saw the Commander-in-Chief later that morning, 28 August, the latter stated that it was his own order, and 'emphasised the necessity for it by refusing to accept, what he called, my optimistic view of the situation'.[2] Smith-Dorrien's biographer, Brigadier General C. Ballard, who was with 15th Brigade during the retreat, found it surprising that Smith-Dorrien should react so strongly. While commanders in the 4th Division (i.e. Snow and Hunter Weston) might view the order with impatience, Ballard observed, their men had only marched around forty miles. Other units had travelled much further: the 3rd Division, for example, had marched 114 miles by the 27th. In consequence, Ballard argued, they 'were prepared to sacrifice personal baggage, ammunition, and even

---

2   Smith-Dorrien, *Forty-Eight Years*, pp. 416–17.

rations, provided they could use the wagons to save their stragglers'. Ballard believed that if the matter 'had been put to the vote opinions would have been very evenly divided'.[3]

Notwithstanding this judgement, the fact that the order elicited such strong reactions from the commanders of a corps, a division, and a brigade, all in the field, indicates how dramatically different their perception of events was to GHQ's – an impression reinforced by the exchange between Smith-Dorrien and the Commander-in-Chief quoted above. General Snow, in particular, was adamant that the order should not have been issued, and, given that his troops had suffered the heaviest losses at Le Cateau, this casts doubt on Sir John French's claim that Smith-Dorrien's force had been broken by the battle.

---

3   Ballard, *Smith-Dorrien*, pp. 187–9.

APPENDIX 4

DISTANCES MARCHED BY THE BRITISH EXPEDITIONARY FORCE, 20 AUGUST–5 SEPTEMBER 1914

	I Corps		II Corps		III Corps	
	1st Div.	2nd Div.	3rd Div.	5th Div.	19th Inf. Bde	4th Div.
August 20	8.5	-	2	-	-	-
21	13	-	21	15	-	-
22	22.5	20	17	15	-	-
Total	44	20	40	30	-	-
August 23	[-]	22	5	3	7	-
24	17	14	15	10	13	-
25	15.5	24	25	24	19	6
26	15	16	14	15	40	21
27	23	15	17	23		10
28	21	20	27	20	17	20.5
29	rest day	2	25	4	rest day	12.5
30	10	23		12	15	14
31	18	12	15	15	19	15
September 1	19	19	15	12	14	11.5
2	18.5	21	13	14	13	9.5
3	16.5	18	10	18	22	17.5
4	11.5	8	rest day	rest day	rest day	rest day
5	15	16	16	16	14	14
Total	200	230	197	186	193	151.5
Grand total	244	250	237	216	193	151.5

Notes

1. Distances are given in miles and 'represent the bare minimum done on the roads': 'In many cases, on certain days, particular units greatly exceeded the distances given.'
2. The 4th Division and 19th Infantry Brigade came under the aegis of III. Corps on 30 October.

3.   The figure of twenty-one miles given for the 4th Division on 26 August combines the distances marched *to* its Le Cateau positions from the vicinity of Solesmes on the night of 25–26 August (8¾ miles), as well as *from* those positions on the 26th (12¼ miles).

Source: *MO, 1914*, v. 1, p. 542.

APPENDIX 5

LOSSES OF THE BRITISH EXPEDITIONARY FORCE, 23–27 AUGUST 1914

	I. Corps		II. Corps						
	1st Div.	2nd Div.	3rd Div.	5th Div.	4th Div.	19th Bde	Cav'ry	Total	%
Sun 23rd	9	35	1,185	386	-	17	6	**1,638**	11.1
Mon 24th	42	59	557	1,656	-	40	252	**2,606**	17.6
Tues 25th	32	230	357	62	65	36	123	**905**	6.1
Weds 26th	61	344	1,796	2,366	3,158	477	15	**8,217**	57.3
Thur 27th	826	48	50	76	58	108	14	**1,180**	7.9
Unit totals	970	716	3,945	4,546	3,281	678	410	**14,546**	
%	6.7	4.9	27.1	31.2	22.6	4.7	2.8		
Corps totals	1,686		8,491		4,369				
%	11.6		58.4		30.0				

Notes

1. These figures do not include those missing who later returned to their units. They are based on: *MO, 1914*, v. 1, 'Note IV', p. 238, and Smith-Dorrien, *Forty-Eight Years*, p. 411. There is a small discrepancy between these two sources over the losses at Le Cateau (i.e. the combined total of II. Corps, 4th Division, 19th Infantry Brigade, and Cavalry, *but not* I. Corps). These are given as 7,812 in *MO, 1914*, v. 1, p. 191, n. 1 – the figure that is agreed by Smith-Dorrien, and which is given in most accounts. But elsewhere in *MO, 1914*, v. 1 it is given as 8,077 ('Note IV', p. 238). The difficulty arises over the losses of the 5th Division, which Smith-Dorrien gives as 2,366 (the figure used above), but *MO, 1914*, v. 1, gives as 2,631 ('Note IV', p. 238). Smith-Dorrien notes that of his total '2,600 were taken prisoners'.

2. On 23 August (the battle of Mons) and throughout the following day the 4th Division was en route to the front.

3. During the battle of Le Cateau the 4th Division, the 19th Infantry Brigade, and Allenby's cavalry acted under II. Corps, but for the purposes of this table they have been treated independently.

APPENDIX 6

THE BRITISH ORDER OF BATTLE, HILL 60 AND SECOND YPRES, APRIL–MAY 1915

3rd Division: GOC Major-General J. A. L. Haldane
  7th Infantry Brigade: GOC Brigadier General C. R. Ballard
    3rd The Worcestershire Regiment
    1st The Duke of Edinburgh's (Wiltshire Regiment)
    Hon. Art. Company (TF)
    4th Prince of Wales's Volunteers (South Lancashire Regiment) (TF)
    2nd Prince of Wales's Volunteers (South Lancashire Regiment)
    2nd The Royal Irish Rifles
  8th Infantry Brigade: GOC Brigadier General A. R. Hoskins
    2nd Royal Scots
    2nd The Suffolk Regiment
    4th The Duke of Cambridge's Own (Middlesex Regiment)
    1st Gordons
    4th Gordons (TF)
  9th Infantry Brigade: GOC Brigadier General W. Douglas Smith
    1st Northumberland Fusiliers
    1st Lincolnshire Regiment
    10th King's (TF)
    1st Royal Scots Fusiliers
    4th Royal (City of London) Fusiliers
  RFA Brigades: XXIII. (107th, 108th, and 109th Batteries); XLII. (29th, 41st, and 45th Batteries); XL. (6th, 23rd, and 49th Batteries); XXX. Howitzer (128th and 129th Batteries)
  RGA: 5th Mountain Battery
  Engineers: 56th and 1st Cheshire (TF) Field Companies
  Mounted Troops: C Squadron, North Irish Horse; Cyclist Company.

4th Division: GOC Major-General H. F. M. Wilson
  10th Infantry Brigade: GOC Brigadier General C. P. A. Hull
    1st Royal Warwickshire
    1st Royal Irish Fusiliers
    2nd Seaforth Highlanders(Ross-shire Buffs, The Duke of Albany's)
    2nd Royal Dublin Fusiliers
    7th Princess Louise's (Argyll and Sutherland Highlanders) (TF)
  11th Infantry Brigade: GOC Brigadier General J. Hasler
    1st Prince Albert's (Somerset Light Infantry)
    1st Hampshire
    1st The East Lancashire
    1st The Rifle Brigade
    London Rifle Brigade (TF)
  12th Infantry Brigade: GOC Brigadier General F. G. Anley
    1st The King's Own
    2nd The Lancashire Fusiliers
    5th Prince of Wales's Volunteers (South Lancashire Regiment) (TF)
    2nd The Royal Irish
    2nd The Essex
    2nd The Monmouthshire (TF)
  RFA Brigades: XIV. (68th and 88th Batteries); XXIX. (125th, 126th, and
      127th Batteries); XXXII. (27th, 134th, and 135th Batteries)
  RGA: 2nd Mountain Battery
  Engineers: 9th and 1st West Lancashire (TF)
  Mounted Troops: A Squadron, Northamptonshire Yeomanry; Cyclist
      Company

5th Division: GOC Major-General T. L. N. Morland
  13th Infantry Brigade: GOC Brigadier General R. Wanless
      O'Gowan
    2nd The King's Own Scottish Borderers
    1st Queen's Own Royal West Kent
    9th The London (Queen Victoria's Rifles) (TF)
    2nd The Duke of Wellington's (West Riding)
    2nd The King's Own Yorkshire Light Infantry
  14th Infantry Brigade: GOC Brigadier General G. H. Thesiger
    1st The Devonshire
    1st The Duke of Cornwall's Light Infantry

5th The Cheshire (TF)

1st The East Surrey

2nd The Manchester

15th Infantry Brigade: GOC Brigadier General E. Northey

1st The Norfolk

1st The Cheshire

6th King's (TF)

1st The Bedfordshire

1st The Dorsetshire

RFA Brigades: XV. (52nd and 80th Batteries); XXVIII. (122nd, 123rd, and 124th Batteries); XXVII. (119th, 120th, and 121st Batteries); XXX. Howitzer (130th Battery)

Engineers: 59th Field Company; 2nd The Home Counties (TF) and 1st The North Midland (TF) Field Companies

Mounted Troops: C Squadron Northamptonshire Yeomanry; Cyclist Company

27th Division: GOC Major-General Thomas D'Oyly Snow

80th Infantry Brigade: GOC Brigadier General W. E. B. Smith

2nd The King's Shropshire Light Infantry

3rd The King's Royal Rifle Corps

4th The King's Royal Rifle Corps

4th The Rifle Brigade

Princess Patricia's Canadian Light Infantry

81st Infantry Brigade: GOC Brigadier General H. L. Croker

1st The Royal Scots

2nd The Cameron Highlanders (Queen's Own)[1]

2nd The Gloucestershire Regiment

1st Princess Louise's (Argyll and Sutherland Highlanders)

9th The Royal Scots (TF)

9th Princess Louise's (Argyll and Sutherland Highlanders) (TF)

82nd Infantry Brigade: GOC Brigadier General J. R. Longley

1st The Royal Irish

2nd The Royal Irish Fusiliers

2nd The Duke of Cornwall's Light Infantry

1st The Leinster

---

1   This battalion was lent to the 5th Division, and was at Hill 60.

1st The Cambridgeshire (TF)

RFA Brigades:[2] I. (11th, 98th, 132nd, and 133rd Batteries); XIX. (39th, 59th, 96th, and 131st Batteries); XX. (67th, 99th, 148th, and 364th Batteries); VIII. Howitzer (61st Battery)

Engineers: 17th Field Company, RE; 1st and 2nd Wessex (TF) Field Companies, RE

Mounted Troops: A Squadron Surrey Yeomanry; Cyclist Company

28th Division: GOC Major-General E. S. Bulfin

83rd Infantry Brigade: GOC Brigadier General R. C. Boyle

2nd The King's Own

1st The King's Own Yorkshire Light Infantry

5th The King's Own (TF)

2nd The East Yorkshire

1st The York and Lancaster

3rd The Monmouthshire (TF)

84th Infantry Brigade: GOC Brigadier General L. J. Bols

2nd The Northumberland Fusiliers

2nd The Cheshire

12th The London (Rangers) (TF)

1st The Suffolk

1st The Welch

1st The Monmouthshire (TF)

85th Infantry Brigade: GOC Brigadier General A. J. Chapman

2nd The Buffs (East Kent Regiment)

2nd The East Surrey

3rd The Duke of Cambridge's Own (Middlesex Regiment)

8th The Duke of Cambridge's Own (Middlesex Regiment) (TF)

3rd The Royal (City of London) Fusiliers

---

2   The field artillery of both the 27th Division and the 28th, the next to be formed, originally consisted of three brigades, each with three four-gun batteries, which were created by expanding the nine six-gun batteries brought home from India. In March each of the brigades was augmented by a fourth battery, constituted in some cases by reducing six-gun batteries to four-gun (*MO, 1915*, v. 1, p. 11 and n. 2).

RFA Brigades: III. (18th, 22nd, 62nd, and 365th Batteries); CXLVI (75th, 149th, 366th and 367th Batteries); XXXI. (69th, 100th, 103rd, and 118th Batteries); VIII. Howitzer (37th and 65th Batteries)

Engineers: 38th Field Company, RE; 1st The Northumbrian (TF) Field Company, RE

Mounted Troops: B Squadron, Surrey Yeomanry; Cyclist Company

50th (1st Northumbrian) Division (TF): GOC Major-General Sir W. F. L. Lindsay

149th Infantry Brigade (1st Northumberland): GOC Brigadier General J. F. Riddell

4th Northumberland Fusiliers
5th Northumberland Fusiliers
6th Northumberland Fusiliers
7th Northumberland Fusiliers

150th Infantry Brigade (1st The York and Durham): GOC Brigadier General J. E. Bush

4th The East Yorkshire
4th The Green Howards
5th The Green Howards
5th The Durham Light Infantry.

151st Infantry Brigade (1st The Durham Light Infantry): GOC Brigadier General H. Martin

6th Durham Light Infantry
7th Durham Light Infantry
8th Durham Light Infantry
9th Durham Light Infantry

RFA Brigades: I. Northumbrian, II. Northumbrian and III. Northumbrian (all 15-pounders); IV. Northumbrian (5-inch Howitzers)

Engineers: 2nd Northumbrian Field Company, RE

Mounted Troops: A Squadron, Yorkshire Hussars; Cyclist Company

1st Canadian Division: GOC Major-General E. A. H. Alderson

1st Canadian Brigade: GOC Brigadier General M. S. Mercer

1st (Western Ontario Regiment)
2nd (Eastern Ontario Regiment)
3rd (Toronto Regiment)
4th Battalion

2nd Canadian Brigade: GOC Brigadier General A. W. Currie
    5th Battalion (Western Cavalry)
    8th Battalion (Winnipeg Rifles)
    7th Battalion (1st British Columbia Regiment)
    10th Battalion (10th Canadians)
3rd Canadian Brigade: GOC Brigadier General R. E. W. Turner, VC
    13th Battalion (Royal Highlanders of Canada)
    14th Battalion (Royal Montreal Regiment)
    15th Battalion (48th Highlanders of Canada)
    16th Battalion (Canadian Scottish)
Canadian Field Artillery Brigades: I. (1st, 2nd, 3rd, and 4th Batteries); II.
    (5th, 6th, 7th, and 8th Batteries); III. (9th, 10th, 11th, and 12th
    Batteries) (all three brigades having 4-gun batteries)
RFA Brigade: CXVIII. Howitzer (458th and 459th Batteries)
Canadian Field Companies: 1st, 2nd, and 3rd Companies.
Mounted Troops: Service Squadron, 19th Alberta Dragoons; Cyclist
    Corps.

Lahore Division: GOC Major-General H. D'U. Keary
    Ferozepore Brigade: GOC Brigadier General R. G. Egerton
        Connaught Rangers
        57th Wilde's Rifles
        4th London (TF)
        9th Bhopal Infantry
        129th Baluchis
    Jullundur Brigade: GOC Brigadier General E. P. Strickland
        1st Manchester
        47th Sikhs
        4th Suffolk (TF)
        40th Pathans
        59th Scinde Rifles
    Sirhind Brigade: GOC Brigadier General W. G. Walker, VC
        1st The Highland Light Infantry
        4th The King's (S.R.)
        15th Sikhs
        1/1st Gurkhas
        1/4th Gurkhas

RFA Brigades: V. (64th, 73rd, and 81st Batteries); XVIII. (59th, 93rd, and 94th Batteries); XI. (83rd, 84th, and 85th Batteries); XLIII. Howitzer (40th and 57th Batteries)

Engineers: 20th and 21st Field Companies, RA; 3rd Sappers and Miners

Pioneers: 34th Sikh Pioneers

Mounted Troops: 15th Lancers

1st Cavalry Division: GOC Major-General H. de B. de Lisle

    1st Cavalry Brigade: GOC Brigadier General C. J. Briggs

        Queen's Bays

        5th Dragoon Guards

        11th Hussars

    2nd Cavalry Brigade: GOC Brigadier General R. L. Mullens

        4th Dragoon Guards

        9th Lancers

        18th Hussars

    3rd Cavalry Brigade: GOC Brigadier General W. H. Greenly

        15th Hussars

        19th Hussars

    RHA Brigade: VII. (H, I and Warwickshire (TF) Batteries)

    Engineers: No. 1 Field Squadron, RE

2nd Cavalry Division: GOC Major-General C. T. McM. Kavanagh

    3rd Cavalry Brigade: GOC Brigadier General J. Vaughan

        4th Hussars

        5th Lancers

        16th Lancers

    4th Cavalry Brigade: GOC Brigadier General Hon. C. E. Bingham

        6th Dragoon Guards

        3rd Hussars

        Oxfordshire Hussars (Yeomanry)

    5th Cavalry Brigade: GOC Brigadier General Sir P. W. Chetwode

        2nd Royal Scots Greys

        12th Lancers

        20th Hussars

    RHA Brigade: III. (D, E, and J Batteries)

    Engineers: No. 2 Field Squadron, RE

3rd Cavalry Division: GOC Major-General Hon. J. H. G. Byng
  6th Cavalry Brigade: GOC Brigadier General D. Campbell
      3rd Dragoon Guards
      1st Royal Dragoons
      North Somerset Yeomanry
  7th Cavalry Brigade: GOC Brigadier General A. A. Kennedy
      1st Life Guards
      2nd Life Guards
      Leicester Yeomanry
  8th Cavalry Brigade: GOC Brigadier General C. B. Bulkeley-Johnson
      Royal Horse Guards
      10th Hussars
      Essex Yeomanry
  RHA Brigade: XV. (C, K, and G Batteries)
  Engineers: No. 3 Field Squadron, RE

Source: *MO, 1915*, v. 1, pp. 370–4.

APPENDIX 7

'HULL'S ATTACK', 24–25 APRIL 1915

At 6.30 p.m. on 24 April General Plumer received orders from Sir John French to restore the line near St Julien, which had been broken during successive German attacks beginning before dawn. Around 8.00 p.m. Lieutenant General E. A. H. Alderson, CO of the Canadian Division, gave orders for the operation known as 'Hull's attack' – after Brigadier General C. P. A. Hull, CO of the 10th Brigade, who was chosen to command it. Alderson's Operation Order No. 10 ran as follows:

1. By orders of the Corps commander a strong counter-attack will be made early to-morrow morning in a general direction of St. Julien with the object of driving the enemy back as far north as possible and thus securing the left flank of the 28th Division.

2. Br.-General Hull commanding the 10th Brigade will be in charge of this counter-attack.

3. The following troops will be placed at the disposal of Br.-General Hull for this purpose, viz.:

     10th Infantry Brigade, York and Durham Brigade; K.O.Y.L.I. and Queen Victoria's Rifles of the 13th Brigade, 1st Suffolks and 12th London Regiment of the 28th Division, 4th Canadian Battalion, and one battalion of the 27th Division.

4. The O's C. these units will report for instructions at 9 p.m. to-night to General Hull, whose Hqrs. will be at the road junction in I.l.c. and d. up to midnight.

5. The Northumberland Brigade and Durham Light Infantry Brigade of the Northumbrian Division, forming the Corps

reserve and now at Potijze, can be called upon for support by Gen. Hull.

6. The first objectives of the attack will be Fortuin (if occupied by enemy), St. Julien and the wood in C. 10. and 11. After these points have been gained, General Hull will advance astride of the St. Julien-Poelcappelle road and drive back the enemy as far north as possible. All units holding the front line of trenches will follow up the attack and help to consolidate the ground gained.

7. The C.R.A. Canadian Division will arrange for artillery support of the counter-attack and get into touch with the C.R.A.'s of the 27th and 28th Divisions regarding all possible artillery support from these Divisions.

8. The counter-attack will be launched at 3.30 a.m.

9. Divisional hqrs. will remain at the Chateau de Trois Tours near Brielen.

C. Romer, Colonel,
General Staff

8 p.m.

Note

1. The grid points in part 4 indicate a position west of the canal just north of Ypres; those in part 6 indicate Kitchener's Wood. Source: *MO, 1915*, v. 1, p. 395

Appendix 8

British/Canadian and German Losses at Second Ypres

British and Canadian Losses at Hill 60 and Second Ypres, 22 April–31 May 1915

Unit	Officers K.	Officers W.	Officers M.	Other ranks K.	Other ranks W.	Other ranks M.	Total
1st Cavalry Division	17	59	9	151	638	329	**1,203**
2nd Cavalry Division	4	7	-	36	180	17	**244**
3rd Cavalry Division	31	60	3	273	1,057	194	**1,618**
4th Division	87	224	36	1,566	5,476	3,470	**10,859**
5th Division	71	209	13	1,068	5,478	1,155	**7,994**
27th Division	55	166	13	1,122	4,980	927	**7,263**
28th Division	97	300	98	3,177	5,548	6,313	**15,533**
50th Division	40	121	25	596	2,963	1,459	**5,204**
Canadian Division	65	104	39	1,672	1,822	1,767	**5,469**
Lahore Division	34	162	1	357	2,780	554	**3,888**
Totals	501	1,412	237	10,018	30,922	16,185	
	2,150			**57,125**			**59,275**

German losses before Ypres, 21 April–30 May 1915

Unit	Officers K.	Officers W.	Officers M.	Other ranks K.	Other ranks W.	Other ranks M.	Total
XXIII. Reserve Corps	66	127	18	1,610	6,429	2,342	**10,592**
XXVI. Reserve Corps	91	210	9	2,243	8,878	1,414	**12,845**
XXVII. Reserve Corps	56	207	5	1,656	6,268	460	**8,652**
XV. Reserve Corps	25	44	2	590	2,131	52	**2,844**
Totals	238	588	34	6,099	23,706	4,268	
	860			**34,073**			**34,933**

Note

1. These tables are based on the figures given in *MO, 1915*, v. 1, pp. 356, 358. They *do not* offer an exact comparison of like with like: the *XXIII. Reserve Corps*, for example, was mostly engaged against the French (not the British or Canadians), while the losses of detachments of the *XXII. Reserve Corps* and *Marine Corps* are not included in the German figures; in addition, the Germans did not always count as casualties the 'lightly wounded'; and the British–Canadian figures include the fighting at Hill 60, which the German figures may not.

APPENDIX 9
STATISTICS

1. The size and marching depth of an infantry division in the Expeditionary Force

The six infantry divisions of the original Expeditionary Force each consisted of three brigades. In addition to these brigades there were divisional troops, including: mounted troops (cavalry and cyclist companies); artillery (batteries and ammunition columns); engineers; signals service; army service corps; field ambulances. The full complement of such a division was 18,073 men of all ranks and 5,592 horses, and its marching depth was approximately fifteen miles:

	Men	Horses
Head Quarters	82	54
3 Infantry Brigades	12,165	741
HQ Divisional Artillery	22	20
3 Field Artillery Brigades	2,385	2,244
1 Field Artillery (Howitzer) Brigade	755	697
1 Heavy Battery and Amm. Col.	198	144
1 Divisional Ammunition Column	568	709
HQ Divisional Engineers	13	8
2 Field Companies	434	152
1 Signal Company	162	80
1 Cavalry Squadron	159	167
1 Divisional Train	428	378
3 Field Ambulances	702	198
Total	18,073	5,592

A cavalry division consisted of 9,269 men of all ranks and 9,815 horses, and had a somewhat shorter marching depth of about 11½ miles. In an infantry division there were seventy-six guns (fifty-four 18-pounders; eighteen 4.5-inch howitzers; and four 60-pounders) and twenty-four machine guns (i.e. two per battalion). In a cavalry division there were twenty-four 13-pounders and twenty-four machine guns (i.e. two per regiment).

2. The average age of British divisional / corps commanders (infantry)

Average age at . . .	Division	Corps
5 August 1914	55	56
10 March 1915	53	57
25 September 1915	54	55
1 July 1916	54	54
31 July 1917	51	57
11 November 1918	48	54

3. The weight of an infantryman's kit at the beginning of the war

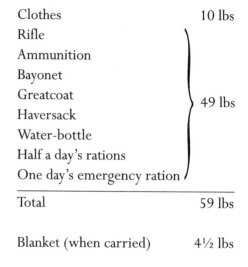

Clothes	10 lbs
Rifle	
Ammunition	
Bayonet	
Greatcoat	49 lbs
Haversack	
Water-bottle	
Half a day's rations	
One day's emergency ration	
Total	59 lbs
Blanket (when carried)	4½ lbs

4. The hour of sunrise and sunset (in London) at selected dates

Date	Event	Sunrise	Sunset
Sunday 23 August 1914	Battle of Mons	4.59	7.07
Wednesday 26 August	Battle of Le Cateau	5.04	7.00
Saturday 5 September	End of the Retreat from Mons	5.20	6.38
Wednesday 19 October	Start of 1st Ypres	6.31	4.59
Sunday 22 November	End of 1st Ypres	7.31	4.01
Friday 1 January 1915	27th Division arrives at St Omer	8.08	3.59
Thursday 22 April	German gas attack at Ypres	4.54	7.04
Tuesday 25 May	End of Second Ypres	3.58	7.56

5. Ports of embarkation and disembarkation

The speed of Britain's mobilisation after war was declared on 4 August 1914 helped to offset the political delays occasioned by the cabinet's need to keep parliament informed of the progress of events, and its determination also not to take any measures that might be construed as provocation towards Germany. General Joffre had planned to open his campaign on 20 August, but the lateness of Britain's declaration meant that the BEF might not be ready to fight until the 26th. Time was saved, however, by the efficiency with which mobilisation proceeded, and this was a function of the thoroughness of the pre-war planning, which was largely the responsibility of Sir John Cowans, the Quartermaster-General between 1912 and 1919. A pre-war census of horses, for example, made it possible to collect within twelve days of mobilisation the 120,000 animals deemed necessary. During the period 9 to 17 August an average of thirteen ships left British ports every day bound for France. They were divided into carriers of four classes: 1) personnel; 2) horses and vehicles; 3) motor transport; 4) stores. The ports of embarkation and disembarkation were as follows:

Port of embarkation	Carried	Ports of disembarkation
Avonmouth	Motor transport and petrol	Havre
Belfast	5th and 6th Divisions	
Cork	5th and 6th Divisions	
Dublin	5th and 6th Divisions	Rouen
Glasgow	A few details	
Liverpool	Frozen meat and motor transport	Boulogne
Newhaven	Stores and supplies	
Southampton	All GB troops	

Sources: Table 1: *MO, 1914*, v. 1, pp. 485–7; Table 2: Ballard, *Smith-Dorrien*, p. 186; Table 3: Robbins, *Generalship*, pp. 214–15; Table 4: *Whitaker's Almanack*, 1914, 1915; Table 5: *MO, 1914*, v. 1, pp. 31–2, and 10 n. 3

A Chronology of the 4th Division, and its Role in the Retreat from Mons July–September 1914

This chronology informs General Snow's narrative of the 4th Division, in particular the battle of Le Cateau, but is in no way comprehensive; it is based largely on the account in *Military Operations, France and Belgium, 1914.Volume I: Mons, the Retreat to the Seine, the Marne and the Aisne, August–October 1914* (1933 edition); all page references are to this work, unless otherwise stated.

28 June (Sunday)
> Assassination in Sarajevo of Archduke Franz Ferdinand, the heir apparent to the throne of Austria–Hungary; Austria blames Serbia for this outrage

6 July (Monday)
> Germany communicates its support for Austria-Hungary

23 July (Thursday)
> Austria delivers an ultimatum to Serbia, in response to which Serbia appeals to Russia for support

25 July (Saturday)
> Serbian army mobilizes against Austria-Hungary

28 July (Tuesday)
> Austria-Hungary declares war on Serbia; the Tsar orders the partial mobilisation of the Russian army

29 July (Wednesday)
> Midday – cabinet agrees to declaration of 'Precautionary Period' in case of war
> 5.00 p.m. – General Snow learns of Precautionary Period at Shorncliffe

30 July (Thursday)
> 6.00 p.m. – Russian government orders general mobilisation

31 July (Friday)

Austria decrees full mobilisation; Germany issues ultimatum to Russia to stop mobilisation; Britain seeks assurances from Germany and France regarding Belgian neutrality – France gives reassurance, Germany does not

1 August (Saturday)

France and Germany begin general mobilisation; Belgian government orders mobilisation in defence of its neutrality

7.00 p.m. – Germany declares war on Russia

2 August (Sunday)

Britain assures France its fleet will 'give all protection in its power' to prevent German hostilities towards French coast or French shipping; cabinet will not go further without first consulting parliament

2.50 p.m. – Territorial Force annual training cancelled

6.00 p.m. – Regular Army manoeuvres cancelled

7.00 p.m. – Germany requests free passage for troops through Belgium; Belgian Government replies that it will resist encroachment from any quarter

3 August (Bank Holiday Monday)

House of Commons: Sir Edward Grey, foreign secretary, makes the case for intervention on the side of France: Britain might conceivably avoid the immediate danger, but at the risk of its future independence

6.45 p.m. Germany declares war on France, falsely alleging a violation of its frontier by French patrols

Night (3/4 August) – it becomes clear that Germany intends to advance in force through Belgium

4 August (Tuesday)

Morning – German cavalry cross Belgian frontier; Britain issues ultimatum to Germany to observe Belgian neutrality

4.00 p.m. – War Office sends by telegraph, *en clair*, the message 'MOBILISE'

6.26 p.m. – 4th Division HQ at Woolwich receives order to mobilise

11.00 p.m. – Britain at war with Germany (midnight, central European time) after ultimatum expires

5 August (Wednesday)

Officially 'the first day of mobilisation'

6 August (Thursday)

Morning – Kitchener becomes secretary of state for war; cabinet sanctions the despatch to France of BEF

9 August (Sunday)

Embarkation of BEF begins (completed by 17th)

14 August (Friday)

BEF entrains to concentration area between Maubeuge and Le Cateau

17 August (Monday)

Sir James Grierson, commander II. Corps, dies in France

19 August (Wednesday)

GHQ informed of despatch of 4th Division to France; battalions employed on lines of communication become 19th Brigade; RFC conducts first reconnaissances from Maubeuge – sees no large bodies of enemy

20 August (Thursday)

Concentration of BEF virtually completed: II. Corps east of Landrecies, with HQ there; I. Corps east of Bohain, HQ Wassigny; Cavalry east of Maubeuge, HQ Aibes; RFC at Maubeuge; at 1.00 p.m. C-in-C issues Operation Order No. 5, ordering BEF to move north of Sambre

Cavalry pushes forward without encountering enemy, but aerial reconnaissance detects massive enemy column at Louvain; German troops enter Brussels; German supreme command believes BEF not yet in France

21 August (Friday)

Patrols of 9th Lancers and 4th Dragoon Guards sight German patrols east of Mons; Smith-Dorrien arrives in Bavai to take command of II. Corps

10.25 p.m. – 4th Division entrains for Southampton from Harrow area (completed by 2.20 p.m. on the 22nd)

22 August (Saturday)

Dawn – C Squadron, 4th Dragoon Guards, fires on German piquet while pushing north from Obourg towards Soignies – the first shots fired by British in the war

Morning, and throughout day – 4th Division crosses to France (mostly Havre–Rouen but also Boulogne) arriving evening/night

10.00 p.m. – French retreat compels C-in-C to abandon planned advance; he accedes to French requests to remain on canal at Mons for twenty-four hours

Midnight – General Snow and 4th Division staff disembark from SS *Cestrian* at Havre

23rd August (Sunday)

BEF takes up positions on angled front approximately twenty-seven miles long, west and south-east of Mons, with flanks exposed

6.00 a.m. – Cavalry before Mons, and 4th Middlesex at Obourg, engage with enemy

8.30 to 10.30 a.m. – von Kluck believes BEF detraining at Tournai: he halts *First Army* for two hours and prepares to wheel westwards

9.00 a.m.– German guns north of Mons shell British positions

c.9.15 a.m. – 19th Brigade detrains at Valenciennes and marches to left flank of canal line

10.00 a.m. – 3rd Division in Mons salient heavily engaged; attack spreads westwards to Condé

Afternoon and night – units in salient and on canal line withdraw, as local conditions dictate, from outpost line to main defensive position 1–3 miles in rear

8.40 p.m. – C-in-C to Smith-Dorrien: 'I will stand attack on ground now occupied by troops. You will therefore strengthen your position by every possible means during night'

Evening – Lanrezac's planned retreat at 3.00 a.m. extends gap between French and British: C-in-C decides his position is untenable

11.00 p.m. – 4th Division HQ leaves Havre, arriving at Amiens early next morning

24 August (Monday)

1.00 a.m. – CGS imparts C-in-C's decision to retire south to line La Longueville–Bavai–La Boiserette; no detailed instructions issued, and corps commanders expected to make arrangements between themselves

2.00 a.m. – Haig learns by telegraph from GHQ of order to retire and that I. Corps to cover retirement of II. Corps; he transmits at once to his brigades

3.00 a.m. – II. Corps belatedly gets message to retire

4.00 a.m. – I. Corps begins withdrawal without difficulty

Dawn – Germans open heavy bombardment against right of II. Corps, extending westwards

5.15 a.m. – general infantry attack developing, delaying retirement of 5th Division especially

8.00 a.m. – 3rd Division begins withdrawal

1.00 p.m. – II. Corps informs I. Corps HQ of delayed retirement of 5th Division; Haig directs his rearguards to conform

2.30 p.m. – Norfolks and Cheshires of 15th Brigade (5th Division), having held off von Kluck's flanking movement, retreat from Élouges much depleted

4.00 p.m. – General Snow reaches Busigny; 10th Brigade and 11th Brigade detrain at Le Cateau, advancing to Beaumont and Troisville respectively; 12th Brigade detrains at Bertry, advancing to Montigny and Ligny; divisional artillery detrains at Busigny and Bohair, forming up along Le Cateau–St Quentin road

6.00 p.m. – at Bavai Smith-Dorrien urges C-in-C to issue orders for early and coordinated retirement

8.25 p.m. – C-in-C's Operation Order No. 7 sends I. and II. Corps down east and west side of Forêt de Mormal respectively, towards 'a position in neighbourhood of Le Cateau, exact positions will be pointed out on ground to-morrow'

25 August (Tuesday)

4.30 a.m. – 4th Division HQ set up at Briastre Church

5.00 a.m. – 4th Division in position around Solesmes: 10th Brigade at St Python; 11th at Briastre; 12th at Viesly

Afternoon – GHQ learns through air reports of concentration of enemy forces at Valenciennes and of infantry marching towards Solesmes

3.00 p.m. – Haig receives GHQ message informing him II. Corps occupying Le Cateau line and asking when I. Corps will be able to take its place in the Inchy–St Benin defensive line

3.00–8.00 p.m. – 5th Division arrives on right of Le Cateau position

5.00–7.00 p.m. – thunderstorm, with heavy rain

5.00 p.m. – General Snow issues Operation Order No. 1, instructing retirement of 4th Division to Le Cateau positions

6.00 p.m. – Smith-Dorrien receives note from Henry Wilson warning him that retirement to be continued

6.00 p.m. – GHQ set up at St Quentin

6.00–7.00 p.m. – 3rd Division arrives at Le Cateau position, around Audencourt and Inchy

6.40 p.m. – GHQ shortens 4th Division front to Fontaine-au-Pire–Wambaix, c. three miles

7.30 p.m. – C-in-C's Operation Order No. 8 continues the retreat south-west next day to Busigny–Le Catelet line

7.30 p.m. – at Landrecies, piquets of I. Corps attacked by German infantry and artillery

9.00 p.m. – Smith-Dorrien receives Operation Order No. 8

25 August (Tuesday) *continued*

9.00 p.m. – 12th Brigade vacates heights above Solesmes

10.00 p.m. – I. Corps telephones GHQ: 'Attack heavy from north-west can you send help?'; Smith-Dorrien replies to GHQ that he cannot

10.00 p.m. – 19th Brigade bivouacs in central square at Le Cateau; 11th Brigade leaves Solesmes

10.15 p.m. – Smith-Dorrien issues orders 'for renewal of retreat' to start *c*.4 a.m.

11.00 p.m. – Allenby's HQ at Beaumont gets GHQ orders to cover continuing retreat; Allenby learns that enemy controls heights around Solesmes, jeopardising retirement from Le Cateau; he proceeds to Bertry to see Smith-Dorrien

Midnight – 10th Brigade, delayed by 3rd Division at Briastre, begins withdrawal south

Midnight – General Snow belatedly gets Operation Order No. 8; he prepares divisional orders, but does not issue to brigades, which are all on the road

Night – General Sordet's Cavalry Corps arrives behind II. Corps' left flank

After midnight – the fighting at Landrecies ends and enemy draws off

26 August (Wednesday)

1.35 a.m. – Haig, from his HQ at Le Grand Fayt, reports situation at Landrecies 'very critical'

2.00 a.m. – Allenby explains to Smith-Dorrien that his cavalry are too dispersed to cover retreat, and that enemy commands high ground around Solesmes; he advises that unless retirement begins 'before daylight' the enemy will be 'upon them before they could start, and it would be necessary to fight'; Smith-Dorrien sends for General Hamilton, GOC 3rd Division – Hamilton states that as many of his units still arriving he cannot move before 9 a.m.; Smith-Dorrien decides to stand at Le Cateau, with 4th Division on left, 5th Division on right, 3rd Division in centre, 19th Infantry Brigade in reserve Cavalry on flanks

2.15 a.m. – 11th Brigade arrives at Fontaine-au-Pire having been delayed by 3rd Division transport at Viesly

3.30 a.m. – Smith-Dorrien dispatches by car to GHQ (St Quentin) a detailed statement of his decision

3.40 a.m. – 10th Brigade arrives in dark at identified village (Cattenières): it is thus in front of outpost line of 4th Division; the brigade moves at once, but transports fired upon shortly after clearing Cattenières

26 August (Wednesday) *continued*

3.45 a.m. – Smith-Dorrien wrongly informed by GHQ that enemy working round south of Landrecies; GHQ confirms orders to continue retirement

Daylight – as 11th brigade stands to arms hostile forces seen advancing from north on Cattenières

4.30 a.m. – 10th Brigade arrives at Haucourt

5.00 a.m. – GHQ gets Smith-Dorrien's 3.30 a.m. message

5.00 a.m. – staff officers sent from 4th Division HQ to ascertain positions of brigades, with intention of issuing orders for continued retirement

5.00 a.m. – II. Corps sends message to GHQ asking that General Sordet be informed of situation

5.00 a.m. (shortly after) – General Snow informed of Smith-Dorrien's decision to fight: Snow agrees to act under him

*c.*5.30 a.m. – Snow sends messages to his brigades to stand on the positions already ordered (i.e. in Operation Order No. 1 of 5.00 p.m. on the 25th)

6.00 a.m. – 1st King's Own, 12th Brigade, suffer heavy casualties in attack from enemy situated between Wambaix and Cattenières; two reserve companies of 1st Warwickshires suffer heavy losses in counter-attack

6.00 a.m. – units of 14th Brigade belatedly receive counter-orders to stand fast – some east of Le Cateau never receive them at all; a dozen German batteries open fire from three miles north-north-east. of Le Cateau on right of line

6.00 a.m. (shortly after) – GHQ prepares written reply to Smith-Dorrien's message, but not sent until 11.05 a.m. as telephone communication established with II. Corps

6.00 a.m. – C-in-C, concerned at prospect of I. Corps retiring south, sends staff officer to I. Corps HQ (arriving 6.00 a.m.) with 'instructions giving [Haig] the alternatives of retiring south-westward on St Quentin, that is towards II. Corps, or in a south-easterly direction to seek shelter with French'; Haig elects to retire due south – confirmed in message timed 10.00 a.m.; 'by this decision direct touch with II. Corps was broken, and not regained until 1st September' (p. 201)

*c.*6.00–6.45 a.m. (*MO, 1914*, v. 1, suggests 'shortly after 6 a.m.' but Smith-Dorrien indicates 6.45 a.m.) – Smith-Dorrien summoned to telephone at railway station near Bertry HQ and explains to Henry Wilson, sub-CGS, impossibility of breaking away

8.45 a.m. – German progress towards Wambaix, round left flank of advanced line, induces retirement of the 12th Brigade across Warnelle ravine

26 August (Wednesday) *continued*

9.00 a.m. – Sordet learns of situation at Le Cateau from C-in-C

11.00 a.m. – enemy's early attempt to turn right flank contained, but Smith-Dorrien has to use two battalions from reserve to reinforce it

11.05 a.m. – C-in-C's written reply to Smith-Dorrien sent to II. Corps: 'If you can hold your ground situation appears likely to improve. . . Although you are given a free hand as to method this telegram is not intended to convey impression that I am not as anxious for you to carry out retirement and you must make every endeavour to do so' (p. 142)

Midday – Smith-Dorrien visits Sir Charles Fergusson at 5th Division HQ; difficulty of disengaging means a decision to retire temporarily postponed

1.00 p.m. – Sordet, near Cambrai, receives Joffre's message requesting him 'not only [to] cover left of British Army, but do more and intervene in battle with all forces at [his] disposal' (p. 185)

1.20 p.m. – 5th Division urgently requests assistance

1.30 p.m. – Sordet orders his Corps to recross Schelde

1.40 p.m. – Smith-Dorrien places remaining reserve at Fergusson's disposal, asking him 'to hold his ground at any rate a little longer, so as to allow preliminary movements of retirement to take effect' (p. 173)

2.00 p.m. – Smith-Dorrien authorises 5th Division to withdraw: Fergusson orders retirement, but this does not reach any battalion 'much before 3 p.m.'; Smith-Dorrien orders 3rd and 4th Divisions to conform; some units, *c*.1,000–2,000 men, never receive order to retire and fight on

2.00 p.m. – General d'Amade's Territorials leave Cambrai after holding off *II. Corps*, thus protecting Smith-Dorrien's left

3.30 p.m. – Joffre visits C-in-C: 'His main interest was that, in spite of heavy losses they had suffered, British should not fall out of line' (p. 200); GHQ retires to Noyon

c.3.30–5.00 p.m. – 11th Brigade repels enemy before Ligny

4.00 p.m. – Sordet's corps fires on German *IV. Reserve Corps* as 4th Division retires on left flank

4.00 p.m. – Smith-Dorrien watches 5th Division pass along road south of Maurois; he likens them 'to a crowd coming away from a race meeting' (Smith-Dorrien, *Forty-Eight Years*, p. 408)

4.30 p.m. – Smith-Dorrien hears Sordet's guns

5.00 p.m. – 4th Division begins to withdraw, just as *IV. Reserve Corps* arrives in force from the direction of Cattenières–Wambaix

5.00 p.m. – enemy artillery fire intensifies on left of line; outflanking movement around Esnes develops

26 August (Wednesday) *continued*

6.00 p.m. – in drizzling rain and fading light enemy's pursuit dies away

6.30 p.m. – Sordet breaks off his action and retires

8.15 p.m. – French liaison officer at GHQ gains impression that BEF is in disarray and II. Corps given up as lost

8.30 p.m. – German guns fire on Audencourt, long since deserted by 3rd Division, which watches from heights south of Clary six miles away

8.30 p.m. – Haig enquires of GHQ: 'No news of II. Corps except sound of guns from direction of Le Cateau and Beaumont. Can I. Corps be of any assistance'; he receives no answer

11.00 p.m. – Haig sends to II. Corps via GHQ the message: 'Please let me know your situation and news. We are well able to co-operate with you to-day, we could hear sound of your battle, but could get no information as to its progress, and could form no idea of how we could assist you.'

11.00 p.m. – isolated parties of several battalions of 4th Division, left behind about Haucourt and Ligny, begin their escape from battlefield

Evening – on arrival at St Quentin Smith-Dorrien finds that GHQ now at Noyon and proceeds there to report on Le Cateau

Night – I. Corps in and around Éstreux; II. Corps, 4th Division, etc., eighteen miles to west, in south-westward retreat to Oise

27 August (Thursday)

1.00 a.m. – Smith-Dorrien reaches Noyon to find GHQ asleep; C-in-C, 'clad in his *robe de nuit*', receives Smith-Dorrien's report: 'he told me he considered I took much too cheerful a view of situation' (Smith-Dorrien, *Forty-Eight Years*, p. 411)

Dawn – British troops begin pouring into St Quentin

5.30 p.m. – 11th and 12th Brigades entrench and rest at Hancourt

8.30 p.m. – C-in-C's Operation Order No. 9: ammunition and impedimenta on wagons to be thrown away and officers and men carried instead

9.30 p.m. – 4th Division marches by night to Voyennes

28 August (Friday)

4.00 a.m. – 4th Division reaches Voyennes; main body of 11th Brigade rejoins

Dawn – almost all of Smith-Dorrien's force south of Somme, thirty-five miles from Le Cateau

c.1.30 p.m. – retirement continues

Night – I. Corps south of Oise and of La Fère; II. Corps, with 4th Division, eleven miles away, north and east of Noyon

29 August (Saturday)

Morning – BEF at overnight positions on Oise, with French Fifth Army to right, and the newly formed Sixth Army on the left; for most of Smith-Dorrien's force a day of rest

Afternoon – Joffre visits GHQ anxious that BEF should remain in line; C-in-C 'equally anxious to withdraw and rest it for a few days'; C-in-C later speaks to staff of making 'a definite and prolonged retreat due south, passing Paris to east or west' (p. 241)

9.00 p.m. – becomes clear that French Fifth Army unable to advance; C-in-C issues orders for further retreat behind the Aisne

Midnight – practically whole of General Smith-Dorrien's force brought south of Oise, with bridges mostly destroyed behind it

30 August (Sunday)

6.00 a.m. – air reconnaissance shows Germans sweeping south over Somme between Ham and Péronne, bearing down on Sixth French Army

7.00 a.m. – C-in-C agrees to Joffre's request to stay in line with French Fifth and Sixth Armies

Midday – C-in-C communicates to Joffre his change his mind: 'I cannot comply with your request to fill gap between Fifth and Sixth Armies' (p. 245)

5.15 p.m. – GHQ issues amended orders for BEF to move south

6.15 p.m. – Operation Order No. 12 unites 4th Division and 19th Infantry Brigade in III. Corps under command of General Pulteney

31 August (Monday)

Aerial reconnaissance reveals that von Kluck's army now turning south-eastwards, after reaching limit of westwards advance; telegrams between GHQ and London reveal C-in-C's determination to withdraw BEF from line to refit

10.00 p.m. – after a flank march through Forest of Compiègne, III. Corps near Verberie, c. five miles from II. Corps, but in touch with French on left

8.50 p.m. – C-in-C issues orders for retreat to continue next day

1 September (Tuesday)

Dawn – engagement at Néry between 1st Cavalry Brigade and German *4th Cavalry Division*

3.00 p.m. – Kitchener arrives in Paris to see Sir John French

7.30 p.m. – Kitchener telegraphs cabinet stating that C-in-C has agreed to 'remain conforming to movements of French army' (p. 264)

2 September (Wednesday)

Marne bridges destroyed on authority of General Joffre

3 September (Thursday)

C-in-C telegraphs Kitchener: 'I fully understand your instructions . . . I am in full accord with Joffre and the French' (p. 264)

4 September (Friday)

10.00 p.m. – Joffre's Instruction no. 6: 'time has come to profit by adventurous position of German *First Army* and concentrate against that Army all efforts of Allied Armies of extreme left. All dispositions will be made during 5th September for beginning attack on 6th.' (p. 543)

5 September (Saturday)

5.15 p.m. – C-in-C's Operation Order No. 17: '. . . enemy has apparently abandoned idea of advancing on Paris and is contracting his front and moving south-eastward . . . Army will advance eastward with a view to attacking . . .' (p. 545)

7 September (Monday)

C-in-C's despatch commends Smith-Dorrien for saving left wing of BEF at Le Cateau (p. 412)

8 September (Tuesday)

7.30 p.m. – C-in-C's Operation Order No. 19: '. . . enemy are continuing their retreat northwards . . . Army will continue advance north to-morrow' (p. 555)

9 September (Wednesday)

8.15 p.m. – C-in-C's Operation Order No. 20: '1 Army to-day forced passage of Marne. . .

General Snow seriously injured in fall with his horse

A Chronology of the 27th Division, and its role in Second Ypres, October 1914–May 1915

This chronology informs General Snow's narrative of the 27th Division, but makes no claims to be comprehensive, in particular with respect to the many actions that comprise the four battles collectively known as Second Ypres. It is based on the account given in *Military Operations, France and Belgium, 1915. Volume I: Winter 1914-1915: Battle of Neuve Chapelle: Battles of Ypres* (1927), to which all page numbers refer, unless otherwise stated.

19 October (Monday)
General Snow returns to England after period of recuperation in Paris

15 November (Sunday)
Snow summoned to War Office by Lord Kitchener – informed on arrival that he is to command 27th Division

19 November (Thursday)
27th Division begins assembling at Winchester

19 December (Saturday)
27th Division marches from Winchester to Southampton for embarkation to France

1 January 1915 (Friday)
27th Division arrives at St Omer

5 January (Tuesday)
27th Division takes over trenches from Kemmel–Wytschaete road north-eastwards to St Eloi, relieving French 32nd Division, over nights of 5/6 and 6/7 January

1–3 February (Monday–Wednesday)

28th Division takes over trenches immediately to left of 27th, from St Eloi to Ypres–Zandvoorde road, relieving French 31st Division, over nights of 1/2 and 2/3 February

18 February (Thursday)

27th and 28th Divisions organised as V. Corps under General Plumer; 83rd, 84th, and 85th Brigades of latter division temporarily relieved in line by 9th (3rd Division), 13th, and 15th (both 5th Division) Brigades

(10–13 March – Battle of Neuve Chapelle)

13 March (Saturday)

Neuve Chapelle offensive closed down through 'fatigue of troops, and, above all, by want of ammunition' (p. 149)

14 March (Sunday)

5.00 p.m. – Germans attack at St Eloi, taking the village, trenches nearby, and 'Mound' from 80th Brigade; counter-attack after midnight recovers village and trenches – part of which have to be given up at daylight

17 March (Wednesday)

Further German attack at St Eloi 'repulsed with great loss' (p. 31)

30 March (Tuesday)

French Tenth Army, to right of BEF, learns from prisoners that large supplies of asphyxiating gas are being kept in cylinders along Zillebeke front

2–8 April (Friday–Thursday)

27th Division moves into salient, occupying sector left of Hill 60 to midway along Polygon Wood

7 April (Wednesday)

Canadian Division assigned to V. Corps from First Army

8–11 April (Thursday–Sunday)

28th Division moves into salient, occupying sector from midway along Polygon Wood to just left of Berlin Wood

15–17 April (Thursday–Saturday)

Canadian Division moves into salient, occupying sector from just left of Berlin Wood to Ypres–Poelcappelle road

15 April (Thursday)

Second Army forwards to GHQ report from its liaison officer with the French indicating imminent use of asphyxiating gas by enemy; senior medical officers in V. Corps discuss gas rumour, but no special action taken

16 April (Friday)

45th (Algerian) Division comes into salient to left of Canadians

Reconnaissance by RFC squadron in light of rumours of impending gas attack reveals nothing out of ordinary, but GHQ learns from Belgian sources that Germans are mass-producing 'mouth protectors . . . against effects of asphyxiating gas' in Ghent

17 April (Saturday)

7.05 p.m. – detonation of mines under German lines signals British attempt on Hill 60; units of the 13th Brigade take the hill and hold it against enemy counter-attacks

18 April (Sunday)

V. Corps issues warning to commanders in salient against enemy action in retaliation for loss of Hill 60; persistent shelling of Ypres by enemy artillery, including seventeen-inch howitzer

20 April (Tuesday)

28th Division HQ moves from Ypres to chateau at Vlamertinghe as a result of shelling of town; of the three British divisions in the salient only the 27th HQ is now based there

21 April (Wednesday)

Inhabitants of Ypres leaving because of shelling; Winston Churchill visits General Snow's HQ

(22–23 April – Battle of Gravenstafel Ridge)

22 April (Thursday)

5.00 p.m. – amid a heavy bombardment of Ypres and the villages to its east, Germans release chlorine gas against the front line around Langemarck held by the French 45th (Algerian) Division; gas is followed by an infantry attack, leading to the collapse of French line from Ypres–Poelcappelle road west to canal around Steenstraat; Canadian Division's left flank entirely exposed

7.00 p.m. – French 'seventy-fives' defending gas-affected area suddenly cease firing

7.30 p.m. – General Snow hears from V. Corps that French right has been 'slightly driven back and that they were organising a counter-attack'

Midnight – 10th Canadians, with 16th Battalion in support, launch successful counter-attack, re-taking Kitchener's Wood; promised French counter-attack fails to materialise

Midnight – enemy attacks sectors held by 27th and 28th Divisions, impeding reinforcement of Canadians' threatened flank

23 April (Friday)

Early morning – 'Geddes' Detachment' and battalions under Brigadier General Turner improvise a defensive line from Ypres–Poelcappelle road towards the canal

2.40 p.m. – Second Army issues orders to V. Corps for a 'general attack between Kitchener's Wood and canal' to begin 3.00 p.m.

2.45 p.m. – artillery opens bombardment in support of attack, which is delayed

4.15 p.m. – O'Gowan's and Geddes' combined assault on enemy lines fails to reach objectives, but advances British positions to some 600 yards from enemy

(24 April–4 May – Battle of St Julien)

24 April (Saturday)

4.00 a.m. – enemy releases thick cloud of gas along 1,000-yard front around apex of Canadian line

9.00 a.m. – General Plumer gives General Snow virtually autonomous command of the corps' reserve around Potijze

1.40 p.m. – 3rd Canadian Brigade obliged to retire and General Snow takes extreme step of ordering 28th Division reserve to Fortuin; with reinforcement from 150th Brigade and Canadians, Fortuin is secured

4.15 p.m. – C-in-C orders Second Army 'at once to restore and hold line about St. Julien' (p. 233) – this is the genesis of 'Hull's attack' at dawn next day

8.00 p.m. – General Alderson gives orders for 'Hull's attack': Operation Order No. 10

(25 April – Gallipoli landings at Cape Helles and Anzac Cove)

25 April (Sunday)

2.45–3.15 a.m. – artillery of 27th and 28th Divisions open in support of 'Hull's attack' at 3.00 a.m., ignorant of its postponement

25 April (Sunday) *continued*

5.30 a.m. – 'Hull's attack' proceeds, but fails to reach objectives

26 April (Monday)

Midday – Second Army's advanced HQ established at Poperhinge; V. Corps HQ also moves that day to Goldfish Chateau, 1½ miles west of Ypres

27 April (Tuesday)

Morning – Smith-Dorrien writes to C-in-C making detailed case for withdrawal to 'GHQ Line' if French 'are not going to make a big push' (p. 401)

2.15 p.m. – CGS telephones Smith-Dorrien: 'Chief does not regard situation nearly so unfavourable as your letter represents . . .' (p. 402)

4.35 p.m. – GHQ sends telegram *en clair* directing Smith-Dorrien to hand over command of all troops in salient to Plumer (transfer effected 5.30 p.m.)

28 April (Wednesday)

7.50 a.m. – GHQ instructs that all troops under Plumer now constitute 'Plumer's Force'

10.00 a.m. – Plumer instructed by C-in-C to 'take such preliminary measures for commencing retirement to-night' (p. 278) to line closer to Ypres

10.00 a.m. (soon after) – French sees General Foch at Cassel, who protests 'vehemently against any thought of withdrawal' (p. 279); French agrees to wait, instructing Plumer to co-operate with planned French attack, but also sending out of salient all non-essential troops and supplies (as Smith-Dorrien had proposed)

29 April (Thursday)

9.30 a.m. – Plumer issues preparatory order for withdrawal over four nights to reduced line: 'the movement will probably commence to-night' (pp. 407–8)

9.30 a.m. – Foch sends notification to Sir John French of postponement of General Putz's planned attack: C-in-C agrees to conform, and keep his endangered troops in the diminished salient

30 April (Friday)

3.00 a.m. – Plumer is informed of Putz's plans for attack; due to begin at 8.00 a.m. it is delayed until 11.15 a.m., and then makes minor gains only

French warns Foch in writing that if attacks that day did not restore French line 'he would that night begin his withdrawal' (p. 285); Foch motors to Hazebrouck and 'at his urgent request' (p. 285) French agrees to a second twenty-four-hour postponement of the withdrawal

1 May (Saturday)

Smith-Dorrien writes to C-in-C asking for an interview on the subject of his command; his letter is unanswered

3.10 p.m. – zero hour of French attack: artillery opens fire but infantry does not leave its trenches; before this is known Foch visits French with news that Joffre has over-ridden him – Ypres sector to be placed on defensive in favour of attacks further south

3.45 p.m. – failure of French attack made known: GHQ orders Plumer to begin withdrawal of troops in east of salient; order received by Plumer 4.00 p.m.

4.00 p.m. – Plumer issues instructions, already prepared, for first stage of withdrawal, to begin at 8.00 p.m.

Night of 1st/2nd May – first stage of withdrawal carried out without incident; Plumer's HQ moved back

2 May (Sunday)

10.45 a.m. – Plumer issues orders for next stage of withdrawal that night

Midday – enemy bombards front held by 4th Division in north of salient

4.30 p.m. – enemy releases gas cloud on three-mile front held by 10th and 12th Brigades; with French and British artillery support, infantry hold line

9.45 p.m. – Plumer confirms orders for withdrawal to continue that night

3 May (Monday)

Dawn – enemy shelling during night becomes persistent and is directed primarily against apex of front near Berlin Wood

7.00 a.m. – long enemy column seen moving westwards towards Passchendaele, indicating imminent attack on 85th Brigade front

11.45 a.m. – Plumer orders final withdrawal of infantry of 27th, 28th, and 4th Divisions, to line Sanctuary Wood front of Hooge–Frezenberg–Mouse Trap Farm–Turco Farm, an average retirement of 4,000 yards; 27th Division HQ moves west of Ypres

3.00 p.m. – threatened German attack develops; enemy gains footing in Berlin Wood, but advances no further, and by 9.00 p.m. attack effectively ended; Plumer proceeds with withdrawal as planned

8.30 p.m. – withdrawal begins of remaining artillery

9.00 p.m. – half of infantry in salient retire

10.30 p.m. – remaining infantry retire to intermediate position, before final phased withdrawal from midnight

4 May (Tuesday)

Early morning – retirement successfully completed, and battle of St Julien effectively ended

5 May (Wednesday)

Germans retake Hill 60, using gas, and withstand a counter-attack that evening from the 13th Brigade, just returned from the salient

6 May (Thursday)

Smith-Dorrien writes to C-in-C, asking again for an interview: 'I have had more to fear from the rear than from the front' (Smith-Dorrien, *Forty-Eight Years*, p. 480)

7.30 p.m. – Smith-Dorrien instructed to hand over command of Second Army to Plumer, and proceed to England next day

7 May (Friday)

6.00 a.m. – 'Plumer's Force' disbanded

(8–13 May – Battle of Frezenberg Ridge)

8 May (Saturday)

7.10 a.m. – intense two-hour bombardment begins of 83rd Brigade front around Frezenberg

*c.*10.00 a.m. – German infantry succeeds, at third attempt, at penetrating 83rd Brigade front

12 May (Wednesday)

Night of 12/13 – 'Cavalry Force' relieves the 28th Division

13 May (Thursday)

3.30 a.m.–1.00 p.m. – incessant enemy artillery fire on front between Hooge and Ypres–St Julien road, held by Cavalry Force and 80th Brigade; 7th Cavalry Brigade forced to retire, but a new line eventually established 1,000 yards in rear of old one

17-19 May (Monday-Wednesday)

27th Division gradually relieved by the 1st Cavalry Divison

(24–25 May – Battle of Bellewaarde Ridge)

24 May (Monday)

2.45 a.m. – gas attack along almost entire length of V. Corps' front, from Turco Farm to south of Hooge

5.00 p.m. – 84th Brigade, the 28th Divisional reserve, counter-attacks

11.00 p.m. – 80th Brigade, from reserve, launches delayed counter-attack in support of 84th, but is forced to retire to 84th Brigade line east of Witte Poort Farm.

26 May (Wednesday)

Night 26/27 – 80th Brigade relieved by 8th Brigade

BIOGRAPHICAL NOTES

An effort has been made to give essential biographical details for everyone mentioned in the text, but it has not been possible to search regimental archives, etc., and so these notes tend to cover only those most prominent. Career details, lists of titles, etc., have of necessity been abbreviated, with the exception of the entry on General Snow. The editors acknowledge their debt to published sources such as *Who Was Who* and the *Oxford Dictionary of National Biography* (*ODNB*).

Allenby, Edmund Henry Hynman (1861–1936). Inspector of cavalry, 1910–14; assumed command of Cavalry Division on outbreak of war, August 1914; succeeded Plumer as commander, V. Corps, 6 May 1915; commander, Third Army, 1915–17; C-in-C, Egyptian Expeditionary Force, 1917–19; conducted victorious campaign in Palestine; appointed field marshal, and cr. 1st Viscount Allenby of Megiddo, 1919; high commissioner for Egypt, 1919–25. Deeply affected by the loss of his son, Michael – an only child, and lieutenant in the RHA – killed in action on Western Front, July 1917. Allenby's report at Le Cateau, early on 26 August 1914, that the enemy was in force close by, and that the Cavalry Division could 'be of little help' in covering II. Corps' retirement, were important factors in deciding Smith-Dorrien to fight.

Allfrey, Captain Henry Irving Rodney (b. 1879). Entered army, 1899; lieutenant, 1900; adjutant, Somerset Light Infantry, 16 November 1907; promoted major, 1 September 1915; General Snow's ADC at outbreak of war, and with him on staff of VII. Corps; later, on staff, Fifth Army.

Balfour, Arthur James (1848–1930). Unionist leader in the Commons, 1891–1911, and nephew of Lord Salisbury, whom he succeeded as prime minister in 1902–5; first lord of the admiralty, 1915–16; foreign secretary, 1916–19; lord president of the council, 1919–22 and 1925–9; cr. Earl, 1922. Balfour affected an air of indifference to many political issues, but critics failed to appreciate his abiding interest in matters of defence.

Barstow, Major John Baillie (1872–1914). Commissioned RE, July 1891; lieutenant, 1894; captain, 1902; killed in action at Bailly bridge, 30 August 1914; he left a wife and four children.

Bulfin, Sir Edward Stanislaus (1862–1939). Commander, 2nd Infantry Brigade, 1913–14; 28th Division, 1914–15; 60th Division, 1915–17; XXI. Corps in Palestine and Syria, 1917–19. Given prestigious command of 2nd Infantry Brigade in June 1913, which he led during opening months of the war; gained 'a reputation among his peers as an outstanding fighting soldier' (Bourne, 'Bulfin', *ODNB*). Commanded newly raised 28th Division during Second Ypres, transferring to Egypt with 60th Division, June 1917. Promoted temporary lieutenant general, August 1917, and given command of XXI. Corps – which, in September 1918, played a key role in Allenby's final offensive in Palestine.

Burnett Hitchcock, Basil Ferguson (1877–1938). Educated at Harrow and Sandhurst (Sword of Honour); joined Sherwood Foresters, 1897; deputy assistant adjutant and quartermaster general, 4th Division, from 1912; DSO, gazetted 9 December 1914, for his action at Haucourt, 26 August, 'for gallantry in rallying troops in disorder and leading them against the enemy, thereby ensuring an orderly evacuation of the village' (Creagh, vol. 2, p. 341); promoted major-general, June 1919.

Churchill, Winston Leonard Spencer (1874–1965). Educated at Harrow and Sandhurst; served with 21st Lancers on Nile Expedition to retake Sudan, 1898; *Morning Post* correspondent in South Africa, 1899–1900; Unionist MP for Oldham, 1900–6 (thereafter, successively, a Liberal, Coalition Liberal, Constitutionalist, and Conservative MP); first lord of the Admiralty, 1911–15; sacked by Asquith, May 1915, he became chancellor of Duchy of Lancaster, before leaving government to command 6th Battalion, Royal Scots Fusiliers, in France, 1915–16; minister of munitions, 1917; held numerous cabinet posts, 1919–29, and returned to Admiralty outbreak of second world war, 1939; prime minister and minister of defence, 1940–5; leader of the opposition, 1945–51; prime minister, 1951–5. Churchill married, September 1908, Clementine Ogilvy *née* Hozier (1885–1977), with whom he had four daughters and one son. The author of many histories, including *The World Crisis* (4 vols., 1923–9).

Cowans, Sir John Steven (1862–1921). Director general, Territorial Forces, 1910–12, and quartermaster general, 1912–19; ex officio, military member of army council; responsible for successful mobilisation of BEF, and later oversaw massive expansion of his department's responsibilities – the corollary of industrialised warfare. Regarded by Lloyd George as 'the most capable soldier thrown up by the War in our Army' (Grieves, 'Cowans', *ODNB*).

Douglas, Charles Whittingham Horsley (1850–1914). Inspector general, Home Forces, 1912–14; CIGS, March–October 1914. A conscientious inspector general, his staff tours 'were regarded as models of their kind' (Spiers, 'Douglas', *ODNB*); became CIGS after resignation of Sir John French; demands of office took a heavy toll of his health, and he died in office, 25 October.

Edmonds, James Edward (1861–1956). Gazetted RE, 1881, after passing out first from RMA, Woolwich; GSO1, War Office, 1909–10; GSO1, 4th Division, 1911–14; later deputy engineer-in-chief, BEF, 1918. Edmonds found General Snow, his commanding officer, 'a formidable and irascible man', but they enjoyed an excellent working relationship, Snow telling him: 'I provide the ginger and you provide the brains' (Falls/Matthew, 'Edmonds', *ODNB*). During the retreat from Mons Edmonds' strength gave way, and after a period of recuperation he was attached to GHQ, where Haig used him 'as a sort of private adviser and father-confessor' (French, *RUSI*, 131:1, p. 60). He retired with the rank of honorary brigadier general. As OC Historical Section, CID, 1919–49, he supervised the official history of the war. Edmonds has been discounted as a malicious gossip, because of his privately expressed but waspish comments about, inter alia, the limitations of Douglas Haig, but he had, by his own admission, 'the clan prejudices of a professional solder'. In the official history at least he had no intention of damaging the reputations of former comrades: 'I am too fond of the old Army to want to do that' he told Liddell Hart in 1930: 'If they weren't intelligent, they were a nice sporting lot' (French, *RUSI*, 131:1, p. 59).

Ensor, Major Howard (b. 1874). Commissioned lieutenant in RAMC, June 1899; served South African War, DSO; deputy assistant director of medical services, 4th Division, August 1914, and later of 3rd Division; later commandant, RAMC School of Instruction, British armies in France.

Eveleigh, Eliott Nial (b. 1890). Second lieutenant, RE, December 1910; lieutenant, August 1913; captain, December 1916; MC and DSO.

Fortescue, Hon. Charles Granville (1861–1951). Gazetted Rifle Brigade, January 1881, and saw service in Burma and Africa before becoming private secretary to secretary of state for war, October 1899; served South African War, 1899–1902 (DSO); brigadier general on staff, Eastern Command, April 1912 to outbreak of war; subsequently with BEF, 22 November 1914 to 25 March 1915; thereafter with Home Forces.

French, John Denton Pinkstone (1852–1925). Served as midshipman, RN, before transferring, 1870, to army; commanded a cavalry division in South African war; as a result of success there promoted substantive lieutenant general, August 1902; the following month given the prestigious Aldershot command (1902–7); inspector general of the forces, 1907–11; CIGS, 1911–14; appointed field marshal, 1913; resigned over 'Curragh affair', March 1914; re-appointed inspector general of the forces, 26 July 1914; informed that he was to be C-in-C, BEF, 30 July 1914; formally resigned this post, 6 December 1915; cr. 1st Viscount of Ypres and of High Lake, 1915; C-in-C of Home Forces, 1915–18; lord lieutenant of Ireland, 1918–21; cr. 1st Earl of Ypres, June 1922. When French landed at Boulogne on 14 August 1914 his force consisted of four infantry divisions and a cavalry division – when he was replaced as C-in-C, roughly seventeen months later, it consisted of three armies. This dramatic expansion illustrates the scale of the problems that French faced, and if, in recent times, there has been greater criticism of his leadership, there has also been more appreciation of the problems that he faced. Immediately after the war French published a memoir, *1914*, which includes an unreliable account of the retreat from Mons, in particular the battle of Le Cateau and its aftermath. The memoir was an attempt at self-justification at the expense of others, notably Sir Horace Smith-Dorrien, and George V was said to have been angered by its 'un-English and ungenerous' nature. Smith-Dorrien was nevertheless among the pall bearers at French's funeral.

Geddes, Augustus David (1866[?]–1915). Colonel of 2nd The Buffs (East Kent Regiment); during Second Ypres Geddes took effective charge of a composite brigade known as 'Geddes' detachment', which played an important role in the defence of the salient; he was killed early on 28 April when a shell hit 13th Brigade headquarters, where he had chanced to spend the night. He was mentioned in despatches, 31 May.

Grierson, James Moncrieff (1859–1914). Director of military operations, 1904–6; commander, 1st Division, 1906–10; GOC Eastern

Command, from 1912. As director of military operations, Grierson was instrumental in promoting closer military ties with France. He was made commander of II. Corps after the outbreak of war, but died of a heart attack near Amiens, 17 August. Kitchener appointed Smith-Dorrien as his replacement, against the wishes of Sir John French, establishing at the outset a major fault line in the high command of the BEF.

Haig, Douglas (1861–1928). Entered Sandhurst, 1884, after Oxford; saw service in India, Sudan, and South African War; director of staff duties at army headquarters, 1907–9; Chief of Staff, India, 1909–12; GOC, Aldershot, 1912–14; Commander, I. Corps, 1914; First Army, 1914–15; C-in-C, Expeditionary Forces in France and Flanders, 1915–19; cr. 1st Earl Haig, 1919; field marshal C-in-C Home Forces, 1919–20. As commander of I. Corps during the retreat from Mons Haig demonstrated a singular determination to keep his force intact, and at a distance from the enemy, until he arrived at ground on which he was prepared to fight. He was able to do this because of the remarkably lax control that Sir John French exercised over his corps commanders, and by the failures of GHQ staff to rectify this. There was no detailed plan of marches, for example, on 24 August 1914, with the result that II. Corps effectively covered the retirement from Mons of I. Corps – the opposite of what the C-in-C had intended.

Haldane, (James) Aylmer Lowthorpe (1862–1950). Cousin of the statesman R. B. Haldane, secretary of state for war, 1905–12. Commissioned into 2nd Gordon Highlanders, 1882, and saw service in India and South African War, 1899–1902; later on staff, Eastern Command, 1909–12; commander, 10th Brigade, April 1912–October 1914; commander, 3rd Division, October 1914–16; commander, VI. Corps, 1916–19; GOC, Mesopotamia, 1919–22; promoted general, 1925. Sir James Grierson considered Haldane 'a first rate brigade commander' who brought the 10th Brigade 'to a high state of efficiency', and General Snow, his divisional commander, also had the highest regard for him, describing him as 'one of the most energetic officers both mentally and physically whom I have ever met . . . He has the confidence of his subordinates and I am fortunate in having in him a brigade commander I can put absolute trust in both as regards loyalty and action' (Scott, pp. 3–4). This confidence was not reciprocated. Haldane considered Snow 'no tactician', and after a staff tour in May 1913 wrote that his chief 'again showed his ignorance of any tactical principles', adding: 'He, however, was quite pleased with himself' (Scott, p. 3). Haldane was 'an excellent example of the type of technocratic general through whose efforts the First World War on the western front was won' (Simpson, 'Haldane', *ODNB*). He was the author of, inter alia, *A Brigade of the Old Army* (1920).

Hamilton, Hubert Ion Wetherall (1861–1914). Entered Queen's Regiment, 1880; OC, North Midland Division, 1911–14; GOC, 3rd Division in France; Hamilton was 'very definite' on the eve of Le Cateau that his men 'could not move before 9 a.m.', a factor that weighed heavily with his close friend Smith-Dorrien (Smith-Dorrien, *Forty-Eight Years*, p. 400). The latter was deeply affected by Hamilton's death, from a shrapnel wound, on 14 October 1914.

Hare, Robert Hugh (b. 1872). Gazetted RA, July 1886; served in South African War (DSO); brigade major, RA, 27th Division, 17 November 1914–26 March 1915; later commander, 83rd Infantry Brigade, British Salonika Force.

Hunter-Weston, Aylmer (1864–1940). Joined RE, 1884, served in South African War, 1899–1901, gaining the DSO for his services there, and notably his raids against the Boers, which Conan Doyle lauded in his history of the war; promoted brigadier general, February 1914, and OC, 11th Infantry Brigade, which he took to France; subsequently GOC, 29th Division at Gallipoli landings, April 1915, and of VIII. Corps, Dardanelles and in France; he retained command of VIII. Corps to the end of the war, in spite of its inconsistent record of performance; elected MP (Coalition) for North Ayrshire, October 1916, while still on Western Front.

Kitchener, Horatio Herbert (1850–1916). Educated at an English boarding school in Switzerland, where he became fluent in French and German, Kitchener served with a French field ambulance in the latter stages of the Franco-Prussian war; commissioned RE, 1871; as sirdar of Egyptian army, 1892, planned and led the 'River war' to retake the Sudan, 1896–8, and was briefly governor general there; cr. 1st Baron Kitchener of Khartoum, 1898; Chief of Staff of forces in South Africa, 1899–1900; C-in-C, 1900–2; cr. 1st Viscount Kitchener of Khartoum, 1902; C-in-C, Indian Army, 1902–9; field marshal, 1909; member of CID, 1910; British agent and consul general in Egypt, 1911–14; cr. 1st Earl Kitchener, 1914;

became secretary of state for war, 6 August 1914; drowned in the sinking, by a mine off Orkney, of HMS *Hampshire*, 5 June 1916. Kitchener's visionary act in creating the 'New Armies' was a direct corollary of his belief that the war would be long, and would require an unprecedented continental commitment from Britain. In order to train the new armies he retained in England some of the officers and NCOs of the original Expeditionary Force, a policy that Henry Wilson regarded as 'scandalous', but which Churchill considered 'the greatest' of the services that Kitchener rendered his country at this time, and one 'which no one of lesser authority than he could have performed' (Brock, *Asquith-Stanley*, p. 215, n. 7). Kitchener proved an awkward cabinet colleague, but he had a clear sense of strategy, and when he learned that Sir John French was contemplating withdrawing the BEF from the line to refit, at the end of August 1914, he travelled to Paris, 1 September, to dissuade him, attending their meeting symbolically attired in his field marshal's uniform.

Liveing, Charles Hawker (b. 1872). Joined RA, 1892, becoming lieutenant, 1895; commanded 135th Battery, XXXII. Brigade, RFA, at outbreak of war; awarded DSO 'For bravery and devotion in withdrawing guns by hand under a heavy fire near Ligny, France, on 26 Aug. 1914' (Creagh, vol. 2, p. 342).

Longley, John Raynsford (1867–1953). Joined East Surrey Regiment, 1887; lieutenant colonel, 1911; colonel, 1914; commander, 82nd Brigade, 27th Division[?]; later served in Macedonia, Egypt, and Palestine; colonel of the East Surrey Regiment, 1920–39.

Macfarlane, Duncan Alwyn (1857–1941). Entered army as lieutenant, 1st West India Regiment, 1882; served in South African war (DSO); CO, Seaforth and Cameron Infantry Brigade (TF), 1911–14; 81st Infantry Brigade, 1914–15; inspector of infantry, 1915–18.

Mildmay, Francis ('Frank') Bingham Mildmay (1861–1947). Successively Liberal, Liberal Unionist, and Conservative member for Totnes Division, Devon, 1885–1922; served, 1914–19 (despatches four times), and, inter alia, General Snow's interpreter during Second Ypres; cr. 1st Baron Mildmany of Flete, 1922.

Milne, George Francis (1866–1948). Brigadier general commanding 4th Divisional Artillery, Woolwich, 1913–14; later GSO1, III. Corps; headquarters staff, Second Army; commander, 27th Division, and XVI.

Corps; from May 1916, C-in-C, British Salonika Force; later appointed field marshal, 1928, and CIGS, 1926–33; cr. Baron Milne of Salonika, 1933.

Montgomery(-Massingberd), Archibald (Armar) (1871–1947). Commissioned into RFA, 1891; entered Staff College, Camberley, 1905; instructor, August 1914; appointed GSO2, 4th Division, August 1914; Chief of Staff to Sir Henry Rawlinson on Western Front, 1914–18, and played a key role in the Fourth Army's success in the decisive final offensive of August–November 1918; deputy Chief of Staff to Rawlinson when latter C-in-C in India, 1920–2; later field marshal, 1935, and CIGS, 1933–6. After General Snow's original GSO1, Colonel J. E. Edmonds, fell sick in August 1914 Montgomery deputised for him, and he became GSO1 to Rawlinson when the latter took over from Snow in September; they forged a successful partnership that lasted virtually to the war's end. Assumed name Montgomery-Massingberd in 1926.

Murray, Archibald (James) (1860–1945). Entered 27th Regiment, 1879; director of military training, general staff, War Office, 1907–12; inspector of infantry, 1912–14; deputy-CIGS, then chief, 1915; GOC, Egypt and Palestine, 1916–17; at Aldershot, 1917–19. As Sir John French's CGS, Murray worked ceaselessly during the Retreat, and fainted from exhaustion while at his desk on the morning of Le Cateau. In January 1915 he was sent back to England to rest. According to one authority Murray 'lacked the moral fibre or physical stamina for his post', the consequences of which were serious: not only was French ill-served, 'but Murray's inability to assert himself left the field clear for [Henry] Wilson' (Holmes, *Field-Marshal*, p. 218). Murray later served as C-in-C in Egypt, 1916–17; he was recalled after the failure of his two offensives against Gaza, March and April 1917.

Plumer, Herbert Charles Onslow (1857–1932). Entered York and Lancaster Regiment, 1876; quartermaster general and third military member of Army Council, 1904–5; GOC, Northern Command, 1911–14; V. Corps, January–May 1915; Second Army, BEF, 1915–17; general, 1916; GOC, Italian Expeditionary Force, November 1917–March 1918; Second Army, BEF, March–December 1918; Army of the Rhine, December 1918–April 1919; field marshal, 1919; governor and C-in-C, Malta, 1919–24; high commissioner for Palestine, 1925–8; cr. Vicount Plumer of Messines, 1929. As QMG Plumer identified himself too closely with the proposed army reforms of the Unionist Party, and with the change of government in 1905 he was ousted: 'from then on he took great care to present himself always as loyal both to his military superiors and to the army as an institution' (Badsey, 'Plumer', *ODNB*). He had rebuilt his career by the outbreak of war, and was Sir John French's choice to succeed Sir James Grierson, commander of II. Corps, who died in France on 17 August. Lord Kitchener, however, sent General Sir Horace Smith-Dorrien instead, and Plumer had to wait until January 1915 before being given a command on the Western Front, with V. Corps. He was the passive beneficiary of French's vendetta against Smith-Dorrien, assuming command – over Smith-Dorrien's head – of all British and imperial troops in the salient on 27 April, and finally replacing him as commander of Second Army on 6 May. Plumer scored a notable success in the attack at Messines, 7–14 June 1917, from which he later took his title. He was popular with his troops and 'appears to have made a genuine effort to plan on the basis of holding his own casualties down', albeit 'not at the expense of jeopardising his own position with his superiors' (Badsey, 'Plumer', *ODNB*).

Prowse, Charles Bertie (b. 1869). Second Lieutenant, Somerset Light Infantry, October 1893; served in South African War, 1899–1902; major, April 1914; awarded DSO, gazetted 3 June 1916; died of wounds when temporary brigadier general of the 11th Infantry Brigade, 1 July 1916.

Pulteney, William Pulteney (1861–1941). Second Lieutenant, Scots Guards, 1881; OC, 16th Infantry Brigade, 1908–9; 6th Division, Irish Command, 1910–14; III. Corps, 1914–February 1918; GOC, XXIII. Corps (home defence), February 1918–April 1919. Pulteney was promoted temporary lieutenant general on 5 August, and given command of III. Corps. He was sent home in February 1918 after the official inquiry into the failure to stem the German counter-attack at Cambrai, 30 November 1917. Contemporaries were surprised that he lasted this long: according to his Chief of Staff in 1917, Charles Bonham-Carter, Pulteney was 'the most completely ignorant general I served during the war and that is saying a lot' (quoted in Stearn, 'Pulteney', *ODNB*).

Rawlinson, Henry Seymour (1864–1925). Entered 60th King's Royal Rifles, 1884; commandant, Staff College, 1903–6; temporary commander, 4th Division, September 1914; OC, Antwerp force (7th Division and 3rd Cavalry Division), October 1914; later GOC, IV. Corps, and Fourth Army; cr. 1st Baron Rawlinson, 1919; commanded forces in Northern Russia, 1919; GOC, Aldershot, 1920; C-in-C of the army in India, 1920. Unemployed and on half-pay at outbreak of war, Rawlinson was made director of recruiting under Kitchener, and in late September was appointed temporary GOC of 4th Division, following General Snow's injury; in October led the abortive mission to relieve Antwerp, falling back with his force to Ypres, where it was centrally involved in the first battle there. Played a key role in the Somme, and the successful counter-offensive of August 1918.

Reed, Colonel Hamilton Lyster, VC (1869–1931). Gazetted to RFA, 16 February 1888, becoming captain 1898; served in South African War, 1899–1902, gaining VC at Colenso, 15 December 1899; on General Staff at army headquarters before the war; General Snow's GSO1 at Second Ypres, where he was wounded, 29 April; appointed temporary brigadier general, June 1915; commanded 15th (Scottish) Division, 1917–19; major-general, 1919.

Robb, Major-General Sir Frederick Spencer (1858–1948). Gazetted to 68th Light Infantry, 1880; assistant adjutant general, army headquarters, 1902–4; GOC, 11th Infantry Brigade and Colchester garrison, 1905–9; major-general in charge of administration, Aldershot, 1910–14; inspector general of communications, BEF, 1914; military secretary to secretary of state for war, 1914–16; in charge of administration, Eastern Command, 1916–19.

Simms, John Morrow (1854–1934). Chaplain; served in Nile Expedition, 1898, and South Africa, 1900–1; principal chaplain, BEF, 1914–20; moderator of the Presbyterian Church of Ireland, 1919–20; MP (CU) North Down (now Co. Down), 1922–31. As principal chaplain Simms exercised a 'gentle if firm rule' during the early stages of the war, when 'the greatest harmony' prevailed. From 1915, after an agitation at home, the pastoral care of the troops was treated on denominational lines, and the number of chaplains in France increased that year and the next. According to the adjutant general 'the numbers were excessive' (Macready, pp. 229–30).

Smith, Frederick Edwin ('F. E.') (1872–1930). Barrister and Unionist MP for Walton, Liverpool, 1906–18; after a brilliant maiden speech, in March

1906, 'F.E.' became one of the leading political figures of his generation; deeply involved in Unionist opposition to the Home Rule movement and reform of the House of Lords in the years before the Great War; solicitor general, 1915; attorney general, 1915–19; cr. Baron Birkenhead, 1919; viscount, 1921; lord chancellor, 1919–22; cr. Earl, 1922; secretary for India, 1924–8.

Smith-Dorrien, Horace Lockwood (1858–1930). Entered 95th Derby Regiment, 1876; one of the few British survivors of the battle of Isandlwana, 1879; GOC, Southern Command, 1912–14; commander, II. Corps, then Second Army, BEF, 1914–15; C-in-C, East African Forces, 1915–16; govenor of Gibraltar, 1918–September 1923. Smith-Dorrien was appointed commander of II. Corps after the sudden death, on 17 August 1914, of Sir James Grierson, and against the wishes of the Commander-in-Chief, who had wanted Herbert Plumer instead. Smith-Dorrien took up his command on 21 August, and two days later his force encountered von Kluck's First Army at Mons. He took the courageous decision to stand at Le Cateau, 26 August, and – though outgunned and outnumbered – his forces delivered the 'stopping blow' that he had intended. In his dispatch of 7 September Sir John French gave to Smith-Dorrien the credit that was his due, but the pre-war rivalries later reasserted themselves, and French pursued his feud against Smith-Dorrien more determinedly than ever. Matters came to a head during Second Ypres when, as commander of Second Army, Smith-Dorrien advocated withdrawing to the shorter 'GHQ Line', once it was clear that the French would not restore their line following the gas attack of 22 April. The C-in-C 'mainly on political grounds, thought otherwise' (*Army Quarterly*, October 1930, p. 10), and on 6 May Smith-Dorrien was ordered to hand over command of Second Army to Plumer and return to England next day. Though he was given future employment, he was denied the opportunities for advancement that came to his peers, as well as the honours and enrichments that came with victory. Defamed in French's war memoir *1914*, published in 1919, he was denied an opportunity publicly to clear his name, but was permitted to put on record his version of events, and with the assistance of George V twenty-eight copies of a privately printed defence were circulated to influential figures in society. The publication of the first version of the official history, in 1922, vindicated Smith-Dorrien, a process subtly reinforced in the revised edition of 1933. His own *Memories of Forty-Eight Years' Service*, published in the year of French's death, contains a dignified defence of his position.

Snow, Thomas D'Oyly (1858–1940). Born at Newton Valence, Hampshire on 5 May 1858, the eldest son of the Reverend George D'Oyly Snow and his wife Maria Jane *née* Barlow; educated at Eton, and St John's College, Cambridge; in 1879 commissioned in the Somerset Light Infantry, then based in South Africa; saw service in Anglo-Zulu war, 1879, and in the Nile campaign, 1884–5, being severely wounded at El Gubat, January 1885; promoted captain, 1887; attended Staff College, 1892–3; in 1895 appointed a brigade major at Aldershot; in 1897 promoted major in the Royal Inniskilling Fusiliers, and on 12 January of that year married Charlotte Geraldine, second daughter of Major-General John Talbot Coke of Trusley, Derbyshire; they had two sons and two daughters; during Nile campaign of 1898 participated in the battle of Atbara; in April 1899 made second in command of the 2nd Battalion the Northamptonshire Regiment, then in India. He thus missed the Second South African War, which proved a learning ground for many of his peers. Promoted substantive lieutenant colonel, he returned to England in March 1903, and in June of that year was promoted colonel, becoming assistant quartermaster general of the Eastern Command. He remained in this command until 1914, and was successively assistant adjutant general (1905); brigadier general, general staff (1906); GOC, 11th Infantry Brigade (1909–10); promoted major-general (1910); and GOC, 4th Division, 1911–14. The 4th Division fought with distinction at Le Cateau, and Snow kept it together during the exhausting retreat. On 9 September he broke his pelvis when he fell with his horse, an injury that troubled him for the rest of his life. Such was the demand for experienced commanders at the front, however, that he was pressed back into service by Kitchener before he was properly well again. In November 1914 he took command of the newly formed 27th Division and in December returned to France. The 27th Division was in the line at St Eloi, south of Ypres, but moved into the salient itself just before the outbreak of the second battle there, 22 April–25 May 1915. Snow was the only divisional commander to remain with his division in the battle zone, keeping his headquarters at Potijze until the great withdrawal on 3 May 1915. His successful role in the defence of Ypres, and in the retreat from Mons, marked him out as an operational commander of experience and nerve, and after the 27th Division was taken out of the line at Ypres he was given command of VII. Corps, which he led for the remainder of his time on the Western Front. Snow was made KCB in 1915 (gazetted 23 June), and KCMG in 1917. On the opening day of the Somme Snow was ordered, by Haig, to mount a diversionary attack on Gommecourt with two divisions – the 46th and 56th. Controversy surrounds this attack and Snow's role in it: what is beyond doubt is that it was a disaster. Arguably Snow sacrificed his subordinate, Major-General the Hon. Montagu-Stuart-Wortley, GOC, 46th Division, to save himself. Snow went on to lead VII. Corps at Arras, April 1917, and Cambrai later that year, when VII. Corps remained on a defensive footing during Third Army's unprecedented breakthrough on 20 November. Snow afterwards repeatedly warned of the danger of a counter-attack on his front, but his warnings were not heeded, and the enemy scored a startling success with its attack on 30 November. Snow helped to coordinate a makeshift defence that stemmed the German advance after the first day, but the failings of British operations at Cambrai later became the subject of an official inquiry, and scrutiny fell on Snow's role. In mid-December he had a long interview with General Byng, and shortly afterwards asked to be relieved of his command: he was by this time increasingly lame, and he recognised that the time had come to appoint someone physically more able. He was promoted lieutenant general in the New Year, in recognition of his 'distinguished service in the field' (*The Times*, 1 January 1918), and arrived back in England on 4 January 1918. On his return he was put in charge of the Western Command, 1918–19. He retired from the army in September 1919 and lived in Kensington, devoting much of his time to charitable work, and becoming chairman of the Crippled Boys' Home for Training. Snow was also colonel of the Somerset light infantry, 1919–29. He died at his home, 3 Kensington Gate, London, on 30 August 1940.

Taylor, F. P. S. (nd). Lieutenant colonel, Army Service Corps, and assistant adjutant and quartermaster general, 4th Division, August 1914.

Turner, Richard Ernest William (b. 1871), VC. Lieutenant, Royal Canadian Dragoons, and served in South African War; created DSO, and awarded VC, both gazetted April 1901 – VC for his action on 7 November 1900: twice wounded, deployed his men, and saved his guns against Boers; in command of the 'Canadian Brigade of Infantry' in European war; created KCMG, 1917, and recalled to England; appointed GOC, Canadian Forces in GB.

Vallentin, Major Henry Edward (b. 1870). Entered RA, February 1889, becoming lieutenant, 1892; as commander of the 27th Battery (XXXII. Brigade, RFA), awarded DSO, 'For bravery and devotion in withdrawing guns by hand under a heavy fire near Ligny, France, on 26 Aug. 1914' (Creagh, vol. 2, p. 326). Two of his sergeants, and five of his gunners, were awarded the DCM for this action. Promoted lieutenant colonel, 30 October 1914, and was later assistant adjutant general at the War Office.

Wilson, Henry Hughes (1864–1922). Entered Royal Irish Regiment, 1884, transferring to Rifle Brigade in same year; director of military operations, 1910–14; promoted major-general, 1913; assistant Chief of General Staff to Lord French, 1914; chief liaison officer with the French, 1915 (and, briefly, 1917); commanded IV. Corps, Béthune, 1915–16; KCB, 1915; GOC, Eastern District, 1917; permanent military representative to allied supreme war council, 1917–18, CIGS, 1918–22; GCB, 1918; field marshal, 1919. A strong Unionist, he was elected MP for North Down, 1922, but was assassinated outside his London home by Irish republicans shortly afterwards. Remembered as one of the ablest staff officers of his generation, he believed in the inevitability of a Franco-German war, and, being a strong Francophile, was instrumental in preparing the British Army for deployment on the Continent alongside the French. On the outbreak of war he became sub-CGS: Sir John French wanted him as his chief, but political considerations prevented this, Asquith in particular distrusting 'the constant intriguing of that serpent Wilson' (Brock, *Asquith-Stanley*, p. 342). Nevil Macready, the adjutant general, recalled that during a particularly dark hour of the retreat, when headquarters were at Noyon, Wilson had 'walked slowly up and down the long room with that comical, whimsical expression on his face habitual to him, clapping his hands softly together to keep time as he chanted in a low tone, "We shall never get there; we shall never get there". As he passed me, I said: "Where, Henri?" and he chanted on: "To the sea, to the sea, to the sea." It was just his way to keep up everybody's spirits, some of the younger members of the Staff not always remembering the golden rule of appearing cheerful under any and every turn of circumstance' (Macready, p. 206).

GLOSSARY

AAG – Assistant Adjutant General

ADC – Aide-de-Camp

ASC – Army Service Corps

BEF – British Expeditionary Force

CGS – Chief of the General Staff

CID – Committee of Imperial Defence

CIGS – Chief of the Imperial General Staff

CO – Commanding Officer

CRA – Commanding Royal Artillery

CRE – Commanding Royal Engineers

Cuirassiers – mounted cavalry, from the French *cuirasse*, or armoured breastplate, originally worn by such troops

DAAG – Deputy Assistant Adjutant General

DADMS – Deputy Assistant Director of Medical Services

DAQMG – Deputy Adjutant and Quartermaster General

DCLI – Duke of Cornwall's Light Infantry

DCM – Distinguished Conduct Medal

DSO – Distinguished Service Order

Gazette, the – the *London Gazette*: official newspaper carrying public notices, including lists of army promotions and honours, which are dated by the issue of the *Gazette* in which they appear – thus 'gazetted'

GHQ – General Headquarters

GHQ Line – defensive line to the east of Ypres at the time of the Second Battle; it ran northwards from Zillebeke Lake, roughly two miles south-east of Ypres, to Wieltje, about two miles north-east, and then curved north-westwards to the Ypres–Langemarck road. It consisted of a series of large redoubts, thirty yards along, placed every 400–500 yards, each garrisoned by around fifty men; eventually the line was connected by fire trenches, the whole being protected by thick wire, with openings at tracks and traverse points; strategically well sited, it had good fields of fire

GOC – General Officer Commanding

GSO – General Staff Officer (GSO1 is General Staff Officer, Grade 1)

HE – High Explosive

heliograph – a signalling apparatus employing a movable mirror to reflect the sunlight in flashes

Hill 60 – highest of the three mounds (the others were the 'Caterpillar' and 'Dump') created when engineers made a cutting through the Ypres ridge for the Ypres–Comines railway, close to Zwarteleen, and approximately two and a half miles south-east of Ypres. It was dubbed 'Hill 60' by the British because of its height in metres, as indicated on contour maps; its elevation made it strategically important, and it was taken by the Germans from the French on 10 December 1914, by the British from the Germans on 17 April 1915, and by the Germans from the British on 5 May 1915

impedimenta – the travelling equipment of an army

KCB – Knight Commander of the Order of the Bath

KOSB – King's Own Scottish Borderers

KRR – King's Royal Rifles

KRRC – King's Royal Rifle Corps

KSLI – King's Shropshire Light Infantry

LI – Light Infantry

metalled road – a smooth road made of stone chippings and tar; much preferred by British troops to pavé (see below)

Menin Gate – gateway on the eastern edge of Ypres leading to Menin, eleven miles east-south-east; tens of thousands of British troops passed through the gate on their way to the front, and in 1927 Field Marshal Lord Plumer unveiled the memorial arch that stands there today, upon which is inscribed the names of nearly 55,000 Australian, British, Canadian, Indian, and South African dead (New Zealanders are remembered on individual memorials throughout the salient)

NCO – Non-Commissioned Officer

OC – Officer in Charge

Ourcq, battle of – beginning 5 September 1914, the prelude to the battle of the Marne, during which General Maunoury's Sixth Army engaged the German *IV Reserve Corps*

pavé – a French or Belgian cobblestone road, painful underfoot during long journeys and consequently loathed by British infantry

PPCLI – Princess Patricia's Canadian Light Infantry

QMG – Quartermaster General

Q Officer – Quartermaster Officer

Q Staff – Quartermaster Staff

RB – Rifle Brigade

RE – Royal Engineer(s)

RFC – Royal Flying Corps

redoubt – an outwork or defensive construct, usually square or many-sided, and without flanking defences

'the Retreat' – specifically, the retreat of the BEF from Mons to the Marne, 24 August to 5 September 1914

revetting – the practice of facing a wall or embankment with supporting masonry, common in fortifications

RFA – Royal Field Artillery

RHA – Royal Horse Artillery

salient, the – the pronounced curve in the front line around Ypres, with the line prescribing a semi-circle bulging north and east; before the opening of Second Ypres, 22 April 1915, the front was over five miles from the town, north-east, but at the end of the battle the salient had contracted greatly, the front then being only two miles north and east of Ypres

Scherpenberg, the – high ground to the north-west of Kemmel

Second Ypres – commonly used collective term for the four battles before Ypres, 22 April–25 May, which are defined by the Battles Nomenclature Committee as: 22–23 April: Gravenstafel Ridge; 24 April–4 May: St Julien; 8–13 May: Frezenberg Ridge; 24–25 May: Bellewaarde Ridge

'seventy-five' (or 'soixante-quinze') – renowned French 75-mm quick-firing gun, highly effective and extensively used by the French army during the First World War; it had an advanced recoil system, which meant that it did not have to be re-aimed during firing, and could deliver fifteen rounds per minute on target

shrapnel – as often used by General Snow, shorthand for 'shrapnel shell', and distinct from 'high explosive': the former exploded above the ground, showering lethal projectiles (sometimes called 'bullets') while the latter generally exploded on, or soon after, contact, with a single devastating explosion; the shells had different tactical uses, and ideally artillery had plentiful access to both – in the early stages of the war the British had plentiful access to neither

Stellenbosching – the arbitrary or abrupt removal of an officer from his command; dates from the Boer War, when victims were sent to the army camp at Stellenbosch

Territorials – see below, 'TF'

TF – Territorial Force, created during the army reforms of 1907 as the main reserve of the regular army; over 300,000 strong, it had the same structure as the regular force, its regiments organised into fourteen divisions, commanded by serving major-generals, with small staffs drawn from the regular army

trench foot/feet – debilitating but preventable illness, sometimes synonymous with frostbite, but often attributable to the wet; according to Nevil Macready, adjutant general in 1914, it 'resulted from prolonged immersion in the cold water with which the trenches were more or less filled'; over 20,000 men were affected, but most were soon cured, and later cases 'were generally traceable to want of supervision and neglect to carry out the precautions laid down' (Macready, *Annals*, p. 227)

Uhlans – generic British term for German cavalry, much in evidence at the beginning of the war

Select Bibliography and Note on Sources

This is a select list of useful secondary sources, although this is not meant to be comprehensive. The first reference to a source in the text is always given in full, but subsequent references to the same source are abbreviated to simply the author's name, or the author's name and a shortened title when multiple titles are involved.

I. Primary sources

The two memoirs presented are based on copies in the Imperial War Museum: i) 'The Story of the 4th Div. B.E.F. Aug. & Sep. 1914 Maj. Gen. T. D'O. Snow C.B.' Box 76/79/1 [5]; ii) '27th Division. Nov. 1914 to June 1915. T. D'O. S.' 76/79/1 [6]. The IWM also holds copies of the two volumes of General Snow's 'Letters from France': volume one, 10 August 1914– 31 December 1915, Box 76/79/1 [3]; and volume two, 1 January 1916– 31 December 1917, Box 76/79/1 [4]. There are, in addition, an account of 'The Desert Campaign 1884-1885, By Lt. T. D'O. Snow, The Somerset Light Infantry...' Box 76/79/1 [1], and a volume of 'Letters from the Soudan – 1898' Box 76/79/1 [2].

We have also made use of the following, in the National Archives: 2nd Essex War Diary, PRO WO/95/1505; 1st Rifle Brigade War Diary, PRO WO/95/1496; Somerset Light Infantry War Diary August 1914, PRO WO/95/1499.

II. Secondary sources

The Army Quarterly, vol. XXI, No. 1, October 1930

Atkinson C. T., *Royal Hampshire Regiment 1914–1918* (Naval and Military Press, Uckfield, E. Sussex, 2004)

Badsey, Stephen, 'Dorrien, Sir Horace Lockwood Smith- (1858–1930)', *ODNB*, OUP, Sept 2004

—— 'Plumer, Herbert Charles Onslow, first Viscount Plumer (1857–1932)', *ODNB*, OUP, Sept 2004

Ballard, C., *Smith-Dorrien* (Constable and Co., London, 1931)

Beckett, I. F. W. and Corvi, Stephen J., *Haig's Generals* (Pen and Sword, Barnsley, 2006)

Bidwell, Shelford and Graham, Dominick, *Fire-power: The British Army Weapons and Theories of War, 1904–1945* (George Allen and Unwin Ltd, London, 1982)

Bird, A., *Gentlemen, We Will Stand and Fight: Le Cateau 1914* (Cromwell, 2008)

Bond, Brian and Cave, Nigel (eds), *Haig: A Reappraisal 70 Years On* (Leo Cooper, Barnsley, 1999)

Bourne, J. M., 'Bulfin, Sir Edward Stanislaus (1862–1939)', *ODNB*, OUP, Sept 2004; online edn, May 2006

Brice, Beatrix, *The Battle Book of Ypres* (John Murray, London, 1927)

Bridges, Lieutenant-General Sir Tom, *Alarms and Excursions: Reminiscences of a Soldier* (Longmans Green and Co., London, 1938)

Brock, Michael and Brock, Eleanor (eds), *H. H. Asquith: Letters to Venetia Stanley* (Oxford University Press, Oxford, 1985); abbreviated in text to *Asquith–Stanley*

Buchan, John, *Francis and Riversdale Grenfell: A Memoir* (Thomas Nelson and Sons Ltd, London, 1920)

Buckland, R. U. H., 'Demolitions carried out at Mons and during the retreat, 1914', in *The Royal Engineers Journal*, vol. XLVI, (March) 1932, pp. 18–39, 220–50

Callwell, C. E., *Field-Marshal Sir Henry Wilson: His Life and Diaries* (Cassell and Company Ltd, London, 1927)

Cassar, George H., *The Tragedy of Sir John French* (Associated University Presses, London, 1985)

Cave, Nigel and Sheldon, Jack, *Le Cateau, 26 August 1914* (Pen and Sword, Barnsley, 2008)

Charteris, John, *At G.H.Q.* (London, Cassell, 1931)

Clutterbuck, L. A. and Dooner, W.T. (eds), *The Bond of Sacrifice: A Biographical Record of all British Officers who Fell in the Great War: Volume I, Aug.-Dec. 1914* (The Anglo-African Publishing Contractors, London, 1916)

Creagh, Sir O'Moore and Humphris, E. M. (eds), *The V.C. and D.S.O.: A Complete Record of All Those Officers, Non-Commissioned Officers and Men of His Majesty's Naval, Military and Air Forces Who Have Been Awarded Those Decorations* (Standard Art Book Co. Ltd., London, 3 vols., c.1924)

Cruttwell, C. R. M. F., *History of the Great War 1914–1918* (Clarendon Press, Oxford, 1934)

Dixon, John, *Magnificent but not War: The Battle for Ypres, 1915* (Leo Cooper, Pen and Sword, Barnsley, 2003)

Edmonds, James E., *History of the Great War Based on Official Documents –
Military Operations France and Belgium, 1914: Volume I: Mons, the Retreat
to the Seine, the Marne and the Aisne, August–October 1914* (Macmillan,
London, 1922; and third edition, 1933); abbreviated in text to '*MO,
1914*, v. 1'.

— and Wynne, G. C., *History of the Great War Based on Official Documents ...
Military Operations, France and Belgium, 1915. Volume I: Winter 1914–1915:
Battle of Neuve Chapelle: Battles of Ypres* (Macmillan & Co., London, 1927)
; abbreviated in text to '*MO, 1915*, v. 1'.

Falls, Cyril, *and Matthew*, H. C. G., 'Edmonds, Sir James Edward (1861–
1956)', *ODNB*, OUP, Sept 2004

Ferris, John, *The British Army and Signals Intelligence during the First World War*
(Alan Sutton for the Army Records Society, Stroud, 1992)

French, David, '"Official but not History?" Sir James Edmonds and the
official history of the great war', *The RUSI Journal* (1986), 131:1,
pp. 58–63

French, John, *The Despatches of Sir John French: I. Mons, II. The Marne, III. The
Aisne, IV. Flanders* (Chapman & Hall, London, 1914)

—*1914* (Constable and Co. Ltd, London, 1919)

Gleichen, E., *Infantry Brigade: 1914* (Leonaur, Driffield, E. Yorkshire,
2007)

Grieves, Keith, 'Cowans, Sir John Steven (1862–1921)', *ODNB*, OUP, Sept
2004; online edn, Jan 2008

Haldane, Aylmer, *A Brigade of the Old Army, 1914* (Edward Arnold, London,
1920)

Hamilton, Ernest W., *The First Seven Divisions: Being a Detailed Account of the
Fighting From Mons to Ypres* (Hurst and Blackett Ltd, London, 1916)

Hildebrand, A., 'Recollections of Sir Horace Smith-Dorrien at Le Cateau,
August, 1914', in *The Army Quarterly*, vol. XXI, No. 1, October 1930,
pp. 15–19.

Holmes, Richard, *The Little Field-Marshal, Sir John French* (Jonathan Cape,
London, 1981)

— *Riding the Retreat: Mons to Marne: 1914 Revisited* (Pimlico, London, 2007)

Holt, Tonie and Holt, Valmai, *Battlefield Guide to the Western Front – North*
(Pen and Sword, Barnsley, 2007)

Hopkinson, E. C., *Spectamur Agendo* (Privately Printed, 1926)

Jeffrey, K., *Field Marshal Sir Henry Wilson: A Political Soldier* (Oxford University
Press, Oxford, 2010)

Kuhl, von, '(1921) The Operations of the British Army, August–September
1914', *The RUSI Journal*, 66:462, pp. 293–303

Lomas, David, *First Ypres 1914: The Birth of Trench Warfare* (Osprey Publishing Ltd, Oxford, 1998)

MacDonald, A., *A Lack of Offensive Spirit: The 46th (North Midland) Division at Gommecourt, 1st July 1916* (Iona, 2008)

Macready, Nevil, *Annals of an Active Life* (Hutchinson & Co., London, 2 vols., c.1924)

Montgomery, B. L., *The Memoirs of Field Marshal Montgomery* (Pen and Sword, Barnsley, 2010)

Osburn, Arthur, *Unwilling Passenger* (Faber & Faber Ltd., London, 1932)

Pottle, Mark (ed.), *Champion Redoubtable: The Diaries and Letters of Violet Bonham Carter, 1914–1945* (Weidenfeld and Nicolson, London, 1998

— and Ledingham, John (eds), *We Hope to Get Word Tomorrow: The Garvin Family Letters, 1914–1916* (Pen and Sword, Barnsley, 2009)

Purdom, C. B. (ed.), *Everyman at War: Sixty Personal Narratives of the War* (J. M. Dent & Sons Ltd., London, 1930)

Robbins, Simon, *British Generalship on the Western Front 1914–1918: Defeat into Victory* (Frank Cass, Abingdon, Oxon, 2005)

Scott, Peter T., *'Dishonoured' The 'Colonels' Surrender' at St. Quentin, The Retreat from Mons, August 1914* (Tom Donovan, London, 1994)

Sheffield, Gary and Bourne, John (eds), *Douglas Haig: War Diaries and Letters, 1914–1919* (Weidenfeld & Nicolson, London, 2005)

— and Todman, Dan, (eds) *Command and Control on the Western Front: The British Army's Experience 1914–18* (Spellmont, Tonbridge, 2007)

Simpson, Andy, 'Haldane, Sir (James) Aylmer Lowthorpe (1862–1950)', *ODNB*, OUP, Sept 2004

Smith-Dorrien, Horace, *Memories of Forty-Eight Years' Service* (John Murray, London, 1925)

— *Smith-Dorrien: Isandlwhana to the Great War* (Oakpast, Driffield, E. Yorkshire, 2009)

Soames, Mary (ed.), *Speaking for Themselves: The Personal Letters of Winston and Clementine Churchill* (Doubleday, London, 1998)

Spears, Major-General Sir Edward, *Liaison 1914: A Narrative of the Great Retreat* (Cassell & Co., London, 2000)

Stearn, Roger T., 'Pulteney, Sir William Pulteney (1861–1941)', *ODNB*, OUP, online edn, Oct 2008

Strachan, Hew, *The First World War: Volume I: To Arms* (Oxford University Press, Oxford, 2003 paperback edn.)

Terraine, John, *Mons: The Retreat to Victory* (Pen and Sword, Barnsley, 1991)

Tomlinson, H. M., *Waiting for Daylight* (Cassell, London, 1929)

Travers, Tim, *The Killing Ground: The British Army, the Western Front and the Emergence of Modern Warfare, 1900–1918* (Allen & Unwin, London, 1987)

Westlake, Ray, *British Battalions on the Western Front, January–June 1915* (Leo Cooper, Pen and Sword, Barnsley, 2001)

Whitaker, Joseph, *An Almanack for the Year of Our Lord 1914* (J Whitaker and Sons, London, 1914)

—— *An Almanack for the Year of Our Lord 1915* (J Whitaker and Sons, London, 1915)

Wirth, Captain Alfred, '(1920) The Battle of Le Cateau', *The RUSI Journal*, 65: 457, pp. 185–7

INDEX

An asterisk indicates that there is an entry in the biographical notes
(pp. 195-208) for the individual in question.